HOUSING: PARTICIPATION AND EXCLUSION

Housing: Participation and Exclusion

Collected papers from the Socio-Legal Studies Annual Conference 1997, University of Wales, Cardiff

Edited by
DAVID COWAN
Department of Law, University of Bristol

Routledge
Taylor & Francis Group
LONDON AND NEW YORK

First published 1998 by Dartmouth and Ashgate Publishing

Reissued 2018 by Routledge
4 Park Square, Milton Park, Abingdon, Oxon OX14 4RN

and by Routledge
605 Third Avenue, New York, NY 10158

Routledge is an imprint of the Taylor & Francis Group, an informa business

A Library of Congress record exists under LC control number: 98003166

ISBN 13: 978-1-138-32031-4 (hbk)
ISBN 13: 978-0-429-45338-0 (ebk)

Contents

List of Figures and Tables

List of Contributors

Helen Carr qualified as a solicitor in 1981 and spent 10 years working at Bradford Law Centre where she specialized in public law and housing law. Since taking up her post at the University of North London she has taught Landlord and Tenant Law and Social Security Law on both professional and academic courses. Her research interests arise out of her experience in practice and in particular she is concerned with the difficulties of tenants in the private rented sector.

David Cowan is a Lecturer in the Law Department at the University of Bristol. He has taught housing law for some time and is author of *Homelessness: The (In-)Appropriate Applicant* (1997), also published by Dartmouth.

Rose Gilroy is a Lecturer in the Department of Town and Country Planning, University of Newcastle. Prior to joining academia in 1988 she was a local government housing officer. Her research has focused on the marginalization of particular groups within housing and planning. Her publications include *Housing Women* (Routledge, 1994) coedited with Roberta Woods.

Gill Hague is a Senior Research Fellow in the Domestic Violence Research Group, located in the School for Policy Studies, University of Bristol.

Simon Halliday is studying for a PhD in the Law School of the University of Strathclyde where he is a Graduate Teaching Assistant. His thesis concerns the impact of judicial review on the administration of homelessness law in local government. He teaches housing law, sociology of law, and law and society. He is coauthor with Peter Robson of *Residential Tenancies* (forthcoming, 1998), W. Green/Sweet & Maxwell.

Andrew Harries is Research Officer in Law and a member of the Centre for Research in Financial and Legal Studies, Sheffield Hallam University. With Peter Vincent-Jones, he has been examining local authority contracting for blue-collar and white-collar CCT services in metropolitan authorities over the past four years, and is currently engaged in a 30 month ESRC-funded project, 'Conflict and Co-Operation in Contracting for Professional Services: A Comparative Study'.

Caroline Hunter is a lecturer in law at the University of Nottingham. She still retains a practice as a barrister specializing in housing work. She has published extensively on housing law and is senior editor of the *Encyclopaedia of Housing Law* and the *Housing Law Reports*.

Martin MacEwen graduated (LLB) from Aberdeen University and worked as a District Officer in the Solomon Islands and then with Dunfermline Town Council and the Race Relations Board in London before returning to his native city at the Edinburgh College of Art to lecture in planning, housing and equal opportunities. He is Director of the Scottish Ethnic Minorities Research Unit and Vice-Principal of the College. Martin has researched and published widely on race and law issues, including *Housing, Race and Law* (Routledge, 1991) and *Anti-Discrimination Law Enforcement* (Ashgate, 1997).

Ellen Malos is a Senior Research Fellow in the Domestic Violence Research Group, located in the School for Policy Studies, University of Bristol.

Judy Nixon is a senior lecturer in housing studies in the School of Urban and Regional Studies at Sheffield Hallam University. She has a particular interest in housing advocacy work and the barriers to justice for the tenants of social landlords.

Nicholas Smith is a Lecturer in the Faculty of Law, University of Leicester.

After graduating from Lancaster University with a First Class Honours degree in Social Ethics, **Hilary Third** began her career in housing working as an outreach worker with homeless families. Having later gained an MA in Housing Studies, she was employed as a Research Fellow in the Centre for Housing Policy at York University. Hilary now works in the School of Planning and Housing at Edinburgh College of Art/Heriot-Watt University, Edinburgh. She has been involved in a wide range of research studies on access to housing in Scotland, several of which have focused on the experiences of minority ethnic groups.

Dr Philip Timms is a Senior Lecturer in Community Psychiatry, Guy's and St Thomas's UMDS. Dr Timms conducted epidemiological research in the 1980s and for the last five years has worked as a consultant psychiatrist with the START team, providing mental health services for homeless people. He has established a computerized clinical information system and is a member of the Public Education Committee of the Royal College of Psychiatrists. He is editor of the 'Help is at Hand' series of leaflets on mental health problems.

Peter Vincent-Jones is Reader in Law and Assistant Director of the Centre for Research in Financial and Legal Studies, Sheffield Hallam University. With Andrew Harries, he has been examining local authority contracting for blue-collar and white-collar CCT services in metropolitan authorities over the past four years, and is currently engaged in a 30 month ESRC-funded project, 'Conflict and Co-Operation in Contracting for Professional Services: A Comparative Study'.

Matthew Waddington is currently a Lecturer in Law at Manchester Metropolitan University. At the time of the SLSA Conference, he was the housing solicitor in the Salford Law Centre and a freelance trainer. He has previously worked as a housing specialist for the Law Centres Federation and as a solicitor in a legal aid private practice.

Lisa Whitehouse is a Lecturer in Law at the University of Hull, with particular interests in property, housing, and company law. Her publications on the mortgage repossession process include 'The Home Owner: Consumer or Citizen?' in S. Bright and J. Dewar, *Law and Land: Themes and Perspectives*, (Oxford University Press, 1998).

Editor's Note

The chapters in this volume were originally delivered as part of the housing stream at the Socio-Legal Studies Annual Conference in 1997. As my introduction states, this was the first SLSA conference to include a stream on housing issues. I am extremely grateful to the conference organizers for allowing us the scope to develop our ideas under the SLSA umbrella. In particular, Phil Thomas provided the spark of inspiration; Anne Mumford and Iain McDonald immeasurably assisted and calmed my panic attacks.

The housing stream operated a collective, non-confrontational approach which we all found extremely helpful in reconsidering our work. The editorial process also operated a collective approach which has influenced the shape, contents and progression of this book. I have learnt from the insights of the contributors as well as from their generosity of spirit. It is hoped that this spirit will continue into the future and influence the direction of housing research as well as the desperate search for the little available funding.

David Cowan

Abbreviations

CCT	Compulsory Competitive Tendering
CRE	Commission for Racial Equality
DoE	Department of Environment
DoH	Department of Health
DLO	Direct Labour Organization
DSO	Direct Service Organization
HANK	Housing Academics' Network
SEMRU	Scottish Ethnic Minorities Research Unit

Introduction

DAVID COWAN

Crossing Boundaries

Since its inception, the Socio-Legal Studies Association annual conference has consistently provided a forum for debate about current issues. However, one unfortunate omission has been a lack of focus on critical, socio-legal debate(s) around housing. The 1997 conference, at Cardiff Law School, radically altered this position. Under the overall theme of 'Crossing Boundaries', a vibrant housing stream came into being, causing debate and constructive argument on housing issues to be located at the forefront of the socio-legal studies movement, rather than as a subsumed topic. It was my pleasure to coordinate the stream as well as provide a conduit for the collective editorial policy which has governed these contributions.[1]

Fifteen papers were delivered on housing issues at the 1997 conference, 11 of which appear in this volume as a representative sample, or snapshot, of current research being undertaken on housing issues.[2] The general theme of the conference was pursued by reference to two apparently contradictory aims of the government then in office – 'participation' and 'exclusion'. The conference papers eloquently showed that these aims often, somewhat paradoxically, overlapped. Thus, each paper suggested a dynamic process, shaped by its context(s). In terms of the organization of the book, therefore, there could be no neat structural pattern. However, as each contributor generally began their analysis from one or other standpoint, this was the organizing force. It may therefore be helpful to the reader if the first two sections of this Introduction discuss how I and we have constructed these sub-themes for the purposes of this book, as well as fitting the various chapters into different constructs of these themes.

However, the general theme was also pursued in a number of other ways. Thus, the personnel of the housing stream reflected differing traditions within and outside the housing movement. In addition to a group of housing academics within law departments (representing the diversity within the University structures and academics at different stages in their careers), the housing stream hosted papers from the Scottish Ethnic Minorities Research Unit (SEMRU), a law centre solicitor, a mental health voluntary organization, a Domestic Violence Research group, as well as from a Department of Town Planning. Some of these people were, perhaps, surprised to be asked to give a paper at the conference, either because their primary interest was in a direction not explicitly related to the housing movement or because their legal knowledge was minimal (although the latter proved not to be the case). Each paper, nevertheless, cast a new light on housing issues, and the different perspectives generated considerable comment and discussion. It was notable also that many of the sessions were attended by those whose interest in housing was marginal. It is hoped that this will also be reflected in the readership of this collection.

Not only does this tell us something about the reach of housing issues, but it also should provide a method for reconsidering the notion of 'housing law'. For far too long, housing law has played a minor role in law schools. It is regarded as an optional subject with little coherence, marginalized by most law schools in their drive for commercialism. The 1997 conference brought some of these issues to the fore (leading to the setting up of a Housing Academics Network – 'HANK' – on the internet,[3] as well as other conference opportunities for us all to meet again[4]) and the third section of this Introduction expands upon my personal philosophy within this debate.

Shortly after the conference, the most significant event for a generation occurred with the unmourned near destruction of the Conservative party and its loss of office. The Thatcher and Major administrations' populist housing policies have radically reoriented housing policy, finance, and tenure. Much of that reorientation has had contradictory results. So, for example, the need to increase the numbers of accommodation units, finally identified in a 1996 White Paper, was met soon after with a (further) drastic cut in the budget available to housing organizations. Furthermore, the melt-down of the public sector has caused an overlap with the housing association movement but, after the Housing Act 1988, this has left totally different types of tenancy affecting each sector. The new New Labour government swept into power amidst much optimism, particularly in the housing world (see, for example, Blake, 1997). The New Labour manifesto made many significant pledges relating to housing, and recent pronouncements from the Minister without Portfolio, Peter Mandelson, have suggested that the new government will organize a cross-departmental group to eliminate social (and therefore also housing) exclusion. The final section of this chapter broaches the tricky subject of the future for housing.

Participation

'Participation' was chosen as one of the themes of the housing stream because it seemed, like no other concept, to provide a unifying socio-historical, as well as socio-legal, element to the study of housing. The concept also seemed to embody the very essence of housing law, which should be concerned with redressing the inequalities of bargaining power between provider and recipient/ purchaser of housing. Participation, either on collective or inter-agency or individual bases, is concerned with the appreciation of, and responses to, such inequalities.

Participation has a variety of different meanings and levels which depend upon the context in which the concept is used. Furbey et al. suggest that it 'is a slippery concept, raising questions of power, ideology and influence in public policy-making and service delivery' (1996, p. 251). In one sense, each housed person 'participates' in housing, for they take part in, and subject themselves to, the housing process. This individualized *experience* of housing has, in retrospect, been a particular influence in the individualized *response* to housing (see Cole and Furbey, 1994, pp. 212–32):

> The problem is expressed succinctly by Saunders in his remark that, even though council housing may constitute, ... , an example of 'collective consumption' in that it is an item of consumption where provision has been supported by the state, the acute politicisation of housing and mass action does not occur because the dwellings are 'consumed individually' (Cole and Furbey, 1994, p. 159; see also pp. 150–62).

Nevertheless, one of the (many) paradoxes of the Conservative government's radical housing policies was that their individualized responses in fact partly gave rise to collective action (see Woodward, 1991). Whilst collective participation has taken place by tenants at different times and for different reasons over the course of this century (Partington, 1981), what has been different over the past 18 years has been the level of cohesion of tenants' groups as well as the correlation between funding-dependence and participation ('collective participation' below). Government policy, particularly in the late 1980s and early 1990s, also either encouraged or obliged housing agencies to work together. Again, this could not be regarded as a new development but perhaps reflected the failure of the state to cope with the upward spiral of housing need (see Darke and Darke, 1979; Cowan, 1997). This collection has several papers which are concerned with this theme (see 'inter-agency participation' below). Finally, the issue of social justice within housing is considered within this collection (see 'individualized participation' below). The Woolf report on *Access to Justice* made several trenchant criticisms of housing law and procedure (1996, ch. 16). This collection spreads the net wider to embrace the mortgage repossession process as well as ordinary, but confusing, concepts of housing law.

Collective Participation

The first context of participation reflects the growing desire to empower council tenants to participate effectively in the processes of governance affecting their environment. For much of the twentieth century, council tenants have been regarded as objects of the state's largesse with little role to play in the development of localized policies other than through the indirect method of voting. For example, housing allocation, design and construction, agreements, repairs were all the preserve of the local state which, subject to central controls of different devices, rendered these objects of state support the powerless. Public sector tenants, to use Hirschman's concepts, had no 'voice' and, equally, were unable to 'exit' (1970). Much space has been devoted to analysing the methods of 'exit', devised by successive Conservative governments of the 1980s and 1990s, from local authority and other forms of tenure (the following is a small sample: Forrest and Murie, 1991; Woodward, 1991; Balchin, 1996, ch. 8; Hughes and Lowe, 1995, ch. 2).

However, little emphasis has been placed in the available material on 'voice' until more recently (see, for example, Cole and Furbey 1994, pp. 212–32; Burns et al., 1994, esp. ch. 6; Hoggett, 1997; Hoggett and Hambleton, 1987; Foley and Evans, 1994; Karn et al., 1997). The central concern of the New Right was to provide mechanisms which would force the break-up (or down) of the State monopoly of council housing. Constantly revivifying methods of exit were, at the same time, conjoined to new and individualized methods of complaining about services. So, for example, the promise of the *Citizen's Charter* (Cabinet Office, 1991) was more privatization and individualized rights which, in turn, would provide choice and accountability. In order to retain their tenants' loyalty (Hirschman, 1970), authorities were forced into a greater programme of tenant involvement in the policy process (cf. Karn et al., 1997). Furthermore, central controls on local authority expenditure provided an incentive to local authorities to gain large scale exit from their control, either through what became known as large scale voluntary transfers or through Housing Action Trusts (see Mullins et al., 1992). In order to accomplish these types of transfer, tenants' votes were needed, even though this was not quite the intention of the Thatcher governments, which saw these methods of exit as the best way of breaking the state 'monopoly' on housing. So, local authorities were forced to consult with, and provide information to, their tenants. The power relationship between these two bodies was indelibly altered (see Atkinson and Cope, 1997, pp. 208–19).

Participation has been an important element in the UK planning process at least since the Skeffington Committee Report in 1969 (see, for example, McAuslan, 1975, ch. 2; 1980, chs 1 and 2), and for longer in the USA. Research has provided a useful ladder through which participation can be gauged (see Arnstein, 1969 (USA); Burns et al., 1994, ch. 6 developing the ladder as an analytical tool in the UK). Such ladders are helpful analytical tools but must not be used simplistically for there is a complex interaction between each rung of the ladder. Thus, that developed by Burns et al. represents a much more complex reality of intertwining concepts. The value of such tools is put in this way:

> The ladder juxtaposes powerless citizens with the powerful in order to highlight the fundamental divisions between them. In actuality, neither the have-nots nor the powerholders are homogeneous blocs. Each group encompasses a host of divergent points of view, significant cleavages, competing vested interests, and splintered sub-groups. The justification for using such simplistic abstractions is that in most cases the have-nots really do perceive the powerful as a monolithic 'system,' and powerholders actually do view the have-nots as a sea of 'those people,' with little comprehension of the class and caste between them (Arnstein, 1969, p. 217).

Arnstein's ladder of participation described a process of 'therapy' and 'manipulation' the objective of which 'is not to enable people to participate in planning or conducting programs, but to enable power holders to "educate" or "cure" the participants' (at pp. 217 and 218–9). In other words, these are methods through which the powerful control the powerless and result in non-participation. Burns et al. provide four examples of this in their ladder: civic hype; cynical consultation; poor information; customer care (at pp. 164–6). The perceived need of local authorities to push large scale voluntary transfers through voting resulted in a cynical consultation and poor information being provided to tenants, which lawyers would see as breaching fiduciary duty (see Mullins et al. 1992; and for fiduciary duties, see generally Martin, 1993, ch. 20 and specifically in the context of local government, Loughlin, 1996).

Gilroy's chapter in this volume suggests that consultation became better during the 1980s as both local and central government became tuned into lower capital funding levels and rising rents. Participation was, in reality, a sop to increase tenant satisfaction in this context. Local government was therefore forced into dreaming up more inventive solutions. Nevertheless, in spite of the better organized consultation, housing officials were still uni-dimensional and thought only in terms of housing without the more contextual, environmental considerations such as poverty, discrimination, and continuing economic 'restructuring'. So, schemes had 'given people central heating which they cannot afford to use; car parking spaces when they had no car to park and children's play areas which they could not let their children use because of stranger danger'. Generally, it was not until the 1990s that this was redressed. Vincent-Jones and Harries' chapter adds a further layer to this analysis. Despite the ever-increasing methods of exit, local authority tenants remain a huge body which must, in order to play an effective role in the process of Compulsory Competitive Tendering, rely on small groups of tenants. However, these groups can negate the process of participation if they themselves do not encourage the participation of other tenants: 'The term "mafia" was used to describe the powerful position of some [tenant] groupings.'

Arnstein's next grouping – 'degrees of tokenism' – involved information, consultation, and placation through which 'citizens may indeed hear and be heard. But under these conditions they lack the power to ensure that their views will be *heeded* by the powerful' (at pp. 217 and 219–21 – original emphasis). So, the rights to information and consultation given to tenants under the Thatcher/Major regimes specifically excluded those rights in relation to rent-setting which, ultimately, was controlled by central government. Burns et al. suggest that citizen participation is enhanced through: high quality information; genuine consultation; effective advisory boards; limited decentralized decision-making; partnership; and delegated control (at pp. 166–74). Vincent-Jones and Harries' chapter suggests that a benevolent use of each of these can result in the benevolent exercise of essentially privatizing measures, which genuinely respond to tenants' fears and demands.

The first two chapters in this volume add another factor, particular to the groups with which they deal: training. Whilst there is some disquiet about the types and nature of training, expressed within academic writing (see esp. Furbey et al., 1996), Gilroy's chapter suggests that any training must respond to the needs and economic marginality of tenants. That chapter sees the training process as a crucial determinant which has yet to be approached satisfactorily. Vincent-Jones and Harries note that tenant representatives had to qualify by attending training courses. Other chapters similarly suggest that training is a key to participation. Timms' analysis of relationships between voluntary and state sectors depended upon quality training in order to facilitate participation between these groups.

The concern about training, though, is that housing professionals and others, in their attempts to proselytize, simply create new examples of themselves. Thus, training can often be perceived as an inculcation of professional ideologies, forming part of 'professional growth, aggrandizement and self interest' (Cohen, 1985, p. 167). The transmogrification required causes the Self to become Other and simply extends the net of bureaucracy as explanations are given which justify the old failures and do not speak of better futures (see, for example, McCulloch, 1997). In other words, in order to give the ability to participate in policy- and decision-making, training can simply reproduce the trainer unless it is rooted in the demands of the community. It may well be that the best trainers are the trainees themselves through their own collective experience and evaluation.

The final rungs on Arnstein's ladder of participation represent 'degrees of citizen power', beginning with partnership, delegated power and citizen control (at pp. 217 and 221–4). Vincent-Jones and Harries' chapter suggests that the compulsory competitive tendering process can provide power to collective groups of tenants given that the necessary contextual conditions exist prior to the exercise taking place. In other words, the tenants effectively held a controlling grip on the process of devising the process, choosing the contractor, and then evaluating the contractor's performance (see Burns et al.'s discussion of citizen control at pp. 174–9).

Inter-agency[5] Participation

So far, the discussion has been limited to the notion of collective participation within the burgeoning tenants' movement. However, there is an alternative context (touched upon above) for the participatory movement which seems to have been a key in the delivery of central government's policies – state, quasi-state, and voluntary organizations should work together as part of a coordinated solution to housing (and other social welfare) issues. In this sense, participation represents a management solution which central government often seemed to regard as a localized panacea to centralized problems. Criminologists regard the parallel development in crime control processes as a result of the failure of the state to stem the rising tide of crime (Garland, 1996 refers to an expansion of community 'responsibilisation'; see also Pease, 1997) and it might be argued that the same applies to the failure of the state to stem the rising tide of housing need.

These practices have also seeped into housing management, partly through the Home Office (see, for example, in relation to the prevention of racial harassment with particular reference to local authorities, Home Office, 1989), Department of Health (see, for example, with particular reference to community care, DoH, 1990a; and children subject to abuse, see the voluminous Guidance, DoH, 1990b), and Department of Environment (see, for example in relation to racial harassment, DoE, 1991). There is an extensive literature evaluating the effects of these policies in the housing sphere (see Hague et al., 1996; Means and Smith, 1996; McCluskey, 1994; Cowan, 1997, chs 2–7). Bearing in mind that these policies rarely appear in anything other than Guidance or research reports, it is perhaps not surprising that little work has been conducted from a legalistic perspective (although when such matters do appear in legislation, see Cowan and Fionda, 1994, where difficulties are predicted; and the (a-)legalistic results of *R v. Northavon DC ex parte Smith* (1994) 26 HLR 659). Socio-legal research in housing has also tended to eschew this important aspect of policy.

Generally, the available research has discussed the practical difficulties in facilitating this form of participation. In this context, 'participation' is often phrased in different ways which might be compared with those expressed in Arnstein's ladder. For example, the word 'partnership' is sometimes used (see, for example, Kaganas et al., 1995, in the context of the Children Act 1989), which suggests a manipulation of the power differential between agencies. At the same time, it suggests that the agency which has taken primary responsibility in the past will lose that power (which must then be shared with other, alien disciplines) and thus the participative context challenges previous bargaining relationships. My own research suggests that these difficulties can be reflected within actual practice and decision-making (see Cowan, 1997).

Three chapters (Timms, Waddington, and Malos and Hague) in this book have concerned themselves with analysing this alternative strategy. Each does so from a totally different perspective and therefore advances our ability to respond adequately to the issues raised. A further chapter (Smith) also draws attention to recent developments by some local housing authorities in developing area fora as part of their policy on 'Houses in Multiple Occupation'. Whilst these appear to be at an early stage of development, they nevertheless represent a further march in the direction of local participation in policy-setting and performance criteria.

Timms' chapter is an exercise in navel-gazing, for it evaluates a programme in which he has been involved as well as discussing the programme's search for a solution to the problems of inter-agency partnership. This is an extremely welcome advance to our knowledge, not only because of Timms' background (as a consultant psychiatrist), but also because it raises the issue of the voluntary sector which, to my knowledge, has never been discussed in housing socio-legal or legal literature. The latter is a surprising phenomenon because of the huge role foreseen by all political parties for the voluntary sector. As Timms works within the project, it enables him to provide a valuable, personal account of some of the problems caused by this form of participation. The argument is, in many ways, a simple one but nevertheless repays considerable attention: the different organizational structures cause difficulties which can only be surmounted by the adaptation of each agency to the demands of the other. The solution is partly seen to be training. At the SLSA conference, this paper caused much discussion partly because of the novelty of the subject-matter and partly also because of the parallels with the research of many of the participants (including my own).

The two other chapters offer an important contrast, suggesting the differing motivations of central government policy in influencing the development of this form of participation. Garland suggests that the rise of responsibilization has had a concomitant 'in a form of denial which appears increasingly hysterical in the clinical sense of that term' (at p. 459), which has prefaced the move towards harsher, more penal policies. Waddington's chapter in this volume, on the other hand, is able to link the two explicitly. The chapter discusses the invitation extended to local authority homelessness officers to participate with a particular branch of the Home Office in the process of deciding whether a person is an 'illegal' immigrant (although that term has no *de iure* status). As soon as this judicially inspired concept came into being, the invitation to participate was thrust upon local authorities. Waddington suggests that this invitation is cast in terms that a refusal might have negative consequences. Furthermore, the lack of knowledge of immigration law renders housing officers powerless. Hence, the invitation becomes a requirement. As a requirement, it smacks more of the 'conspiratorial model' of inter-agency participation (cf. Sampson et al., 1988), '... potentially having social control and civil liberties implications in terms of greater surveillance of service users and others, and the possible domination of community agencies by the police in particular' (Hague et al., 1996, p. 7).

The chapter from Hague and Malos charts the government's concern with informing and developing a multi-agency approach to 'domestic' violence. This developmental approach has, however, been met by the implacable lust of the Conservatives to destroy long-term housing obligations. In one fell swoop, the Housing Act 1996 dismantled the more positive policies emanating from the Home Office. In other words, the move towards responsibilizing the response to violence to women has effectively been regressed by the exclusionary effects of the new legislation. If nothing else, then, these two chapters illustrate that the motive of the government in their 1996 Act was essentially cost-saving. In the process, responsibilities were to be minimized. Enquiry duties to root out 'illegal' immigrants are stepped up (requiring participation between local and central parts of the state) whilst at the same time responses to those who have had violence inflicted upon them suffer by the withdrawal of local obligations (potentially destroying the moves towards participation which already exist).

Individualized Participation

The third context of participation considered in this book reflects the lawyers' apparent need to individualize not only disputes but also the construction of rights in housing. Consideration therefore revolves around the type of right granted, participation in the judicial process, and the impact of consumerism within this context. It comes as little surprise that this aspect, the traditional domain of housing law, has been most covered by texts on housing law. However, these texts, with one notable exception, normally eschew socio-legal analysis and research, as well as the context. The one exception is Stewart's *Rethinking Housing Law* (1996; discussed in greater depth below) and the repercussions of that text are fully evident in two of the three papers in this section. These papers enable us to provide an alternative slant to housing *law* and in this way advance the thesis that the study of housing law needs to escape the limitations of a simple black letter approach (best summed up by the fact that, currently on my bookshelf, there are six casebooks on housing law). The best example of black letter housing law comes in the (usually interminable) chapters on the law of landlord and tenant, supposedly representing one of the major sources of housing law issues. This is usually presented in entirely legalistic fashion with references to 'the usual legal sources'. In doing so, they thus display a contextual and empirical ignorance.

Rarely, if at all, in those texts is reference made to the difficulties inherent in the individual's participation in the judicial process when things go wrong and the landlord seeks possession. Hunter and Nixon's findings in their chapter suggest that this process is similar to a cattle market and needs to be compared with the better served, and more private, judicial process of mortgage repossession. The chapter expands on their earlier research (Nixon et al., 1996) in significant ways. For example, it is interspersed with comments from several

District Judges, which suggest that the ability of the tenant or home owner to participate in the proceedings is severely undermined by the supposed arbitrators' preconceptions as well as by the procedures involved. Participation is, therefore, used in this context as *due process*.

The results of this study should, in my view, be read in tandem with the more mainstream research on ideal-type appeal mechanisms (see, for example, Sainsbury, 1993; 1994; Sainsbury and Eardley, 1991; also the influential work of Mashaw, 1983). This suggests that such mechanisms should produce accurate decisions and be conducted fairly – that is, promptly, impartially, participatory, and accountably. As Sainsbury suggests, '[t]he important point is that procedures should provide opportunities, or even facilitate participation [with or without the applicant being present], and not discourage it or present obstructions' (1993, p. 304). Hunter and Nixon's chapter suggests that participation of many of the applicants in their study was actively discouraged and obstructed by both the procedures and some arbitrators.

Housing law texts will also provide a conceptual discussion of the thin distinction in law between a lease and a licence. The discussion is usually illuminated by reference to the numerous judicial decisions on the subject and also, if we are lucky, to its relevance to security of tenure (the statutory method of regulating the relationship between landlord and tenant[6]). Carr's chapter provides an alternative focus, arguing that housing lawyers need to rethink this distinction by reference to the purpose of the person or organization which grants the right. It is argued that the distinction causes practical problems partly because it is so wafer-thin (different advisers will provide different solutions) and partly because organizations grant rights without intending to do so. This is an argument with which I have much sympathy (see Cowan 1992; 1993; an argument extrapolated by Hill, 1996) and which, I believe, reflects the housing law experience. Hitherto, the law in this area has been dominated by *property law* approaches which question whether a particular agreement creates a property or personal right. In housing, however, such a question is irrelevant – the only real issue is whether a person is (or should be) entitled to statutory protection. So, the cases simply answer an irrelevant question and, in the process, produce the most ridiculous, convoluted, and unnecessary body of law.

Whitehouse's chapter focuses on the mortgage market and repossession rates. It argues for a more consumerist approach on both counts, using and developing the findings from an empirical project. The complexity of the law in this area (part of the obfuscation of land lawyers) masks an important empirical fact which Whitehouse explores. Mortgage companies effectively operate a cartel through non-publication of repossession policies, non-information through overly complex agreements, as well as limited and uneven self-regulation. All of these factors simply exacerbate the apparent inequality of bargaining power inherent in the mortgage relationship between those who want and those who have.

When reduced to this level, the situation resembles the landlord and tenant relationship. That relationship has been subjected to regulation, through statutory security of tenure provision and rent control, for most of this century. Owner-occupation, a minority tenure choice, has generally been left to market forces with occasional resort to legal processes when inequalities became too apparent. However, in 1997, about 70 per cent are now owner-occupiers, the majority of whom require a mortgage, in a largely unregulated 'market' or cartel. Whitehouse argues that a response to the research findings should reflect a consumerist approach, developing recent European law output (in itself, an important facet of the more recent legal regime affecting housing).

Exclusion

Social exclusion has been one of the most important angles of recent empirical research, part of the emphasis of which derived from the ESRC's research programme. This collection however provides a more specific emphasis on housing exclusion. Indeed, even the earlier chapters, which provide a potentially positive analysis of housing participation, provide classic examples of housing exclusion. For example, Gilroy's chapter concludes by showing the marginalization of tenants on a local estate and questioning the processes which require them to participate in the new programmes. Vincent-Jones and Harries' chapter suggests the pitfalls of participation through indirect processes, which can lead to an equally less pluralistic environment as existed prior to the CCT programme. My own work has attempted to show how the requirement or exhortations for agencies to work together can equally result in exclusion when these relationships break down (Cowan, 1997, chs 2–6). It is important, then, to keep the notion of exclusion in perspective. Often, when we discuss housing exclusion, we do so through a consideration of exclusion *from* housing. This collection provides ample proof of exclusion occurring *within* housing, or amongst the housed.[7] Equally, the processes of exclusion take place in a more complex environment than is usually discussed (for an extrapolation of these contexts in terms of youth and the so-called 'underclass', see MacDonald, 1997).

Two further examples of the complexity of this form of exclusion are provided in this collection. MacEwen and Third's chapter provides an illuminating discussion of housing tenure choice (or lack of it) in relation to Scotland's ethnic minorities. A significant portion of Scottish ethnic minorities occupy housing they own. Most commonly, this is presented as the success of Thatcher/Major housing policies in encouraging this tenure choice. However, MacEwen and Third expertly uncover a more intricate web of exclusion from other housing tenures which have forced ethnic minorities into a tenure which is usually unrepresentative of their need for housing. This web is made up of housing design which does not reflect the make-up of ethnic minority familial relationships, allocation policies which exclude, little ethnic monitoring (which results in an inability to respond), and no housing associations specifically designed for ethnic minorities.

Smith's chapter suggests the exclusion of those accommodated in houses in multiple occupation. This is reflected by the types of people who occupy the housing who are, in housing terms, the most marginalized (for example, those who are not entitled to housing benefit or whose housing benefit has been reduced, and the homeless for whom this type of accommodation has judicial approval[8]). The occupants within this accommodation have few enforceable rights and local authorities which seek to enforce the statutory duties, for example to ensure that the landlord provides appropriate methods of escaping from fire, often find that their attempts are scuppered by delays between issuing statutory notices and the court process.

The more traditional arena of housing research is that which considers exclusion from housing (the classic example of which is provided by Loveland, 1995). Three chapters in this collection take this as their primary theme. Halliday's research is most closely related to that of Loveland, although focused differently in terms of the 'impact' of judicial review on homelessness decision-making as well as considering the process of conducting fieldwork. The case law in this area has been subjected to widespread criticism because it has tended to narrow considerably the reach of that legislation (predicted as early as 1974: James, 1974; see also, Loveland, 1996; Cowan, 1997; Hunter and Miles, 1997). Thus, rather than provide an extrapolation of the rights of the homeless, case law has pursued a negative, exclusionary thesis dependent upon stereotypes and ideological errors. Halliday attempts to show how one authority's experience of case law has impacted upon its own administration of the legislation. So, the concentration is upon the first hand experience of judicial review. This essay also discusses the problems and pitfalls of this type of research project; this is particularly valuable because so little discussion is given over to this in published housing research.

Waddington's chapter shows how inter-agency participation can be used as an exclusionary device, sometimes with the most tragic consequences (such as the death of Joy Gardiner). Waddington's analysis shows a hitherto unrecognized aspect of the judiciary's exclusionary emphasis in the housing sphere, through tracing the development of a category known as 'illegal immigrants' for which there is no legal basis whatsoever. The development of this concept has been mirrored by an escalation of control by Home Office officials who should be irrelevant to the purposes of housing decision-making but whose web is now weaved around practically all aspects of welfare policy. Housing officers, in this context, become part of the immigration service. One point made by Waddington came as a surprise to me but my own investigation provides corroborating evidence. The point is that hardly any material on immigration exists in textbooks covering either the law or policy of housing. This is a surprising omission, to say the least, and it is hoped that Waddington's chapter will at least provide the basis for treatment within these textbooks.

The final chapter in this volume is given over to a discussion of the Housing Act 1996 in the context of violence to women. Hague and Malos have been at the forefront of the debate concerning issues of access to housing in this context (1993a; 1993b) as well as pursuing the 'multi-agency' debate (1996). The Home Office has been involved in pursuing the latter approach with the Department of Environment not far behind. However, the 1996 Act has turned the clock back more than a decade with its ignorance of the general requirements of women who are abused. Superficially, the Act in fact did much with the repeal of the awkward and exclusionary distinction between violence inside and violence outside the home (the former being a situation where the female was deemed homeless, the latter not). However, a deeper analysis of the provisions suggests that much of the positive work will be undone, largely through the ignorance of the policy-makers. Whilst the New Labour government has tinkered with the system, they have nevertheless left the Conservative's primary structure and strategy intact. The paper begins with a poem which all of those who attended the final housing session at the conference will remember – a moving, inspiring, emotional enjoinment that requires all of us involved in the housing movement to take action.

Housing Law – a Call to Arms

I am a so-called academic lawyer engaged in teaching and researching housing issues within a law department. My primary focus therefore is law and, not unnaturally, my concern is specifically centred around housing law issues. Part of the reason why I asked to organize a housing stream at the SLSA conference in 1997 was to provide a showcase for socio-legal research in housing law. Another part was to stimulate a debate upon the way in which housing law is taught in law schools. This debate has not really occurred in the field of housing, although the 1970s witnessed a debate on the subject of Welfare Law, a not unrelated subject (Partington and Jowell, 1979). In law schools, the study of housing law has often taken place from a 'black letter' perspective. This means that students are inculcated in the legal ethic of housing law, but do not (or rarely) encounter a contextual approach(-es).

Part of the problem lies in the available material, of which the 1990s have witnessed a proliferation. Within this collection, the positivist, black letter legal tradition dominates, although occasionally one can spy attempts to provide some contextual analysis (see, for example, Bright and Gilbert, 1995). Part of the reason may be that housing law is a relatively new addition to law schools. Textbooks have been written to reflect upon, inform, and analyse the housing law which is practised. The first such book was a mammoth achievement, bringing together whole streams of law (Arden and Partington, 1983). Its current development into an encyclopaedic loose-leaf version reflects the ever-expanding law on housing (Arden, Hunter and Partington, 1994). What follows is not a criticism of this brand of housing law; rather, it is an attempt to develop the way in which we approach housing law within the academic community.

Even when an attempt was made to expand the reach of housing law through a combination of authors from different perspectives – law and policy – the result was that the authors 'embraced th[e black letter] temptation at most opportunities' (Hughes and Lowe, 1995; Cowan, 1995, p. 668). The massive expansion of socio-legal studies and the study of 'law in context(s)' (as to which, see Thomas, 1997, ch. 1) has led to a much broader acceptability of this type of research. Other subjects have sought to build on this research by incorporating these movements within their approaches to text book writing (for two such examples, see Sanders and Young, 1994; Parkinson, 1993). Housing law has, however, remained stubbornly outside this new tradition. One reviewer of a recent casebook (Madge, 1996; reviewed in the *New Law Journal*) even argued that housing law had no intellectual core and was simply a practitioners' device or label.

This is a myth designed by housing practitioners to illustrate the depth of housing practice and I strongly dissent from it. The recent acceptability of the law of restitution can assist us in the development of a conceptual model. Birks argues that the law of restitution is based upon 'unjust enrichment at another's expense' which triggers a restitutionary response (1986, p. 16). He then goes on to refine this broad, general concept essentially through a consideration of each word.[9] Housing law might adopt a similar methodology through sociological analysis of the broad general concept of 'inequality of bargaining power' which would prove equally complex to that used in restitution.[10] The mismatch between supply and demand for housing means that, when the processes of law intervene, it should redress this unequal balance. If it does not, then we need to consider why not. For example, those with superior bargaining power are those who also influence the scope of intervention of the law.

However, such an analysis is overly simplistic (see, for example, Nelken's influential study of landlords and the development of anti-harassment legislation: 1983). After all, the outmoded concept of long leases, which have enabled certain dukes to remain powerful, has been severely curtailed by recent legislative intervention (causing one such duke to refuse to make further contributions to the Conservative party). The various chapters in this book suggest that this broad concept of inequality of bargaining power hides behind it many complex interactions (see also Beale, 1983). Abandoning the concept as impractical as well as incapable of fulfillment would enable us to provide a deeper analytical approach to the relationship between class and housing law. In turn, this relationship is (or might be) reflected in the production of housing, tenure choice, as well as economic power (see Ball, 1983; Morris and Winn, 1990). Whether or not one agrees with this, the time has now come for the development of a new tradition of research in housing law which, to be successful, will require some critical use of theoretical analysis. When we are able to do this, it will provide an illuminating coherent critique of legislation, judicial decision, policy and practice.

The first glimpse of a new tradition of writing on housing law was provided by Stewart (1996) whose work, in my view, has provided the foundations for the most exciting developments in housing law teaching. Stewart's concentration on the regulatory framework enabled a coherent, enlightening approach to the subject to be within our grasp. Eschewing the standard chapter headings which usually concentrate on landlord and tenant, the book was able to provide an analysis of housing which went beyond the ordinary legal materials. This meant that the concluding chapter was able to make hard-hitting points about some futures of housing law. It is not surprising, therefore, that this work is regularly cited in this collection. It is hoped that this collection will also lessen the scope of the challenge facing us as the acceptability of socio-legal studies has become more dominant. The depth of research into housing issues within this collection suggests that the transition into law teaching must happen shortly.

We must not stop there, though, for housing is a marginalized subject within law schools. This collection suggests that housing law issues reach into other subjects within the law curriculum, as one should expect given that the study of law is often portrayed as a continuum split into convenient modules. Housing law is an amalgam of different traditions, extending into public law (Gilroy, Halliday, Hunter and Nixon, Waddington), contract law (Harries and Vincent-Jones), property law (Whitehouse, Carr), family law (Hague and Malos) and so on. Each chapter in this collection actually challenges many of the established subjects in some way or other – it is up to us to ensure that these other subjects take this into account.

Some Futures

The discredited Conservative governments have left behind them a wreckage that is housing policy. The most evocative academic expression of this wreckage was Professor Loveland's comment that the retention of the homelessness legislation, in the light of the lack of supply of housing, was 'an exercise in legislative deceit' (1995, at p. 331). The New Labour government has immediately made three curative changes to the unwavering ideological position adopted by the Conservatives in relation to housing. First, they have sought to restrain the privatization of housing management through compulsory competitive tendering; second, they will release some of the capital gained from the right to buy sales; third, they have already restored the 'reasonable preference' given to statutorily homeless people under the Housing Act 1985 regime.

These are therefore exciting times for housing researchers although many research questions remain just that – questions. For example, how much difference will the extra money coming into the housing system make to the supply of low-cost accommodation or will the majority of the money be spent on repairing the decrepit state of much of the stock? Even if it is the former, how much difference will it make to the lack of available accommodation? If the latter, then Loveland's comment remains as true now as it did before. What is to be done about the deregulated private rented sector or should it be left to rot as the outmoded form of housing tenure it is? Should tenants be trained and paid to participate in their housing management? Should local authority and housing association tenants be subjected to different protective regimes? Should the mortgage market remain un/self-regulated? Should immigration policy exclude so many from the housing that they need? There are so many more questions but a common theme is whether the un/self-regulatory schema of the Conservatives can meet the housing needs of the majority of the population. It is no surprise that after only a few months, there is much work yet to be done.

Notes

1 Most of the essays have been circulated to each contributor for their comments, which have been forwarded on to the author direct.
2 The others have mostly been published elsewhere, either as part of wider collections or as part of books in their own right: Partington, forthcoming; Mullen et al., 1997; Cowan, 1997.
3 The site can be found at http://home.hands-on.ltd.uk/matthew/acad.htm.
4 The housing stream will, it is hoped, be a regular stream within the SLSA conference.
5 I have used the term 'inter-agency' here because it best sums up the research results considered in the subsequent chapters below. However, I readily acknowledge the difficulties in this terminology and that, in certain circumstances, the phrase 'multi-agency' describes the reality more appropriately: see Hague et al., 1996.
6 In the public sector, this distinction must be between the landlord and tenant or person with exclusive possession – see Housing Act 1985, s. 79(4).
7 The phrase 'housing exclusion', I would argue, is meaningless without analysis. In this respect, it requires to be reconstructed in the same way as the phrase 'community care' (see Cowan, 1995, pp. 214–7). Other examples of exclusion within housing can be found, for example, in the notorious 'introductory' or probationary tenancy regime under which those granted tenancies can be excluded seemingly on the whim of those around them – they thus live in fear of exclusion.
8 *R v. RB Kensington and Chelsea ex parte Ben-el-Mabouk* (1995) 27 HLR 564.
9 Thus, it is argued that there are certain 'unjust' factors – such as a mistaken payment, duress, undue influence – which lead to the restitutionary response.
10 I do not wish to suggest that this is the sole governing ideology of housing law, although it is the one which I personally most favour.

Bibliography

Arden, A., Hunter, C. and Partington, M. (1994), *Housing Law*, Sweet and Maxwell, London.
Arden, A. and Partington, M. (1983), *Housing Law*, Sweet and Maxwell, London.
Arnstein, S.R. (1969), 'A Ladder of Citizen Participation', *Journal of the American Institute of Planners*, July, pp. 216–24.

Atkinson, R. and Cope, S. (1997), 'Community Participation and Urban Regeneration in Britain' in P. Hoggett (ed.), *Contested Communities*, Policy Press, Bristol.
Balchin, P. (1996), *Housing Policy – An Introduction*, Routledge, London.
Ball, M. (1983), *Housing Policy and Economic Power*, Methuen, London.
Beale, H. (1983), 'Inequality of Bargaining Power', *Oxford Journal of Legal Studies*, vol. 6, pp. 123–36.
Birks, P. (1986), *An Introduction to the Law of Restitution*, Oxford University Press, Oxford.
Blake, J. (1997), 'All Change at the Top', *Roof*, May/June, 5.
Bright, S. and Gilbert, G. (1995), *Landlord and Tenant – The Nature of Tenancies*, Oxford University Press, Oxford.
Burns, D., Hambleton, R. and Hoggett, P. (1994), *The Politics of Decentralisation*, Macmillan, Hampshire.
Cabinet Office (1991), *Citizen's Charter*, HMSO, London.
Cohen, S. (1985), *Visions of Social Control*, Polity Press, Cambridge.
Cole, I. and Furbey, R. (1994), *The Eclipse of Council Housing*, Routledge, London.
Cowan, D. (1992), 'A Public Dimension to a Private Problem', *Conveyancer*, pp. 285–93.
Cowan, D. (1993), 'Lease Licence Distinction: Changing Emphases', *Conveyancer*, pp. 157–64.
Cowan, D. (1995), Review of Hughes, D. and Lowe, S., *Social Housing Law and Policy*, *Public Law*, pp. 668–9.
Cowan, D. (1997), 'Doing the Government's Work', *Modern Law Review*, Vol. 60, pp. 276–85.
Cowan, D. (1997), *Homelessness: The (In-)Appropriate Applicant*, Dartmouth, Aldershot.
Cowan, D. and Fionda, J. (1993), 'New Angles on Homelessness', *Journal of Social Welfare and Family Law*, pp. 403–16.
Darke, J. and Darke, R. (1979), *Who needs Housing?*, Macmillan, Hampshire.
Department of Environment (1994), *Racial Incidents in Council Housing: The Local Authority Response*, HMSO, London.
Department of Health (1990a), *Caring for People: Community Care in the Next Decade and Beyond*, HMSO, London.
Department of Health (1990b), *The Children Act 1989 Guidance and Regulations*, HMSO, London.
Foley, B. and Evans, K. (1994), 'Tenant Control, Housing Co-operatives and Government Policy', *Local Government Studies*, Vol. 20, pp. 392–411.
Forrest, R. and Murie, A. (1991), *Selling the Welfare State*, Routledge, London.
Furbey, R., Wishart, B. and Grayson, J. (1996), 'Training for Tenants: "Citizens" and the Enterprise Culture', *Housing Studies*, Vol. 11, pp. 251–69.
Garland, D. (1996), 'The Limits of the Sovereign State: Strategies of Crime Control in Contemporary Society', *British Journal of Criminology*, Vol. 36, pp. 445–69.
Hague, G. and Malos, E. (1993a), *Domestic Violence: Action for Change*, New Clarion Press, London.
Hague, G. and Malos, E. (1993b), *Domestic Violence and Housing*, Womens' Aid Federation.
Hague, G., Malos, E. and Dear, W. (1996), *Multi-Agency Work and Domestic Violence*, Policy Press, Bristol.
Hill, J. (1996), 'Intention and the Creation of Proprietary Rights: Are Leases Different?', *Legal Studies*, Vol. 16, pp. 200–18.
Hirschman, A.O. (1970), *Exit, Voice and Loyalty*, CUP, Cambridge, Mass.

Hoggett, P. (ed.) (1997), *Contested Communities*, Policy Press, Bristol.
Hoggett, P. and Hambleton, R. (eds) (1987), *Decentralisation and Democracy*, School for Advanced Urban Studies, University of Bristol, Bristol.
Home Office (1989), *The Response to Racial Attacks and Harassment: Guidance for the Statutory Agencies*, Home Office, London.
Hughes, D. and Lowe, S. (1995), *Social Housing Law and Policy*, Butterworths, London.
Hunter, C. and Miles, J. (1997), 'The Unsettling of Settled Law on "Settled Accommodation"', *Journal of Social Welfare and Family Law*, Vol. 19, pp. 267–90.
James, D.C. (1974), 'Homelessness: Can the Courts Contribute?', *British Journal of Law and Society*, Vol. 1, pp. 195–201.
Kaganas, F., King, M. and Piper, C. (1995), *Legislating for Harmony – Partnership under the Children Act*, Jessica Kingsley, London.
Karn, V., Lickiss, R. and Hughes, D. (1997), *Tenants' Complaints and the Reform of Housing Management*, Dartmouth, Aldershot.
Loughlin, M. (1996), *Legality and Locality*, Oxford University Press, Oxford.
Loveland, I. (1995), *Housing Homeless Persons*, Oxford University Press, Oxford.
Loveland, I. (1996), 'The Status of Children as Applicants under the Homelessness Legislation – Judicial Subversion of Legislative Intent?', *Child and Family Law Quarterly*, Vol. 8, pp. 89–104.
McAuslan, P. (1975), *Land, Law and Planning*, Weidenfeld and Nicolson, London.
McAuslan, P. (1980), *The Ideologies of Planning Law*, Pergamon Press, London.
McCluskey, J. (1994), *Acting in Isolation: An Evaluation of the Effectiveness of the Children Act for Young Homeless People*, CHAR, London.
McCulloch, A. (1997), '"You've Fucked up the Estate and Now You're Carrying a Briefcase"' in P. Hoggett (ed.), *Contested Communities*, Policy Press, Bristol.
McDonald, R. (ed.) (1997), *Youth, "the Underclass", and Social Exclusion*, Routledge, London.
Madge, N. (1996), *Housing Law Casebook*, Legal Action Group, London.
Malpass, P. and Murie, A. (1994), *Housing Policy and Practice*, Macmillan, Hampshire.
Martin, J. (1993), *Modern Equity*, Sweet and Maxwell, London.
Mashaw, J. (1983), *Bureaucratic Justice*, Yale University Press, New Haven.
Means, R. and Smith, R. (1996), *Community Care, Housing and Homelessness – Issues, Obstacles and Innovative Practice*, Policy Press, Bristol.
Morris, J. and Winn, M. (1990), *Housing and Social Inequality*, Hilary Shipman, London.
Mullen, T., Scott, S., Fitzpatrick, S. and Goodlad, R. (1997), *Tenancy Rights and Repossession Rates in Theory and Practice*, Scottish Homes, Edinburgh.
Mullins, D., Niner, P. and Riseborough, M. (1992), *Evaluating Large Scale Voluntary Transfers*, HMSO, London.
Nelkin, D. (1983), *The Limits of Legal Control*, Academic Press, London.
Nixon, J., Smith, Y., Wishart, B. and Hunter, C. (1996), *Housing Cases in County Courts*, Policy Press, Bristol.
Parkinson, J.E. (1993), *Corporate Power and Responsibility*, Clarendon, Oxford.
Partington, M. (1981), 'Collective Bargaining' in A.C. Neal (ed.), *Law and the Weaker Party*, Professional Books, London.
Partington, M. (forthcoming), 'Regulating the Administration of Housing Benefit – the (Ir)Relevance of Judicial Review' in T. Buck (ed.), *Judicial Review and Social Welfare*, Cassells, London.
Partington, M. and Jowell, J. (1979), *Welfare Law and Policy*, Francis Pinter Limited, London.

Pease, K. (1997), 'Crime Prevention' in M. Maguire, R. Morgan and R. Reiner (eds), *The Oxford Handbook of Criminology*, Oxford University Press, Oxford.

Sainsbury, R. (1993), 'Administrative Justice: Discretion and Procedure in Social Security Decision-Making' in K. Hawkins (ed.), *The Uses of Discretion*, Oxford University Press, Oxford.

Sainsbury, R. (1994), 'Internal reviews and the Weakening of Social Security Claimants' Right of Appeal' in G. Richardson and H. Genn (eds), *Administrative Law and Government Action*, Clarendon Press, Oxford.

Sainsbury, R. and Eardley, T. (1991), *Housing Benefit Reviews*, HMSO, London.

Sampson, A., Stubbs, P., Smith, D., Pearson, G. and Blagg, H. (1988), 'Crime, Localities and the Multi-agency Approach', *British Journal of Criminology*, Vol. 28, pp. 479–93.

Sanders, A. and Young, R. (1994), *Criminal Justice*, Butterworths, London.

Stewart, A. (1996), *Rethinking Housing Law*, Sweet and Maxwell, London.

Thomas, P. (1997), 'Socio-Legal Studies: the Case of Disappearing Fleas and Bustards' in Thomas, P.A. (ed.), *Socio-Legal Studies*, Dartmouth, Aldershot.

Woodward, R. (1991), 'Mobilising Opposition: The Campaign against Housing Action Trusts in Tower Hamlets', *Housing Studies*, Vol. 6, pp. 44–56.

1 Bringing Tenants into Decision-Making

ROSE GILROY

Introduction

Over the past two decades, as public funding for housing declined, Conservative central government policies favoured greater involvement in management by tenants and made some local authority funding for estate improvement conditional on their involvement. While in some localities the process has advanced further with the introduction of innovative management partnerships between landlords and tenants, everywhere the tenor has been shifting from viewing tenants as passive recipients of landlord bounty to customers or partners. This movement has not been confined to local authorities. Within the housing association movement, some associations have taken tenants onto management committees and have invested in training tenants to make them more effective participants. Against this background of gradual shifts in culture there have been major urban regeneration mechanisms such as City Challenge and Single Regeneration Budget through which tenants have been renamed as stakeholders and have been called upon to become decision makers alongside local authority officers and business people. This chapter explores the legal, managerial and policy changes that have contributed to this growth in participation and finally considers the potential of tenant participation to be a vehicle for social inclusion.

Defining Participation

The discussion begins with the vexed question: what is tenant participation? In the late '80s alone the following all seemed possible definitions:

> the involvement of tenants in decisions which affect their housing (Community Development Housing Group, 1986);

> It means devolving real control over policy and resources at the local level, leading to programmes which are better targeted and more suited to tenants requirements and indeed resulting in a strengthening of local responsibility and democracy (Lord Ancram, 1986, quoted in Grayson, 1996, p. 55);

> A two-way process involving sharing of information and ideas, where tenants are able to influence decisions and take part in what is happening (IoH/TPAS, 1989, p. 19);

> The councillors defined tenant participation as providing tenants with information about council policy, the majority of staff thought it meant consulting with tenants before decisions were made and the tenants saw it as being involved in decisions about housing policy and the provision of the service (Platt, Piepe and Smyth, 1987, p. 1);

> ... we use the terms consultation and control. Other phrases are trotted out in writings on this subject, such as 'participation' or 'involvement', but it is not always clear what is meant by them. Control is used ... to refer to the actual structural right to take a decision and is a stage beyond consultation (Bartram, 1988, p. 9).

From this we might agree that 'participation' is a slippery and essentially dynamic concept. It raises questions of power, ideology and influence in public policy-making and service delivery. 'Its shifting meaning reflects the varying values and interests held by different stakeholders and the influence which they can wield in establishing their preferred definition' (Furbey, Wishart and Grayson, 1996, p. 251).

The history of tenant participation in the UK is the story of how values have shifted so that we have moved from consultation to control, at least, in terms of what is possible in law and for which good practice models exist. This discussion begins by sketching in the major legal changes that have contributed to the increase in tenants' power.

The Legal Framework for Participation in Management

The interest of government and the housing profession in tenant participation began in the late 1950s. The Central Housing Advisory Committee (1959) advocated the benefits of a better relationship between tenants and local authorities. In 1968 a government circular on council rents recommended greater tenant consultation and in the same year a private member's bill was introduced which proposed setting up an advisory committee with tenant representation in each local authority. Though this failed, many local authorities were responding through the introduction of tenants' charters to the general groundswell of opinion that, as landlords, they should be less remote. This concern may have sprung from the 1974 radical restructuring of local government which created large bureaucracies with all their attendant problems. It may also be that the growing scepticism over the architectural solutions of 'experts' (Ronan Point, the dissatisfactions with tower blocks and the dinosaur estates heavily criticized by Alice Coleman, 1988) created a space where the voice of everyday experience could be heard. It was in the late '70s that the demand for participation came to the fore, mobilizing around the issue of collective and individual rights for tenants. There was pressure from below by tenants who had grown in power through the rent strikes of the '70s. Support for tenant participation from above came as central government sought various ways to promote tenant involvement (Furbey et al., 1996). Motivations were not the same. Kay, Legg and Foot (undated) put together a powerful argument that economic pressure was the catalyst for cross-party support of the introduction of tenants' legal rights. They argue that the recession and the implications for public spending meant that the problems of housing shortage and the quality of existing stock could no longer be addressed by large injections of public money. Giving tenants greater rights, central government felt, would increase their individual sense of responsibility, increase collective satisfaction and improve the effectiveness of housing management. Tenants' rights, then, were to be a panacea in the face of fewer capital schemes, pressure on rents and undoubted, future discontent from tenants.

The National Tenants Organisation, established in 1977, proposed a charter of rights, part of which, in the following year, was set within the Labour government's Housing Bill introduced in 1979. The coming to power of a Conservative government in that year saw most of these rights enshrined in the Housing Act 1980 with the addition of the first of the Conservatives' exit strategies: The Right To Buy. Thereafter, legislation came thick and fast with every piece of housing legislation giving extra rights to tenants and seeking to alter the power relationship between local authority landlords (as opposed to housing association landlords) and their tenants. Figure 1.1 outlines the main points of the legislation as it touched upon tenants' rights. It also attempts to analyse these according to whether they give increased rights; voice (that is a channel or arena for tenants to express dissatisfaction and create change from within); or exit routes (whereby tenants might express their dissatisfaction

Legislation	Details	Voice/exit
Housing Act 1980	introduction of secure tenancies	
	make improvements without permission	
	take lodgers without permission	
	limited succession with permission	
	some sub-letting allowed	
	information about allocations policies	
	consultation with tenancies on an area- and authority-wide basis	voice
	Right to buy	**exit**
Housing and Planning Act 1986	**right for tenants to take over management via co-ops or EMBs**	**exit**
	section 16 grants for tenants' groups to build up to take-over	**exit**
	right for landlords to assign their stock (LSVT)	**landlord initiated exit**
Housing Act 1988	**Tenants Choice**	**exit**
	Housing Act on Trusts	**government initiated exit**
Local Government and Housing Act 1989	annual report with performance indicators given to tenants	voice
Leasehold Reform, Housing and Urban Development Act 1993	**Tenants' Right to Manage**	**exit**
Housing Act 1996	**Right to Acquire for housing association tenants**	**exit**
	introductory tenancies	loss of rights

Figure 1.1 Legislative approach to tenants' involvement in housing management

by moving from one landlord to another) (Hirschmel, 1970; Jensen, 1995). The figure also sets out whether these new options apply to individual tenants or to tenants collectively.

The Housing Act 1980, in the main, gave tenants basic individual rights surrounding their contract with their landlord. However, there was also the right to be consulted on an area and authority wide basis which was important in bringing the landlord into contact with a collective voice on area improvement issues which might affect many households, such as children's play facilities, car parking, and landscaping. However, one of the most important collective concerns for tenants – the level of rents – was specifically excluded from consultation though in practice some local authorities have gone beyond the law and consulted with tenants on rent rises (Bartram, undated).

The main point for which this Act will be remembered is the introduction of the Right to Buy, which can be described as an individual exit route though it is doubtful whether any purchaser has bought because of a desire to escape local authority control (Murie, 1995). While the Act gave a right it did not confer equal access to it for council tenants. Many of those now in the social housing sector lack the waged income to purchase (Gilroy, 1994). Many others live in undesirable property in areas which have become war zones, where the concept of making such a major personal investment would be economically unsound. Clearly such an exit mechanism only works for a particular cohort of tenants. Other routes were needed for those without economic power.

The Housing and Town Planning Act 1986 gave local authority landlords the right to assign the management of their stock to an agent and through this came two different exit routes. The first of these was the opportunity for tenants as a group to become the agent and take over the management of their estates through a tenants' management co-op. A new middle route also emerged at this time called an Estate Management Board, a legally constituted partnership between officers and tenants to jointly decide policy and its implementation on a given estate. This new model acknowledged the desire of many council tenants to stay with the local authority but at the same time to break away from the monolithic bureaucracy (Bell, Bevington and Crossley, 1990, p. 97). For the first time, training and development grants were made available for tenants' groups through section 16 of the Housing and Planning Act 1986 but these were targeted only at those who were looking to take over stock or management of stock. They were not intended to be a general pump priming fund to empower tenants to come together as a collective in a dialogue with their landlord. Central government was interested in encouraging 'exit' in any form but not 'voice'.

The second exit route was the opportunity for local authorities to seek a 'voluntary transfer' of all their housing stock to another landlord, usually a housing association. While local authorities, at first, overlooked this, it became more attractive as central government revealed the main planks of the 1988 Act which many housing providers saw as the hammer which would finally fragment local authority housing. These authorities, concentrated at first in the Conservative held southern district councils, began to set up housing associations and divest their stock to them (known as Large Scale Voluntary Transfer or LSVT). In this process tenants had the right to be consulted and the right to vote for or against the proposed switch. Early ballots saw a largely negative response from tenants but as the financial implications of the 1989 Local Government and Housing Act became apparent, with indications of higher rents and lower investment, more tenants saw the wisdom of moving themselves and their homes into the housing association sector (Cole and Furbey, 1994). It would be fair to say that Conservative central government was taken by surprise (though no doubt delighted) by this windfall increase in their primary housing objective – to dismantle the power of local authorities by reducing the scale of their property holdings. In practice, the mechanism merely operated to transfer housing stock from one bureaucracy to another.

An added impetus to local authorities to talk with their tenants was given by the Housing Act 1988 which created two new exit options: Tenants' Choice and Housing Action Trusts (HATS). Tenants' Choice gave local authority tenants only (not housing associations) the right to choose to replace their landlord with another (such as a housing association or a commercial company) or to become more directly involved in the running of their property by taking on the ownership and management (tenants' cooperative, neighbourhood housing association, tenant companies).

While presenting an exciting range of choices on paper, few tenants' groups felt motivated enough or dissatisfied enough to seek out alternative landlords and only two estates (both in Westminster) went down the route of tenant buy-outs via tenants' companies and neighbourhood housing associations. The dismal lack of response ultimately caused the tenants' choice mechanism to be 'mothballed' after only two years and repealed in the Housing Act 1996.

The announcement that Housing Action Trusts would be set up in estates around the country chosen by central government was greeted, not with apathy, but with great hostility. In these particular neighbourhoods, it was proposed that the local authority stock would be transferred to the ownership of a quango which would independently make decisions about improvement and management. Animosity was fuelled by the arrogance of government ministers who denied tenants the right to vote on the grounds that their understanding of the policy was incomplete. Finally forced to concede a right to vote on the introduction of each HAT, central government was caught unawares by the collective anger and unanimous rejection of the proposals (Woodward, 1991).

These two exit routes were, from government's point of view, failures to hit the target. Tenants did not flock to change their landlord; indeed, they demanded the right to stay. However, from the perspective of the tenants' movement, the major retreat by central government on Housing Action Trusts was a great victory for collective action. A number of tenants' federations, like those in Kirklees and Sandwell, were developed during this period of campaigning, as was the Estate Management Board in Belle Isle in Leeds and hundreds of other tenants' associations and federations. Hulme tenants having successfully defeated the HAT proposal for their estate forced major concessions and changes to the redevelopment and future management of their notorious deck access estate (Grayson, 1996).

In fact the Housing Corporation had foreseen this reaction and had suggested that tenants use the legislation, not as an exit route but as a mechanism for increasing their 'voice'. It is interesting to note that the Housing Corporation imagined that the opportunity for power through Tenants' Choice would galvanize tenants while the true catalyst was their disempowerment through Housing Action Trusts.

> It may be that after you have considered the options under Tenants' Choice you come to the conclusion that you want to stay with the council but want to try to work with them to provide an improved service. If that is what you and your neighbours want, you will need to talk to the council about what sort of improvements they might be prepared to discuss with you. ... As for what improvements to services might be possible, some councils and tenants have set up consultative committees to consult tenants about how their homes are run, and sometimes to give tenants a share in making some kinds of decisions. Others have gone further and set up tenant management co-operatives or estate management boards through which tenants play a direct part in running and managing their own homes. Councils might be prepared to talk to you about one of these special management arrangements. Alternatively, they might be prepared to offer you an improved service – faster repairs, say, or more regular maintenance – while leaving management arrangements as they are. You have nothing to lose by asking them (Housing Corporation, 1988, p. 11).

Since 1988 there has been a more muted approach by central government which has concentrated on increasing accountability to tenants. This mood can be seen in the 1993 Leasehold Reform, Housing and Urban Development

Act which paved the way for Compulsory Competitive Tendering. In drawing up the specification for contracts, local authorities are obliged to involve tenants who may take a bigger role through the Right to Manage, though this is only on those council estates where there are properly constituted tenant management organizations. These can take the form of either Estate Management Boards or tenant management cooperatives in their constitutional make up, but are more like co-ops in that tenants assume direct responsibility for day-to-day management and repairs (Best, 1996). To date no tenants' organization has taken on the right to manage.

It might seem from this brief outline of the legislation, that the path to greater participation is paved with failed legislation and seemingly attractive rights which cannot be implemented or tenants simply do not want. It could also be stated that tenants have found a stronger voice out of their opposition to attempts to force their exit. Central government badly misjudged their mood through their own lack of consultation with tenants or their representative bodies The discussion now turns to consider changes in management and the impact this has had on landlord style and tenant expectation of involvement.

Involvement Through Management Change

Equally important in extending the involvement of tenants, has been the moves to decentralize the management of housing and to push decision-making further down the officer hierarchy. This movement grew from the Priority Estates Projects, a brainchild of the Department of Environment, which advocated bringing management closer (literally and metaphorically) by placing an estate office on a difficult-to-let estate. Central to their vision was the concept of tenant consultation and participation in any improvements and in the management of the estates. It should be noted that the concept of management involvement was confined to finding joint solutions to shared problems of rubbish dumping and antisocial behaviour rather than tenants taking on any major responsibility for management. The PEP model gained widespread publicity in the 1980s for its success in increasing tenants' satisfaction, reducing voids, rent arrears and turnover as well as overall gains in economy and efficiency (Emms, 1990).

This good practice model led to many large authorities (and some national housing associations) creating a network of decentralized offices often beginning on their problematic estates but then spreading the benefits out across their general stock. The main rationale behind this move to decentralization was the growth in concepts such as consumerism and customer care rather than a concern to shift the base of power from town halls to tenants. However, the simple act of bringing officers and tenants closer together, and enabling officers to see the everyday lives of local people, undoubtedly did help promote greater understanding and an opportunity for tenants to make their views known with a better chance of being heard.

While consumerism (a managerial model) has been the most widely used, there are examples of politically driven models (Hoggett and Hambleton, 1987). Collectivism, a model creating a transfer of power, has been seen in Tower Hamlets where council services were decentralized to neighbourhood offices with neighbourhood committees, as well as in the Middlesbrough model where more than 15 years ago local community councils with elected resident representatives were instituted. In these examples, concepts of getting closer to the people, meant empowering frontline staff, ensuring that decision-making was more transparent and increasing the opportunities for tenants to input into decisions. Introducing new opportunities for tenants' voice demanded that the relationship between the housing manager and the resident be redefined. The extent to which it has, is unclear.

A survey of 60 large local authorities in the north of England showed that Chief Housing Officers had identified certain priorities for decentralization: improved service delivery, increased accessibility, improved public relations, increased staff/tenant contact (Cole, Windle and Arnold, 1990). The study demonstrated that devolving decision-making to lower ranks of management was sixth in the list of priorities. Devolving power to tenants was also very low, though 21 of the 60 authorities had tenants on consultative committees and five had tenants on the housing committee. We might conclude that managerial rather than political objectives were paramount. Nevertheless, many in local government saw the political benefits of strengthening local bases of support in the face of central government attack (Gilroy and Williams, 1991).

Involvement Through Estate Regeneration

So far we have looked at two prongs of the fork: the increasing legislative framework around the management of housing and the managerial changes within housing. This section considers the changes brought about by involving tenants in the improvement of their homes and their neighbourhoods.

The 1980 Housing Act gave tenants the right to be consulted on an individual and collective basis about physical improvements such as those brought about by modernization programmes. Forward thinking local authorities were already working in this way but it is through clashes over capital spending that many tenants' groups came into being. One of the country's largest housing associations recalls that one of its most successful and longest standing tenants associations grew out of a low grade revitalization which brought tenants into conflict with the landlord.[1] Once their demands were met, the tenants' group found that they had created a bond among themselves which remains, though energies are now directed at social events. In the same vein, in Calderdale, tenants campaigns over unfit housing created the Tenants' Federation which has grown into a nationally respected body (Grayson, 1996).

In the mid 1980s the Conservative government which had concentrated its legislation on giving voice and exit routes to tenants in management issues began to look at the possibilities of capital programmes as vehicles to give greater power to tenants. This was done not through legislation but through new urban regeneration policies.

The first of these was Estate Action in the mid 1980s. Estate Action was a housing focused vehicle for regeneration which demanded that tenants be party to all proposals about the estate. Cynically we might observe that it was the need to secure funding that promoted many local authorities to make their first serious overtures to tenants rather than any 'hearts and minds commitment' to openness (Wheeler, 1996). Nevertheless, through this programme many initiatives were born including the Bell's Farm agreement discussed below which presents another model for other estates to follow.

Like many other estate action programmes, the primary aims at Bell's Farm in York were to improve property and create real physical change. Unusually, the project pledged itself to the belief that all of these improvements could act as a better catalyst for changing the reputation of the estate if complemented by a flexible approach to community involvement. As Cole and Smith (1996) observe, viewed as an exercise in the physical improvement of dwellings and the environment, the project was successfully executed. A more tantalizing question was the extent to which the physical refurbishment had an ancillary effect on residents by extending their opportunities for longer term involvement, changing the image of the area, and instilling a new sense of self belief and confidence. This raised issues about the sustainability and overall control of the estate. Tenants had worked hard for a long period of time to bring about their changes within the Estate Action programme and there was no great desire to take on the job of estate management. However, very strong support was given by residents to the idea of adapting the notion of 'a customer contract' for the estate as a way of ensuring their continuing influence over service levels and standards. This steered a middle way between a fully fledged form of management – such as a tenant co-operative or the Estate Management Board which would eat up too much tenant time – and simply reverting back to the position before the project by handing total control back to the local authority and other agencies involved in service provision.

The Estate Agreement (part of this is shown as Figure 1.2) was a way of formalizing resident influence over local services through a partnership with local agencies. Such an agreement does not and cannot confront issues of inequality, polarization and poverty which lie behind the problems faced by estates like Bell's Farm. It is not a substitute for basic financial investment in housing, nor a panacea in the growing armoury of regeneration initiatives, but it can help residents secure a degree of continuing influence over local service provision. This is particularly important at the present time when tenants fear that services may become increasingly complex and fragmented in their mode of delivery in the future (Cole and Smith, 1996) .

Following Estate Action, regeneration underwent something of a sea change of emphasis away from housing based programmes to a more holistic approach. Too many regeneration schemes, in the past, had given people central heating which they could not afford to use; car parking spaces when they had no car to park and children's play areas which could not be used because of stranger danger. It was becoming increasingly clear in the 1980s that the problems of particular housing estates had grown beyond the scope of any housing solutions. Certain council estates and large housing association estates had deteriorated from being merely unpopular or difficult to let/difficult to live in neighbourhoods to being places associated with those now termed 'the socially excluded'. Places characterized by failure; property that few people aspired to live in; property which no one aspired to own, lived in by those who could not get employment or credit (Gilroy and Speak, 1998). A recognition of the broad failure to do anything but pathologize the worst estates led to a new institutional focus upon partnership and the process of creating change through which multiple problems might be tackled.

The first of these holistic programmes was the shortlived City Challenge which created two bidding rounds for projects (the first rounds of City Challenge ended their five year life on March 27th 1997). Change was to be achieved by strategies which focused on the barriers people faced in getting a job: namely education, training support, and increasing the local levels of skills and confidence which are essential if the long term jobless can begin to think about finding a job.

STREET AND ENVIRONMENTAL CLEANING

This leaflet tells you how we clean your streets, snickets and open spaces and how with your co-operation we'll keep your estate looking tidy.

It gives you information about

- What we do to keep your streets clean and the gullies clear
- What we do to keep paths clear of weeds
- How you can help to keep the estate clean
- How to let us know if there is a problem
- How we work with the Residents' Association

Aims

We will:

- Keep the estate clean and tidy
- Set high standards for street cleaning, let you know what they are and review them with you
- Improve links between residents, Environmental Services, the Estate Manager and the Estate Worker
- Respond to complaints quickly

What do you clean?

We clean the streets, pavements, snickets, play area, social hall grounds and open spaces in Bell Farm. We also empty gullies.

How well will my street be cleaned?

The cleaning team visits to check all the streets in Bell Farm every Thursday. If they are dirty they will clean them. We use mechanical sweepers or someone with a brush to do the cleaning depending on which is the most appropriate.

If your street has not been cleaned to your satisfaction please let us know by phoning the **Hotline 636000** (answer phone outside normal hours) and we'll sort the problem out. We'll phone you back by the end of the next working day to let you know what action we'll be taking.

Our Cleansing Inspector Noel Sturgeon checks the work each Friday.

We will also carry out a joint inspection with the Estate Worker and residents every month, usually on the last Friday at 10.30am.

How often do you clean the open spaces?

The open spaces like the Beck area and play area are checked every week and cleaned as required.

How often do you clean the gullies?

We clean the gullies twice every year. We'll let you know in advance through your local newsletter FAB NEWS when this work will be carried out.

Bell Farm Estate Agreement

What about weeds on footpaths and snickets?

We will spray all weeds on footpaths, snickets, the Bull Ring and Kirkham Avenue play area a minimum of twice a year between April and October. We only use weed killers that are not harmful to the environment or your health. We will let you know when this work is being done through your local newsletter FAB NEWS.

Who provides the regular skip?

Bell Farm Residents' Association provide skips for rubbish each Wednesday the times and location of the skip is published in your local newsletter Fab News. They are paid for out of the Estate Improvement Budget for the area. If your skip doesn't arrive on time phone the Estate Manager tel. 613161 ext. 1278. **Please don't overfill the skip or dump rubbish after the skip has been removed.**

What information will you provide to the residents association?

We'll provide information to the Residents'Association every quarter about :-

- Standards and levels of street cleaning achieved over the last quarter
- Number of instructions issued to the cleaning team to put things right
- Number of complaints received and use of the Hotline

We will attend the open meetings when requested to answer any queries about our service and performance.

We are also happy to give talks to children at local schools and other groups. We will provide equipment for a "community clean up day," such as plastic sacks, protective gloves and a skip, to the Residents' Association or other voluntary groups each year.

How can I help?

- Please make sure your car is off the street on the usual cleaning days and when we come to clean the gullies
- Please don't drop litter or dump rubbish - use the litter bins and skips
- Please don't overfill the skip
- Join the monthly inspections
- Use the Hotline 636000 if you have a problem

What if I am not happy about the service you provide?

Talk to Noel Sturgeon the Cleansing Inspector when he inspects the area or telephone him on 613161 ext. 1543.

Bell Farm Estate Agreement

Figure 1.2 Extract from Bell's Farm Agreement *Source*: reproduced from Cole and Smith, 1996

As important as the strategies and the measurable outcomes was the building of a new institutional mechanism through which local people in these communities could be heard and their voice have an impact on decisions. One of the problems faced by these communities, judged by central government, was democratic deficit brought about by lack of motivation, poor confidence levels and impenetrable local bureaucracy (Davoudi and Healey, 1995). Far from being viewed as a sector which had brought decision-making out to the people, local government was very much seen as part of the problem. These new mechanisms brought together a unique three-way partnership of local government, the community and the business sector (Davoudi, 1995). The impacts of City Challenge are still unfolding but there seems to be agreement on the real difficulties faced by local government, in particular, in making the cultural changes necessary to give space for the voices of others to be heard. In many cases other partners have had to learn the style and language of local government quickly or be lost along the way. There is little sense of partners consciously looking for new partnership forms which might respond to their unique set of circumstances and desires of communities. By way of defence, it should be noted that the need to move along a time-limited programme does not sit easily with finding new forms of discourse or styles of running meetings and arriving at decisions.

The City Challenge approach may be viewed as a return to concepts of community development which cut across agency boundaries. They take as their starting point not the service deliverer but the problems experienced in everyday life such as crime or lack of jobs (Blackman, 1995). The attraction of such an approach is the recognition that the bureaucratic approach of the past has left many problems unaddressed because they did not fit with the responsibilities of any one department. Another community development feature is that:

> A local authority deliberately stimulates and encourages groups of people to express their needs, supports them in their collective action and helps with their projects and schemes as part of an authority's overall objectives (AMA, 1993, p. 10).

City Challenge presented local people with greater opportunities than ever before of being involved in regeneration but its emphasis on quick decisions and outputs flew in the face of evidence that working with demoralized communities and enabling them to be able to enter the arena of discussion as any other than weak players, takes time. The lack of monitoring of the process of City Challenge (as opposed to the outcomes) also may have served to undermine the idea that government was interested in focusing on the dual aims of sustainable regeneration backed with a sustainable new process.

The latest urban regeneration mechanism is the Single Regeneration Budget which aims to provide a flexible, locally responsive source of support for initiatives to improve local areas and enhance the quality of life of local people by tackling need, stimulating wealth creation and improving competitiveness. This is to be achieved by encouraging local partners to come together to plan a strategic approach to these needs and priorities (van Zjil, 1994, p. 22). As with City Challenge before it, there is a feeling that the strong emphasis on the involvement of local people may only be a top down gesture as communities are brought into the process too late to be anything more than a rubber stamp for major projects and an influence on minor matters.

Tenants Take Over?

Social housing tenants in this country have been offered the right to buy their dwellings. For those unable or unwilling to purchase, other exit mechanisms have been created. Indeed the inventiveness of central government in trying to lure tenants away from local authorities has been startling. These schemes have focused on helping tenants take over their estates, if not as owners, then at least as managers or joint managers.

Tenants on the poorest estates in Britain are now presented with the added opportunities to have their say through new partnership mechanisms for regeneration. For those without employment or hope of it this might be seen as a useful road to structuring time and finding a sense of purpose – a kind of active citizenship in lieu of economic opportunities. But these are people whose energies are often eaten up with the daily struggle of making ends meet and keeping their children out of crime. Housing managers in the north east talk of council estates which are full of unemployed people who have no sense of purpose; of places where the spirit is gone (Gilroy and Williams, 1991). Evidence from one social housing estate in Newcastle (Table 1.1) demonstrates the drain of economic power.

The country's largest housing association with 25,000 properties in management has only eight per cent of tenants who are not eligible for some welfare benefit. However, figures alone, do not capture the despair of modern times:

> The world economy in its present form, has, as one of its major products marginal

people – the unemployed, the under employed, the disenfranchised – people who lack ... a sense of belonging and having a recognised role (Harman, 1993, p. 1069).

Table 1.1 Social residualization of a Newcastle council estate: socioeconomic group of the economically active population

	1981 (%)	1986(%)	1991(%)
Professional/managerial	27	3	2
Junior non manual	33	30	15
Skilled manual	20	32	26
Semi/unskilled manual	20	35	57

Source: Blackman, 1995, p. 155

This draining away of wealth and identity to be replaced with messages of failure raises many impediments to landlords wishing to promote tenants' voices whether for the need to gear in funding or simply the desire to stop the rot by building some strength inside the community. Simply getting tenants groups together is difficult as those who recognize, within themselves, gifts of being able to mobilize others ask why they should use these skills for the benefit of the community but for no wages. An alternative would be to stand for office as a councillor and be paid at least an attendance allowance. Research into a community development trust in Newcastle (Wood et al., 1995; Gilroy, 1996) revealed that it was only older people who would take on the role of community director and spend their time in decision making. Those of working age were hungry for jobs and saw very limited worth in community work when it was not valued by exchanging time and labour for money. Those who advocate a housing plus and holistic approach to the problems of particular estates must acknowledge that the degree of difficulty in implementing these strategies increases all the time. It may be that the financial base of tenant and citizen organizations needs radical restructuring to enable them to pay 'reasonable honoraria' to their leaders for their time-consuming efforts (Arnstein, 1969, p. 221). It may be that a radical shift in values is needed so that we have a new society which does not hang identity on paid work but allows other roles to develop and be valued. It may be that paid citizenship is the way forward so that people may take on community activist roles but with financial rewards we have come to see as synonymous with being valued.

However, an alternative perspective raises doubts about this thinking, at least in respect of housing:

> Do these arrangements just siphon us off from more appropriate activities? We're concerned with how our lives can be improved. Should we be getting involved in services at all? In many cases they are the wrong kind of response to our needs (Beresford and Croft, 1993, p. 143–4).

A case of the powerful controlling the protests of the powerless. The issue is not just confined to the UK. In the US there is also a move to increase the involvement of tenants with again the ultimate goal that tenants will take over the ownership, or at least the management, of their dwellings. As in this country, many researchers are sceptical of this new movement and believe that resident management is a way of diverting attention from the serious state of public housing and from the responsibility of government to provide decent housing for the poor (Peterman, 1996). Others in the US argue that management is a technical task best left to professionals and that residents would take greater benefit from focusing their energies on personal growth issues or on important community concerns such as education, crime and programmes for young people (Peterman and Young, 1991).

Writing now in a time of new central government it is unclear in what direction housing policy may develop. de Groot, writing in 1992, suggested that Labour local authorities faced a fundamental problem under Conservative control:

> To be able to deliver urban regeneration policies in the last decade of the century it is necessary to address the complex of 'people issues'. Housing, health, community safety, education and above all community involvement are now central to the language of regeneration. The fly in the ointment for Labour local authorities has been that the community involvement has to be in the image of the government view of community and individualistic consumer choice (p. 205).

It may be that there will be a new emphasis on collective rights and collective voice given weight through legislation and/or funding. It is possible that tenants will be encouraged to take on greater responsibility backed by training and that they will be encouraged to consider this a step on the road to waged work.

Whatever shape tenant participation might take, it has become clear from the last two decades that paying attention to the process of involvement is as critical as aiming to a stated outcome:

> Democracy articulated as process and structure is crucial. The key questions are: what structures and procedures exist to facilitate people's involvement in

decisions, provide them with adequate information and ensure the quality and equity of decisions? (Hill, 1994, p. 249).

The real challenge is that we cannot 'bolt on' citizen involvement. The injection of involvement will really only be successful if it is recognized that the whole process will change whether it is planned to change or not (MacAuslan, 1975, p. 97). To create real opportunities for empowerment, those in control need the confidence and humility to manage the process. This demands greater knowledge of the lives and experiences of people in marginalized communities. It also demands a new skill base which enables housing managers and others in governance to help communities build a voice (Wilson, 1997). However, without more funding for social housing, all these endeavours may be viewed as sops. For the future we need participative governance in our housing alongside, not instead of, funding and the political will to improve the quality of social housing.

Note

1 Author's own research involving discussions with providers of social housing in the north east of England.

Bibliography

Arnstein, S. (1969), 'A Ladder of Citizen Participation', *Journal of the American Institute of Planning*, July, pp. 216–224.

Association of Metropolitan Authorities (1993), *Local Authorities and Community Development: A Strategic Opportunity for the 1990s*, Association of Metropolitan Authorities, London.

Bartram, M. (undated), *Consulting tenants – Council Initiatives in the late 1980s*, Community Rights Project, London.

Bell, T., Bevington, P. and Crossley, R. (1990), 'Estate Management Boards – a Way Forward for Tenants', *Housing Review*, Vol. 39, 4, pp. 95–8.

Beresford, P. and Croft, S. (1993), *Citizen Involvement: a Practical Guide for Change*, Macmillan, Basingstoke.

Best, R. (1996), 'Successes, Failures and Prospects for Public Housing Policy in the United Kingdom', *Housing Policy Debate*, Vol. 7, 3, pp. 535–62.

Blackman, T. (1995), *Urban Policy in Practice*, London, Routledge.

Cole, I. and Furbey, R. (1994), *The Eclipse of Council Housing*, Routledge, London.

Cole, I. and Smith, Y. (1996), *From Estate Action to Estate Agreement*, The Policy Press for Joseph Rowntree Foundation, Bristol.

Cole, I., Windle, K. and Arnold, P. (1990), *Understanding Decentralisation*, Sheffield City Polytechnic, Sheffield.

Coleman, A. (1988), *Utopia on Trial*, Hilary Shipman, London.

Community Development Housing Group (1986), *But will it fly, Mr Wright?*, TPAS, Glasgow.

Davoudi, S. (1995), 'City Challenge: the Three Way Partnership', *Planning, Practice and Research*, Vol. 10, 3–4, pp. 333–44.

Davoudi, S. and Healey, P. (1995), 'City Challenge: Sustainable Process or Temporary Gesture', *Environment and Planning C: Government and Policy*, Vol. 13, pp. 79–95.

de Groot, L. (1992), 'City Challenge: Competing in the Urban Regeneration Game', *Local Economy*, Vol. 7, 3, pp. 196–209.

Emms, P. (1990), *Social Housing: A European Dilemma?*, School for Advanced Urban Studies, Bristol.

Furbey, R., Wishart, B. and Grayson, J. (1996), 'Training for Tenants: Citizens and the Enterprise Culture', *Housing Studies*, Vol. 11, 2, pp. 251–69.

Gilroy, R. (1994), 'Women and Owner Occupation in Britain: First the Prince and then the Palace?' in R. Gilroy and R. Woods (eds), *Housing Women*, Routledge, London.

Gilroy, R. (1996), 'Building Routes to Power: Lessons from Cruddas Park', *Local Economy*, Vol. 11, 3, November, pp. 248–58.

Gilroy, R. and Speak, S. (1998), 'Barriers, Boxes and Catapults: Social Exclusion and Everyday Life' in A. Madanipour, G. Cars and J. Allen (eds), *Social Exclusion in European Cities: Processes, Experiences and Responses*, Jessica Kingsley, London.

Gilroy, R. and Williams, R. (1991), 'Community Involvement in Neighbourhood Regeneration: A British Perspective' in R. Altermann and G. Cars (eds), *Neighbourhood Regeneration: an International Evaluation*, Mansell, London.

Grayson, J. (1996), *Opening the Window*, TPAS and Northern College, Salford.

Harman, W. (1993), 'Rethinking the Central Institutions of Modern Society: Science and Business', *Futures*, pp. 1063–70.

Hill, D. (1994), *Citizens and Cities: Urban Policy in the 1990s*, Harvester Wheatsheaf, London.

Hirschmel, A. (1970), *Exit, Voice and Loyalty*, Harvard University Press, Cambridge, Mass.

Hoggett, P. and Hambleton, R. (1987), *Decentralisation and Democracy: Localising Public Services*, Occasional Paper 28, School of Advanced Urban Studies, Bristol.

Housing Corporation (1988), *Tenants' Choice: The Choice is Yours*, The Housing Corporation, London.

Institute of Housing and Tenants Participation Advisory Service (1989), *Tenant Participation in Housing Management*, IoH and TPAS, Coventry/Salford.

Jensen, L. (1995), 'Challenges to Citizenship', *Scandinavian Housing and Planning Research*, Vol. 12, pp. 177–94.

Kay, A., Legg, C. and Foot, J. (undated), *The 1980 Tenants Rights in Practice*, The Housing Research Group, City University, London.

MacAuslan, P. (1975), *Land, Law and Planning*, Weidenfield and Nicolson, London.

Murie, A. (1995), 'Tenants' Choices: Sales, Transfers and Trusts' in R. Pinto (ed.), *Developments in Housing Management and Ownership*, Manchester University Press, Manchester.

Peterman, W. (1996), 'The Meanings of Resident Empowerment: Why just about Everybody Thinks it's a Good Idea and What it has to do with resident Management', *Housing Policy Debate*, Vol. 7, 3, pp. 473–90.

Peterman, W. and Young, M. (1991), *Alternatives to Conventional Public Housing Management*, Voorhees Centre for Neighbourhood and Community Improvement, University of Illinois at Chicago.

Platt, S., Piepe, R. and Smyth, J. (1987), *Heard or Ignored*, National Federation of Housing Associations, London.

van Zjil, V. (1994), 'Update on Single Regeneration Budget', *Housing Association Weekly*, 15 July.

Wheeler, R. (1996), 'Empowerment and Citizenship', *Local Government Policy Making*, Vol. 22, 4, pp. 3–8.

Wilson, P. (1997), 'Building Social Capital: A Learning Agenda for the Twenty-first Century', *Urban Studies*, Vol. 34, 5– 6, pp. 745–60.

Woodward, R. (1991), 'Mobilising Opposition: the Campaign against Housing Action Trusts in Tower Hamlets', *Housing Studies*, Vol. 6, 1, pp. 44–56.

2 Tenant Participation in Contracting for Housing Management Services: A Case Study

PETER VINCENT-JONES AND ANDREW HARRIES

Introduction

As compulsory competitive tendering (CCT) is abolished and replaced with a less prescriptive duty on the part of local authorities to demonstrate 'best value' in the provision of public services,[1] local authorities are considering how far competitive tendering and associated contractual practices should be voluntarily retained. From a socio-legal perspective, the interest in housing management CCT lies in the potential of contracting to improve the quality of both the service and the relationships involved in its provision.[2] Where services are to be provided by the authority's own workforce, the question for the future is whether *voluntary* contracting has any special contribution to make as compared with other initiatives that do not depend on any such quasi-legal arrangement between the authority as client and the internal provider.[3]

In this paper we examine, with reference to a case study of internal provision of housing management services in a metropolitan authority in the north of England, the impact of contractual governance with particular regard to the tenant interests of collective participation, accountability, quality, and redress for poor performance. The main argument developed on the basis of the case study evidence is that contracting may, in appropriate circumstances, both be compatible with and help facilitate tenant participation and inclusion in the housing management process.

CCT and Contracting for Housing Management Services

The effect of competitive tendering, whether compulsory or voluntary, is to create a contractual relationship between local authority client and the service provider. Regardless of whether the winning bidder is the internal direct service organization (DSO) or an external contractor, the relationship is 'contractual' (Walsh and Davis, 1993).[4] The rights and responsibilities of the parties are set out in contract documentation, which typically specifies the task and provides for variation, monitoring, defaults, remedies, liquidated damages, disputes, and rectification for poor performance. The empirical evidence of CCT for blue collar services confirms that the contract tends to form a significant basis for the *ex post* management and adjustment of the relationship (Vincent-Jones and Harries, 1996a, 1996b). An internal DSO contract tends in practice to be observed and enforced by the parties as if it were legally binding. The absence of separate legal personality on the part of the provider and hence of *legal* enforceability makes no difference in this connection. There is usually no contractual relationship of any kind in respect of CCT services, however, between client/contractor and external consumer. As the public consumer is not privy to the CCT contract, no contractual rights are acquired. Instead, the relationships are legally governed mainly by public law.

The Secretary of State determined by statutory instrument in 1994 the housing management functions[5] that could only be carried out by local authorities provided they had previously been subject to competitive tendering.[6] The purpose of compulsory competition is to ensure, for the substantial number of social tenants who remain within the public sector and who are thereby insulated from full market forces, that quasi-market efficiencies are obtained through 'quasi-privatization' of management functions (Hughes and Lowe, 1995, p. 43). Legislation requires tenants to be consulted in the making and managing of CCT housing management contracts.[7] Those tenants likely to be affected must be informed of proposed standards and terms, and of the identities of managers. The views of such tenants must be taken into account before the finalization of any contract. Local authorities are further required to make appropriate arrangements for tenants to make known their views on the conformity of service standards to contractual specifications, and to take into account such views prior to decisions on enforcement of standards.[8]

The legal and quasi-legal relationships involved in 'internal' contracting for housing management services are illustrated in Figure 2.1. Contracts (which remain legally unenforceable) between local authority clients and DSOs must

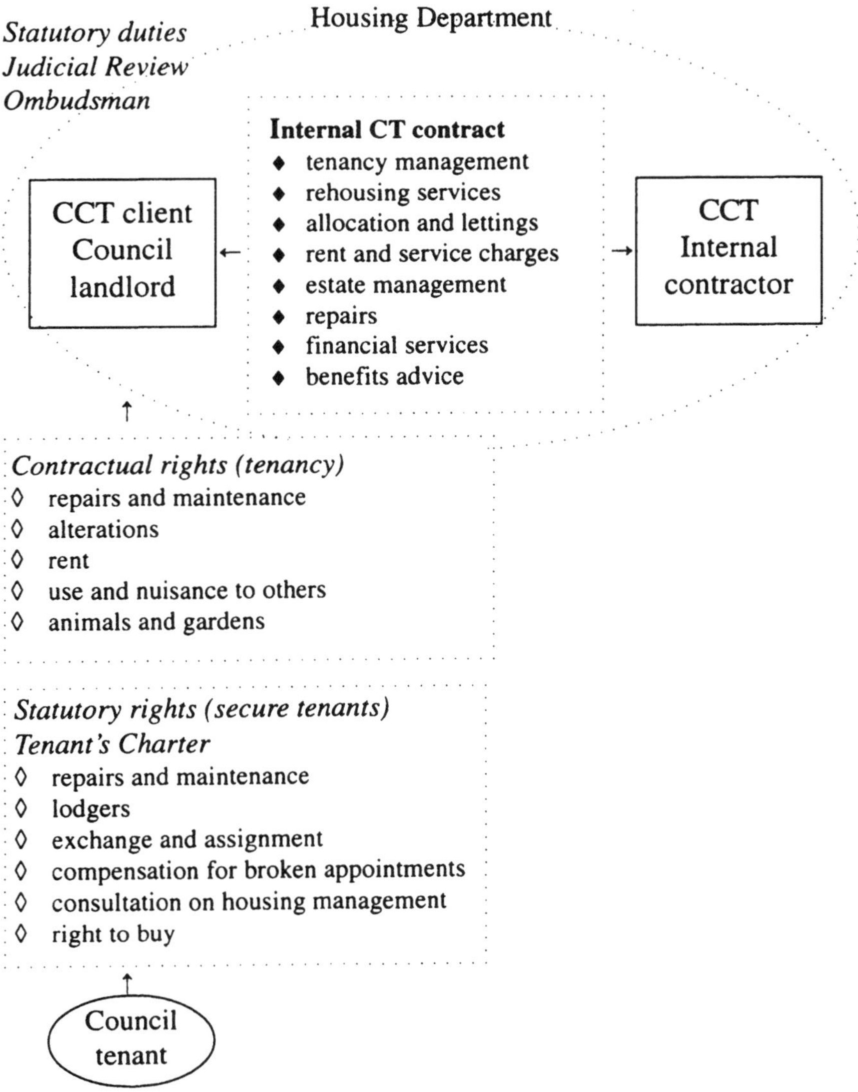

Figure 2.1 Compulsory competitive tendering for Housing Management Services in Northern Metropolitan – legal and quasi-legal relationships

cover the defined activities, which are: housing applications and allocations; assignments of tenancies; informing tenants of terms of tenancies and enforcement of such terms; collecting rents and service charges; provisions for negotiating and payment of arrears; arrangements for the vacating of dwellings at the end of tenancies; inspecting vacant properties and assessing works required before re-letting, and ensuring the work is carried out and reports made; taking steps to secure voids against vandalism and trespass; taking steps to remove unlawful occupiers; assessing the condition and maintenance requirements of common parts of property; assessing repair queries and ensuring the carrying out of relevant works; carrying out surveys of the condition of property and checking occupation; assessing compensation issues under 'right to repair' legislation; operating reception and security services provided at the entrance to local authority housing; taking action to control disturbances; and dealing with neighbour disputes and with dispute resolution agencies.[9] Whilst not privy to the CCT contract, the tenant enjoys contractual rights exercisable against the local authority landlord through the tenancy agreement, typically covering repairs and maintenance, rent, nuisance, and general conditions of use. The tenant also enjoys statutory 'tenant's charter' rights under the Housing Act 1985 concerning repairs and improvements, lodgers, exchange and assignments, compensation for broken appointments, the 'right to buy', and consultation on housing management issues; under these and other public law provisions the tenant may have legal redress through judicial review, ombudsman and complaints systems.[10]

If it is clear that the CCT contract cannot be legally enforced by the tenant, legislation nevertheless gives tenants a significant potential role in housing management at various stages in the contracting process. In order to assess the effectiveness of the new system of contractual governance, it is necessary first of all to identify the various dimensions of the tenant interest in housing management.

The Tenant Interest in Housing Management

One of the main aims of Conservative policies over the past sixteen years has been to facilitate exit for both council landlords and their tenants from the public into the private sector. The free market approach to housing problems sees the satisfaction of needs ideally resulting from a myriad of privatized purchasing choices and decisions (Hoggett, 1990, p. 46; Barnes and Prior, 1995; 1996). However, given the relative failure of the right to buy, Housing

Action Trust and Large Scale Voluntary Transfer schemes to achieve a significant reduction in the public sector's role in the provision of social housing, the attempt to further the consumer interest of council tenants has involved the imposition of proxies for market forces, for example through CCT, satisfaction surveys, and performance management and appraisal schemes (Hoggett, 1996; Clapham and Satsangi, 1992; Kemp, 1995; generally see Hirschman, 1970). But it remains doubtful whether this combination of consumer voice, legal rights and compulsory competition does justice to the full range of the tenant interest in social housing. With specific regard to housing management, four dimensions of this interest may be distinguished: collective participation and political voice; accountability and trust; quality and participation in service specification and provision; and individual redress and remedies for poor performance.

Collective Participation and Political Voice

Public service users have a dual identity, as both consumers of particular services and citizens with a general interest in public service provision (Lewis, 1996, p. 175; Barnes and Prior, 1996, p. 54). As citizens, 'users have a voice in decision-making about the production of public services as well as their consumption' (ibid.). The fundamental problem with consumerism in the context of public services is the supposition of a relatively passive and reactive consumer role. A narrowly conceived 'supermarket' view (Clapham and Satsangi, 1992) of consumption downplays the political nature of citizenship, and the role of the citizen in the process of government (Prior, Stewart and Walsh, 1995; Docherty, 1993). Unlike more mundane services such as buildings cleaning and refuse collection, housing management is likely to be particularly entwined with the core local democratic values (decent housing for all, respect for cultural diversity, combating discrimination and disadvantage) which the council may have been elected to serve. As will be seen below, this element is well captured in the DSO's central commitment, in its Quality Plan for housing management in Northern Metropolitan, to 'a public service within a local democracy'. The idea of collective voice, however, may be taken to extend beyond involvement in the local electoral process to include tenant input in local housing policy via Tenants' Associations and other consultative and participatory fora.

Accountability and Trust

Tenants have a strong interest also in the accountability of the council landlord and the client and contractor parties directly involved in housing management provision. Although there are various mechanisms for the accountability of social landlords (Hughes and Lowe, 1995, pp. 149–65), these remain of a very general nature from the viewpoint of the specific needs of tenants in respect of housing management. Many public service managers may concede that the introduction of contracting has improved accountability *within* the organization, but accountability to the public is more problematic (Deakin and Walsh, 1996, p. 42). The last 25 years have seen the displacement of traditional electoral accountability by a more managerialist vision (Stoker, 1996), with an increased emphasis on financial accounting (Seal and Vincent-Jones, 1997). The greater the involvement of tenants in the contracting process, the more likely there is to be proper client/contractor accountability. Closely connected with accountability in practice is likely to be the phenomenon of tenant trust. Barnes and Prior (1996, p. 54, emphasis supplied) have argued that:

> Public welfare services function both at an individual level (in the face to face interactions between providers and users through which services are produced and consumed) and a collective level (in the aggregate social outcomes that are the outcomes of public services and in which people have an interest as citizens). *Institutions should be generating trust at both levels.*

The institutional framework for public trust has components of dialogue, competence, participation, openness, accountability, and negotiation (p. 55). These components of trust might be investigated in relation to housing management.

Quality and Participation in Service Specification and Provision

If service efficiency denotes the rate at which inputs/resources are converted into outputs, service effectiveness concerns the extent to which objectives are achieved. Such objectives need to be assessed, and effectiveness evaluated, from the viewpoint of the consumer as well as the service producer (Kemp, 1995, p. 783). As has already been indicated, the private sector model of the consumer tends to be one in which (as in manufacturing) production occurs independently of consumer input. In the case of housing management and other public services, however, an important dimension of quality might be the extent of participation or *co-production* (Llewellyn and Saunders, 1996). Whether the ideal form of management envisaged by the New Right is a company reporting to and seeking the views of tenants who are seen as 'shareholders', or an authority 'retailer' offering complaints mechanisms to tenant consumers (Hughes and Lowe, 1995, p. 163), the consumer role remains essentially passive or reactive. Some commentators have argued that the delivery of a high quality housing management service is dependent upon tenant participation and involvement (MacGilp, 1995, p. 34); 'greater customer involvement produces better services' (Walker and Williams, 1995, p. 490). Many housing experts see CCT as a possible means of improving service quality (Docherty, 1993), and as providing mechanisms for going beyond the tenant participation initiatives of the 1980s (Parkin, 1994). Whilst the 'tenant's charter' under the Housing Act 1985 provides a minimum statutory framework of individual rights to information and consultation, local authorities have in practice had considerable discretion in the arrangements they may make for tenant representation, with the result that the overall impact of the charter appears to have been limited (Loveland, 1992; Hughes and Lowe, 1995, p. 163). Some authorities, however, have long histories of tenant participation initiatives aimed at improving service quality, voluntarily adopted as part of broader decentralization programmes (Goodlad, 1994). If CCT may lead to increased efficiency through clearer and better contractual specification, it also offers the prospect of improved quality where tenants have been involved in determining service standards and play a part also in management of the service. Interpersonal trust between service users and providers should be high where such conditions obtain.

Redress and Remedies for Poor Performance

The most individual aspect of the tenant interest in housing management concerns the direct impact of service delivery on particular persons or households, and is seen especially clearly in cases of poor contractor performance. Here effectiveness may be judged according to the speed and adequacy with which service problems are addressed or rectified. Where such redress is not possible and/or where the tenant's interest has been affected in such a way that financial compensation is appropriate, then the question of remedies also needs to be considered.

The main research question addressed in the case study of housing management in Northern Metropolitan is whether the contracting mechanism has anything specific to contribute to the satisfaction of these tenant interests, over and above what has already been achieved by traditional and more recent tenant participation schemes. In answering this question, it will be argued that the impact of the new contractual arrangements cannot properly be evaluated other than in the historical context of the development of housing management services within this authority.

Housing Management in Northern Metropolitan Pre-CCT

Northern Metropolitan is a metropolitan city council in the north of England serving a population of over half a million people. For all but two of the last 50 years the council has been Labour-controlled and strongly committed to socialist policies. The number of council tenancies has diminished from a peak of over 90,000 to around 72,000 in 1997. Two distinct periods involving different styles of housing management may be identified in the postwar years prior to the introduction of CCT. From the 1950s until the 1980s highly centralized services were provided within a paternalist ethos. A period of radical restructuring involving greater tenant participation ('going local') began in the early/mid 1980s lasting up to the onset of CCT.

The Paternalist Legacy: 1950 to early 1980s

The standard model for the organization and delivery of housing management services immediately after the second world war was the large, bureaucratic, centralized housing department. In a period of mass council house building, this model was considered the most effective arrangement for administering new developments and managing the large number of new homes. As expansion levelled off and waiting lists fell, tenants became more critical of the support their landlord was providing. The poor organization and coordination of the housing maintenance function in the Direct Works Department became apparent. Housing repairs were an early source of dissatisfaction, with the link between problem, enquiry, response, and quality being obviously visible to increasingly demanding and knowledgeable tenants. Centralized organization was inefficient as well as ineffective, with virtually no record keeping, a haphazard system of allocation of lettings, and an absence of tenant involvement in the design of new homes. Whilst confidence in the housing management service was generally low, tenants were powerless to effect improvements, due to their lack of representation in policy and decision-making processes, and to impenetrable bureaucracy.

The problems identified in Northern Metropolitan in this period were far from unique. Against the background of general tenant dissatisfaction, the incoming Conservative administration in 1979 introduced legislation placing council tenancies on a statutory basis and allowing tenants more control over their housing environment. The Local Government Planning and Land Act 1980 forced works departments to compete against the private sector. Direct Labour Organizations (DLOs) formed in consequence of CCT were compelled to operate more efficiently. Further incentives for improvement in internal service delivery were provided by the Housing and Building Control Act 1984, which allowed tenants to carry out their own repairs and claim the cost back from the council.

'Going Local': Early 1980–90s

The combination of poor service organization, tenant dissatisfaction, declining resources, and the introduction of CCT for 'works' and 'maintenance' functions made policy change inevitable in Northern Metropolitan. Rather than 'contract out' or privatize the housing management service, as many Conservative authorities had done, the decision was made to improve existing public service provision by decentralization or 'going local'. This strategy would save local jobs at a time of increasing unemployment in heavy industry at the same time as rescuing the discredited housing management service. 'Going local' was a pragmatic policy designed to achieve the *functional* goal of improving the 'production' efficiency of existing services, and the *political* goal of increasing local democracy through greater tenant involvement and participation.

In 1982 a five year improvement plan was developed requiring radical changes in the organization of the Works Department. Of equal importance, the housing management service was completely restructured to increase tenant participation in the decision-making process. Greater localization was the key to both changes. Over a three-year period, the management and delivery of housing services were decentralized from the central Housing Department to fifteen housing areas. The Area Office was now the single contact point in the locality for all operational tenant services such as rent collection, arrears, advice, general enquiries, caretaking, rehousing, waiting lists, new allocations, and repairs and maintenance. Strategic services (which provided the framework for operational services) were retained within the central Housing Department and therefore remained subject to corporate control.[11] Internal efficiency was increased through tighter control of resources and improved responsiveness, whilst the tenant as 'consumer' was saved time and expense in queuing and travelling to the town hall to resolve problems and pay rent. Organization through the 15 area offices allowed better coordination with the Works Department and the development of more integrated procedures for repairs and rehousing. Local organization, together with new information technology, also enabled tenants to be better informed and allowed area managers to develop closer relationships with particular tenants and their problems. Area managers were given their own devolved budgets and had considerable autonomy in determining spending priorities. With financial pressures on the council reaching crisis proportions in the 1990s, one method of controlling costs was to make each area manager a cost-centre for their budget. The emphasis now was on instilling financial discipline in area management practice so that overspends could be deducted from the next year's budget.

Alongside improvements in the production of housing management services, a city-wide consultation forum was implemented through the creation of 15 Area Housing Committees having bimonthly meetings. One of the purposes of such consultation, which also involved 'service improvement groups' and a strengthened Tenants' Association network, was to improve existing decision-making and planning processes by allowing tenants to input their on-the-ground expertise. As part of the downward shift in management and participation, a two pence in the pound levy on rents was used to fund and so encourage stronger, more active 'consumer' voice at local level. This could then be fed into the mainstream policy planning and committee systems of the authority. Tenants' views were valued because they helped in the formation of effective policy, so ensuring value-for-money in the eyes of the Audit Commission and rent-paying tenants. In conjunction with the establishment of a Design and Building Services Department, the council was able to make use of tenant inputs in designing a better standard of council housing. Under the new regime, major building and maintenance programmes were discussed with tenants' representatives through project groups based at Area Committee level. For the first time, tenants were involved in planning and implementing housing improvements, and in determining service levels and quality. Many of the capital development and refurbishment projects carried out at this time were highly acclaimed. The more effective dialogue between officers, tenants and councillors led to improved policy development. After the first five years there was general agreement, despite much initial hostility and suspicion, that councillors, officers and tenants had together through the 'local approach to housing' achieved significant improvements in housing provision and management.

Housing Management in Northern Metropolitan Under CCT

The organization of housing management services prior to the introduction of CCT was already decentralized with a clear differentiation of roles, functions and budgets. Tenants' groups had been reorganized so their views contributed to effective service delivery. The introduction of CCT provided a challenge to the 'partnership' that had developed between tenants and the local authority. The following sections describe Northern Metropolitan's response to this challenge and reveal how new contracting practices were used both to enhance the quality of the existing service and to extend tenant democracy and participation. After a brief explanation of how client and contractor functions were separated for CCT, it will be shown how the involvement of tenants in contract specification, tender evaluation, and contract monitoring provided the foundation for cooperative relationships post-award.

The Organization of Client-Contractor Relationships

Four key principles underlay the organization of client-provider relations for CCT. First, the structure had to be resilient to long-term changes in policy and be flexible enough to deliver the council's corporate strategy on staffing and resources for the foreseeable future. Second, the structure had to anticipate the (at this stage) unknown outcome of the competitive tendering process; this meant planning for a DSO win, but building in economies of scale so the loss of smaller contracts could be accommodated if necessary. Third, the structure had to maintain clear lines of responsibility through differentiation of client and contractor functions; this effectively ruled out 'twin-hatted' roles except at Director or Assistant Director level. Finally, the structure had to facilitate cooperative relations between client and contractor, whether external provider or internal DSO.

In mid-1993, two years ahead of the full implementation of CCT, Assistant Directors were allocated separate responsibilities for 'client' and 'provider' functions. Despite the differentiation of roles, the emphasis throughout the planning process was on the contractor arm working in close conjunction with the client side in developing the contract specification, performance indicators, monitoring systems, and service standards. Although this was part of the long planning cycle required for CCT, it also prepared staff for the inevitability of change. Since the Housing Department lacked contracting expertise and experience, a small team under a new assistant director was formed to facilitate cooperation between client and provider in the contract planning process.[12] After consideration of two alternative options for client and contractor organization, one involving a minimalist or 'soft' split and the other involving a radical or 'hard' split, a compromise solution was eventually adopted. Client and contractor functions were allocated to separate divisions, but these remained within the Housing Department. This allowed overall departmental control and harmonization of working practices, and minimized disruption by maintaining interchangeable career paths and a strong common identity and purpose. The choice of a relatively 'soft' separation was influenced by the negative experience of the 'hard' client-contractor split that had been adopted for building cleaning (Vincent-Jones and Harries, 1996a; 1996b). For the year prior to contract letting, client and contractor officers worked together on a 'shadow' basis implementing the proposed contract specification to gain monitoring and general management experience. This reduced the perceived threat of CCT and helped build trust in preparation for competitive tendering, for which the DSO contractor was formally designated Northern Metropolitan Housing Management Services (HMS).

The newly constituted HMS was now required to meet a 'break-even'[13] financial target and to manage its own budgets for building maintenance, sheltered schemes, laundries, telephones, community rooms, repairs at the Area Office, office cleaning, decorating grants to tenants, discretionary payments, grounds maintenance, and disinfestation. Monthly accounts were now submitted to the client, the claim for payment being based on the management fee agreed in the tender for each property for which services were provided. HMS was also required to meet specified performance standards for activities such as letting, arrears and rent collecting, with the client deducting payment for default wherever the standards were not achieved.[14] The overall effect of client-contractor organization following CCT has been to clarify roles and responsibilities and to create a more transparent relationship between payment and performance. Under the pre-CCT regime, budgets had been devolved to area managers but the level of finance and policy goals were very much a central function. Costing was not accurate because the Housing Department as a whole would always balance its overall budget at the end of the financial year. Under CCT, responsibility for cost control has been delegated to HMS, and there are clearer financial links between activities, activity costs, and costed output and standards. This has been beneficial for staff, councillors and tenants, enabling financial crises such as the budget deficit to be managed more effectively.

Planning the Contract

The Area Committee structure developed in the 1980s was unable to meet the greater demands of the new statutorily defined tenant roles of tender evaluation, contract planning and monitoring under CCT. A network of groups and committees was therefore established to increase tenant involvement. In 1991 a city-wide forum was set up, together with a Contract Working Party comprising tenants, officers, and voluntary-sector workers. The working party included representatives from Area Contract Groups (based on housing committee areas) where tenants' views were made known and amendments to proposals made before being voted on at Area Committee level. The contract specification was initially drafted under the auspices of the six Area Contract Groups, each examining one of the DoE defined housing management activities. The brief was simple: define what you currently do, how often you do it, and how you do it. The involvement of all staff, from the most senior managers to the lowest paid manual workers, helped to build client-contractor trust and to create a sense of communal 'ownership' of the contract standard. Once a draft was agreed it was sent to all Area Committees where special one-day meetings were arranged to discuss the document. In all, some 1000 tenant comments were generated and around 75 per cent of these were directly incorporated in the final specification (the remaining 25 per cent being covered by the others, or substantially rewritten, or ruled out on the grounds of legality). In this way trust was engendered between provider and tenant, in addition to that already established between client and provider.

As well as necessitating new participation fora, CCT required training and the development of new skills to enable tenants to make informed decisions at various stages of the contracting process, eight sessions of three training workshops being provided.. Here as elsewhere, Northern Metropolitan adopted a maximalist approach for the implementation of DoE guidance. Information was disseminated through a number of media including a CCT Update sent quarterly to all tenants with their rent statements. Displays were produced for all Area Offices. Officers attended tenants' meetings at their request. A bimonthly newsletter, CCT News, was sent to all Area Committee tenants' representatives, for whom a, special one-day conference was also arranged. The institutions and linkages enabling tenant participation and involvement are illustrated in Figure 2.2.

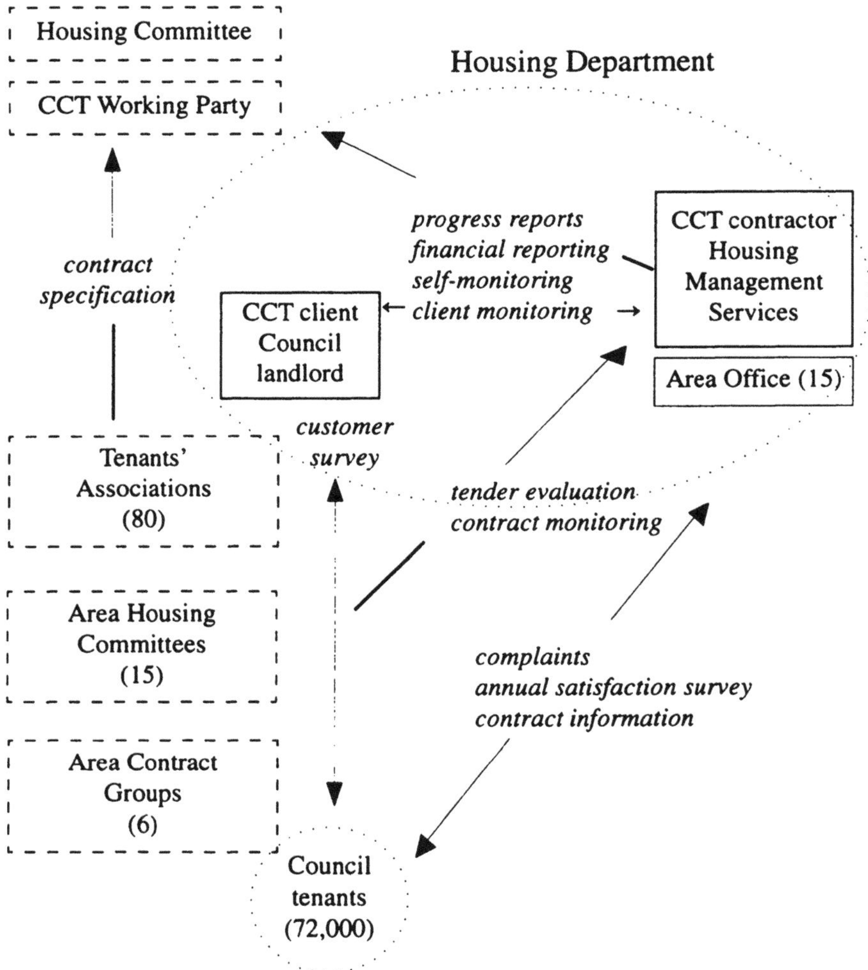

Figure 2.2 Compulsory competitive tendering for Housing Management Services in Northern Metropolitan - tenant involvement and participation

The Contract: Allocation of Client and Contractor Responsibilities

Planning for the delivery of the housing management service is effected through five volumes of documents, comprising Instructions for Tendering, the General Specification, the Activity Specification, the Conditions of Contract, and the Contract Area Profile. Tenant representatives were supplied with an abbreviated but fairly detailed version of the contract specification, which was also made available for public inspection in Area Offices. Individual tenants were informed of key points in leaflets and newsletters.

Under the General Specification, the council client is responsible for housing investment, policy and strategy, whilst the contractor has responsibility for tenancy management, rehousing, allocations and lettings, vacant property management, rent and service charges, estate management, building maintenance, development support, financial services, and benefits administration (para. G1). Payment to the contractor is based on the management fee for each property subject to the contractor meeting performance standards specified in the tender, with deductions for poor performance (para. G2). The contractor is required to consult with tenants and other service users in conformity with legislation and council policy, to arrange and attend at least six committee meetings a year within the Area, and to hold other consultative meetings (para. G4). The contractor is also required to help promote Tenants' Associations, and to give support where appropriate to the establishment of Tenant Management Organizations (TMOs) which may take over some management functions on compliance with certain statutory procedures.[15] The contractor is finally required to observe and implement council policies on health and safety (para. G8) and equal opportunities (para. G9).

The Activity Specification requires the contractor to observe and implement council policy regarding tenancy conditions, nuisance and neighbour disputes, harassment, succession, assignments, unlawful occupations and squatting (para. A1). The specification also covers rehousing (para. A2), letting and management of empty property (para. A3), rent and other payments (para. A4), estate management (para. A5), building maintenance (para. A6), and benefits administration (para. A9). The Contract Conditions comprise 36 clauses and 41 pages and provide for variations, bonds and guarantees, transfer of undertakings, confidentiality, health and safety, agency, indemnity and insurance, security, assignment and subcontracting, cooperation with the local ombudsman, default, termination, and disputes resolution. The contractor is obliged to provide five Method Statements, covering rent collection and arrears, building maintenance, dealing with antisocial behaviour, generating demand for difficult-to-let properties, and quality planning.[16]

Tender Evaluation

A new Contract Group (distinct from the Area Contract Groups which had already played a part in planning the specification) comprising three client officers, three members of the Housing Programme Committee, and three Area Committee tenant representatives from each of the first six contract areas was formed in 1994 to oversee the shortlisting and tender evaluation process. There was no separate shortlisting stage since regulations require this only where at least six contractors have expressed an interest, and only four had done so on this occasion. The 18 tenant representatives had to pre-qualify for participation in the group by attendance at training workshops, courses and conferences. Trial evaluation simulations were then conducted in which tenant representatives and councillors formulated questions they would put to contractors, before these were formally agreed and 'scripted' by officers. Further simulation exercises were arranged in which practice was given in interviewing contractors and mock bids were evaluated.

Although the only contractor finally to tender was HMS, its bid was subject to the full evaluation procedure. The technical tasks of checking the tender for accurate pricing and price/quality assessment were carried out by a specially constituted corporate evaluation team. For the purposes of quality evaluation, HMS was then required to make presentations to councillors and tenant representatives from Area Contract Groups in each of the six contract areas. The bid was scored out of a maximum of 1,150 marks, with 13 per cent (150 marks) being awarded solely by tenant representatives for the quality of the presentation. The ten categories scored apart from the presentation were: health and safety; HMS's five Method Statements; and conformity to four corporate criteria of quality assurance, policy and procedure, relationships to service users, and meeting the council's core values. Details of the final points score remain confidential. The general view of the tendering exercise was that, despite the absence of competing bidders in the final stages, the DSO had been motivated to produce a competitive bid which would satisfy the council's cost and quality requirements. Under Phase 1 of the CCT implementation programme, six contracts covering approximately 6,000 properties each were awarded to HMS in April 1996.[17]

Contract Monitoring

In contrast with monitoring arrangements that had been adopted for building cleaning,[18] responsibility for the monitoring of housing management services was shared between the authority client, HMS and tenants. The aim was that monitoring should be cooperative and non-adversarial. The 'active-client' concept required departmental clients, budget holders and ultimate consumers to be regularly involved in the monitoring process. Rather than have a client agency monitor the contract standard on behalf of the departmental client and tenants, the contractor would self-regulate by producing regular progress reports, which would also serve to communicate problems regarding the contract specifications. Self-monitoring by the contractor, which could lead to significant savings in client management costs, could only operate successfully given the climate of trust that had developed in preparation for CCT. The monitoring system was underpinned by principles which emphasized non-duplication of effort by contractor and client in the interests of economy and efficiency. Many 'noncontractual' practices would continue, with the contract specification and terms being used to support existing cooperative practices rather than undermine them.

The quality of HMS's performance is monitored with reference to both the client's prescribed service standards and the contractor's own Method Statements, which became binding on award of the contract. The client monitors the contractor's management procedures and the level and quality of staff and resources in delivering the service, and also carries out customer feedback surveys. HMS is required partially to self-monitor by submitting monthly performance statements, by attending routine client-contractor meetings, and by involving tenants' representatives in performance appraisal through customer surveys. This implies in theory a strong tenant monitoring role. The General Specification lists activities that have to be monitored on a monthly basis. Some of these activities are self-monitored by the contractor, some have to be formally reported to Area Committees, and some have to be reported to a subcommittee of the council's main Housing Committee.[19] This division of labour reflects different client, committee and contractor priorities. For example, the client must account for discrete audit trails and in order to do this requires regular and up-to-date information from the contractor. The reports give details of outputs achieved in comparison with contract standards, and the performance of the contractor in managing client budgets. With regard to tenant accountability, the monthly reports to Area Committees are regarded as particularly important, since they enable scrutiny of client and contractor activities on a regular and frequent basis. The reports include statistics on response times to tenants' requests and to emergencies, time taken for assessments for rehousing, and numbers of repairs reported and completed, allowing tenants to assess the relative performance of HMS in the different contract areas.

The subcommittee of the main Housing Committee also receives financial reports as to the number of variations to the specification and the level of defaults and penalties in compliance with DoE guidelines. Copies of these reports are sent to Area Committees. The purpose of these reports is to provide quantitative information rather than accurate measures of service quality. HMS's Quality Plan (the most important of the Method Statements) is self-monitored. Self-monitoring involves peer group review, local consultation and customer feedback, the production of an annual plan listing target improvements to be made to services, and a system of customer call-backs. Self-monitoring does not present any problems of 'shirking' in the client's view because of the high level of trust between the client, contractor and tenant. The client monitors the nature and level of complaints as an index of the standard of the contractor's performance. Not all complaints reach the client in the first instance; only if the Area Manager fails to produce a satisfactory response or rectify the problem does the client become involved. The available evidence suggests that this procedure has operated successfully to maintain trust, and that 'gate-keeping' by area managers has not resulted in the stifling of complaints to the detriment of tenants.

Tenant Satisfaction and Redress

Case study evidence based on interviews with Area Housing Managers and tenants' representatives suggests an increase in satisfaction with housing management services as a result of the new contractual arrangements. Tenants' expectations have been raised by publicity accompanying CCT and by the availability of more specific service information; there is a general awareness of 'entitlement' to a certain standard of service as laid out in the contract specification. Tenants' representatives know that the contractor's income is dependent upon the quality of its performance, and that they have a role in assessing any improvement or deterioration. The power to 'censure' or sanction poor performance on the basis of clearly established contractual standards has improved the accountability of managers involved in service provision. Individual officers in Area Offices have become more visible and personally accountable. As a result of new agreements with trade unions, HMS now has dedicated teams working in particular areas, usually with one identifiable person as the first contact point for resolving tenant problems. Both client and contractor have become more sensitive to the finer points of 'customer care', even where such qualities are not explicitly specified in the contract documentation. As a result of the greater operational autonomy accompanying CCT, Areas Managers have been able to respond more effectively to tenant demand in their particular areas, for example through weekend opening.

A political impetus to improved service quality has been provided through the network of Tenants' Associations, councillor surgeries, and Area Housing Committees where problems are discussed and resolutions voted upon. Further pressures for improvement in quality come from the threat of 'exit' by tenants from the council housing management service through self-managed Tenant Management Organizations and the right to buy. HMS managers are also under pressure owing to the limited duration of the contract and are aware that the survival of the DSO is dependent upon maintaining service quality and the confidence of both client and tenants.

Customer and satisfaction surveys conducted by both client and contractor provide further performance incentives, in addition to generating performance data. The results of an annual city-wide survey are broken down by area so that Area Managers can use the information to make further service improvements in response to concerns expressed. The best indication of the level of customer satisfaction with the new service has been provided by a general customer survey carried out at the end of 1996, the results of which were considered by the Housing Committee in April 1997. The survey is regarded as significant because it allows direct comparisons to be made with a pre-CCT 'benchmarking' exercise conducted in the Summer of 1995. With a response rate of 74 per cent from a sample of 5,500 tenants polled, the later survey reveals increases in satisfaction with consultation arrangements and involvement in decision-making, from 61 per cent to 84 per cent and from 55 per cent to 78 per cent respectively. Although such data should be interpreted with caution,[20] they do at least indicate, when taken in conjunction with other case study evidence, that contracting may have played a part in increasing tenant participation in the housing management service in this local authority.

Discussion

Although first-phase contracts have been running for little more than a year and it is too soon finally to evaluate the impact of the new arrangements, a generally positive picture emerges from this case study of the implementation of CCT for housing management services in Northern Metropolitan. There is little evidence of the client-contractor antagonisms and associated contractual problems and disputes that have characterized the introduction of CCT for some blue-collar services. A supportive institutional and organizational environment has ensured that the contract has operated within its limits as a governance mechanism. The level of cooperation between client, provider and tenants has been high. Quality has been built into service provision through 'co-production' of the contract specification. The monitoring of service standards has been jointly and cooperatively effected. Trust has been generally maintained in what could have been a difficult period of transition. Overall, the further development of participatory structures under CCT has both increased tenant voice and improved client/contractor accountability.

The principal finding of the case study is that improvements in the quality of relationships and in service effectiveness cannot be attributed simply to the introduction of contracting, but are explained rather by the integration of contracting processes within an already established system and culture of tenant participation. Whereas for other CCT services Northern Metropolitan had adopted a minimalist approach in complying with regulations, in this instance it followed the spirit as well as the letter of the law because CCT policy was seen as congruent with the council's own housing management objectives. From this perspective, the success of contracting for housing management services was the product of a wide variety of influences and inputs from tenants and council officers over a number of years. The key to cooperative and largely satisfactory new relationships has been the seamless manner in which the new contractual mechanism was incorporated within existing management and participatory structures. Such conditions enabled contracting processes to generate additional benefits of increased tenant awareness and involvement in service provision. It follows from this contextual emphasis that other local authorities with different political and cultural traditions may be expected to have had quite different experiences of CCT, with more implementation problems and fewer (if any) overall benefits.

How successful the new arrangements are in satisfying the various dimensions of the tenant interest may be dependent ultimately upon the adequacy of local democratic structures. A fundamental problem remains concerning the representativeness of tenants' organizations. 72,000 council tenants are officially represented through 80 Tenants' Associations and 15 Area Housing Committees. Tenant representatives are predominantly middle-aged, retired or unemployed white people who have been 'playing the game' for many years, and who have their own agenda regarding status, power, and the maintenance of privilege. Even Estate Management Boards and Tenant Management Cooperatives may not be sufficiently representative to reflect the diversity of opinions within an area on contract specification and monitoring issues (Steele and Somerville, 1994). Power struggles and factionalism are rife amongst the 'fiefdoms' of Tenants' Associations and Housing Committees. Some council officers interviewed were cynical about aspects of tenant representation. The term 'mafia' was used to describe the powerful position of some groupings. For example, the Northern Metropolitan Tenants Federation Group represents 20 Tenants' Associations; relations are poor with other Associations that have refused to align with this body. However, whilst under-representation and the lack of effective collective voice in the contract specification and monitoring process may have further disadvantaged ethnic minorities, women and single parents, it is likely that improvements in accountability, service quality and standards for housing management services have benefited all council tenants to some degree.

A further but related problem concerns the adequacy of individual tenants' redress for poor client or contractor performance. Even on the assumption that many problems have been planned out through careful specification and quality assurance, it might be argued that there are no adequate remedies because the obligations contained in the CCT contract are not legally enforceable by individual council tenants. In the search for participation structures that directly involve and empower a greater number of tenants, some local authorities have experimented with 'estate agreements' involving 'semi-contractual' annual arrangements between council landlord and tenants setting out service standards and detailed procedures for planning, consultation, monitoring and tenant redress. According to Steele and Somerville, 'estate agreements could form an important mechanism for establishing a tripartite partnership in housing management with the tenant, the client and the contractor being parties to the agreement' (p. 19). It is doubtful, however, whether such reforms would lead to any significant improvements in housing management services in Northern Metropolitan, or that they could ever wholly satisfy tenants' interests in housing management other than in conjunction with the types of collective participatory fora that have been described in the case study.

Conclusion

The apparently successful experience of contracting for housing management services revealed in the case study may have implications for the survival of internal contractual provision in the new climate of 'best value' after the abolition of CCT. Many local authorities are privatizing or externalizing white-collar services;[21] even Northern Metropolitan, in a major change of policy, has recently decided to externalize a range of information technology, financial and payroll services. However, housing management poses particular problems for market provision because of the close connection with core local democratic values. This relationship might be difficult to maintain through private sector provision, even if this were by a company employing the same workforce on the same terms. If the decision is taken to retain provision in-house, the choice then is whether this should be on the basis of continued quasi-market competition or through a more informal type of hierarchical arrangement. Where quasi-market pressures on in-house agencies are maintained through voluntary competitive tendering, the contract specification and conditions contained in the tender invitation must formally govern the client-contractor relationship post-award. If, on the other hand, there is no tendering process then the rationale for retaining internal 'contractual' relations is reduced, although relationships with some contractual features may continue through service level agreements. Either way, for those who see potential in an alternative 'social democratic variant on the contract state' (Kirkpatrick and Lucio, 1996, p. 7), the experience of CCT may provide a valuable foundation on which to build more efficient and effective housing management provision in future.

Notes

Paper presented to Socio-Legal Studies Annual Conference, Cardiff University, 2–4 April 1997, and the Sixth Quasi-Markets Research Seminar, University of Portsmouth, 10–11 April 1997. We would like to thank participants at both conferences for their contributions, and David Campbell, David Cowan, and Kevin Dowd for comments on previous drafts. The support of the ESRC is gratefully acknowledged (award R000 236416).

1 Written Parliamentary Answer by Hilary Armstrong, Minister for Local Government, 2 June 1997. The abolition of CCT for blue collar (Local Government Act 1988) services would require primary legislation, likely to take around 18 months. CCT for white collar and related services could be more easily dismantled by statutory instrument since this was the means by which the services were added to the compulsory tendering programme.

Even given Labour's commitment to the abolition of CCT, it will be several years before contractual arrangements already entered into come to an end.

2 This focus avoids the more general issue of whether the introduction of CCT and associated quasi-market mechanisms has led overall to increased efficiency. It will be assumed that at least some efficiency benefits have resulted from CCT. According to the left-wing Institute for Public Policy Research, CCT has made local authorities more focused in their objectives and given a boost to thinking on efficiency and innovation (Kelly, 1996). However, the extent of real efficiency gains remains controversial. Even the Audit Commission recognizes that some savings may have been due to influences other than increased competition and the contractual regime, such as changes to specification and improved productivity through large-scale redundancy (Audit Commission, 1995, p. 2). Apparent improvements may have been achieved at the expense also of worsening working conditions, damaging structural disturbances within local authorities, declining service quality, and greater social costs to the economy generally (Auda, 1995), with women bearing the brunt of redundancies, and deterioration in pay and conditions (Escott and Whitfield, 1995).

3 For example, the Association of District Councils and the Association of Metropolitan Authorities, together with the National Federation of Housing Associations, have suggested replacing CCT with a statutory duty for social landlords to produce a Housing Quality Programme, setting out service specifications, costs, and arrangements for securing quality and value for money (Association of District Councils, 1996). Given such alternatives, many councils are considering how far they might abandon contracting culture (Gordon, 1995; Irvine and Garland, 1996).

4 The adoption of 'contract' as a vehicle for the implementation of radical changes in public service provision has involved a significant movement away from its classical 'private law' basis. Contracting may be understood as a process whereby relationships are managed and adjusted according to arrangements specified in contract documentation. Contracting is what managers in an increasing variety of public sector contexts do (Mackintosh, 1993; Vincent-Jones, 1997).

5 Local Government Act 1988 (Competition) (Defined Activities) (Housing Management) Order SI 1994/1671. The specified proportions of housing management work subject to competition are dealt with under SI 1994/2297.

6 Whilst housing management is one of a number of services that have been subjected to CCT, it differs from blue collar services such as street cleaning, refuse collection, and buildings cleaning which apply to 'the public' generally. Housing management has particular consumers – tenants and prospective tenants of public and quasi-public sector housing. Housing management is also different to white collar services such as information technology, finance, personal and legal services – these have consumers (or clients) internal to the authority and are supportive of its public service-providing role. Furthermore, the service is unusual in that it operates in the context of a complex legislative framework of specific rights enjoyed by council tenants. For a detailed account of the law on housing management CCT, see Hunter and Selman, 1996.

7 S.27AA Housing Act 1985, as amended under s.131 of the Leasehold Reform Housing and Urban Development Act 1993 (replacing s.105 of the Housing Act 1985 as regards housing management).

8 S.27A(2) Housing Act 1985.

9 Many local authorities, such as Northern Metropolitan, have included other activities in their tender invitations in the interests of maintaining a comprehensive and integrated service.

10 For an argument as to the inadequacy of existing public law remedies in such cases, and as to the need for constitutional recognition of a 'public services contract', see Lewis, 1996; Harden, 1992.

11 There is no added functional value in decentralizing 'policy' services such as development, implementation and evaluation of city-wide housing policy on investment, allocations, rent levels, waiting list maintenance, assessment of housing need and warden services; or operational support functions such as training, personnel, IT, legal support, and financial management. The ratio of staff retained at the strategic centre to operational staff working in areas was roughly 15.85 per cent. Around 90 per cent of operational staff worked on the benefits administration counter service. Benefits *determination* remained a client function located in area rather than central offices resulting in client and operational staff working side-by-side.

12 This team contained staff already expert in blue-collar CCT under the 1988 Local Government Act. Their brief was to develop the service specification, to extend tenant participation and consultation, and to liaise with unions and other departments to ensure full coordination with planning for white-collar CCT. This team will be disbanded once the final tranche of housing management contracts has been let in 1997.

13 Under DoE Circular 12/94 (Financial Objectives Specifications 1994) the objective of break even is further specified as including 'a capital financing charge of 6 per cent of the value of fixed assets used in the provision of the service'.

14 Whilst an accounting-contracting nexus – whereby payment is adjusted in accordance with performance – exists for housing management just as for blue-collar services (Seal and Vincent-Jones, 1997), the potential for conflict is here reduced by the general absence of contract variations and the preexisting cooperative client-contractor structures around which CCT was implemented.

15 Section 27AB of the Housing Act 1985, as amended by the Leasehold Reform, Housing and Urban Development Act 1993 and the subsequent Housing (Right to Manage) Regulations 1994. There is currently only one TMO in Northern Metropolitan, with one other in the process of formation.

16 HMS's Method Statements were particularly important in those sensitive areas of contact between contractor and tenant that could lead to a deterioration in landlord-tenant relations. For example, collecting rent arrears is a difficult job which must be done in a sensitive manner. The Method Statement functioned in this regard as an assurance to both client and tenants that methods adopted would not create unnecessary conflict or jeopardize the good name of the authority.

17 The contracts were let for a three year term with the option to extend for a further two. The contracts were fixed price based on a management fee for the number of properties visited per month, audited against a monthly monitoring report. Phase 1 satisfied 40 per cent of the 95 per cent tendering requirement. Under Phase 2 a further 30 per cent involving five contracts was let in April 1997, with the remaining 25 per cent having to be let in Phase 3 by 1998.

18 The experience of client-contractor relationships for blue collar services under the 1988 Local Government Act was that the type of monitoring system was an important determinant of *ex post* conflictual or cooperative relations. Aggressive monitoring of services where standards were not clear-cut (even when specified) could usually be technically justified, but almost always resulted in unfair penalization of the contractor – see Vincent-Jones and Harries, 1996a.

19 Self-monitored activities cover: responses to tenants' requests; breaches of tenancy conditions including applications for possession and eviction warrants; numbers of complaints of harassment; emergency response rates; assessments for rehousing; numbers of court orders and injunctions; caretaking standards; numbers of repairs reported, ordered, and completed; and the numbers of benefit applications. Activities that must be regularly reported to the client include: numbers of tenanted and untenanted properties; staff levels; complaints reports; harassment complaints; tenancies terminated; the value of rent arrears; numbers of evictions; and the value of development support.

20 The methodological problems are numerous: the surveys were not independently conducted; the sample sizes and response rates, although very similar, were not identical; and the categories and questions were different in the second survey. Assuming that apparent improvements can be taken at face value, these might be explained by management changes unconnected with the contracting process.

21 Externalization may be achieved through management buy-outs, employee buy-outs, or the setting up of local authority companies, retaining most of the existing workforce, working arrangements and conditions of service – see Spray, 1992; White, 1996.

Bibliography

Auda, R. (1995), 'The Wrong Tool for the Job', *Local Government Chronicle*, 31 March.

Armstrong, H. (1996), *Municipal Journal*, 10 May.

Association of District Councils (1996), *In Place of Housing Management CCT – Housing Quality Programmes*, Consultation Document.

Audit Commission (1995), *Making Markets: A Review of the Audits of the Client Role for Contracted Services*, Audit Commission Bulletin, March, HMSO, London.

Barnes, M. and Prior, D. (1995), 'Spoilt for Choice? How Consumerism Can Disempower Public Service Users', *Public Money and Management*, Vol. 15 (3), pp. 53–8.

Barnes, M. and Prior, D. (1996), 'From Private Choice to Public Trust: A New Social Basis for Welfare', *Public Money and Management*, Vol. 16 (4), pp. 51–7.

Clapham, D. and Satsangi, M. (1992), 'Performance Assessment and Accountability in British Housing Management', *Policy and Politics*, Vol. 20(1), pp. 63–74.

Deakin, N. and Walsh, K. (1996), 'The Enabling State: The Role of Markets and Contracts', *Public Administration*, Vol. 74, pp. 33–47.

Docherty, B. (1993), 'Competing Priorities', *Housing*, June, pp. 23–4.

Escott, K. and Whitfield, D. (1995), *The Gender Impact of CCT in Local Government*, Equal Opportunities Commission, London.

Goodlad, R. (1994), 'Conceptualising "Enabling": The Housing Role of Local Authorities', *Local Government Studies*, Vol. 20 (4), pp. 570–87.

Gordon, P. (1995), 'Questions of Culture', *Local Government Chronicle*, 22 September.

Harden, I. (1992), *The Contracting State*, Open University Press, Buckingham.

Hirschman, A. (1970), *Exit, Voice and Loyalty: Responses to Decline in Firms, Organizations and States*, Harvard University Press, Cambridge, Mass.

Hoggett, P. (1990), 'Modernisation, Political Strategy and the Welfare State: An Organisational Perspective', *Studies in Decentralisation and Quasi-Markets* 2, School for Advanced Urban Studies, University of Bristol.

Hoggett, P. (1996), 'New Modes of Control in the Public Service', *Public Administration*, Vol. 74, pp. 9–32.
Hughes, D. and Lowe, S. (1995), *Social Housing Law and Policy*, Butterworths, London.
Hunter, C. and Selman, A. (1996), *Compulsory Competitive Tendering of Housing Management: Law and Practice in the Management of Social Housing*, Lemos & Crane, London.
Irvine, M. and Garland, D. (1996), 'Putting the House in Order', *Municipal Journal*, 20 September, pp. 20–1.
Kelly, P. (1996), *Municipal Journal*, 23–29 February.
Kemp, P. (1995), 'Researching Housing Management Performance', *Urban Studies*, Vol. 32 (4–5), pp. 779–90.
Kirkpatrick, I. and Martinez Lucio, M. (1996), 'The Contract State and the Future of Public Management', *Public Administration*, Vol. 74, pp. 1–8.
Lewis, N. (1996), *Choice and the Legal Order: Rising Above Politics*, Butterworths, London.
Llewellyn, S. and Saunders, I. (1996), 'Tracking Resource Use in a Welfare Organisation: Needs, Costs and Co-production', EIASM Workshop on *The Role of Accounting in Public Sector Transition*, Stockholm, 7–8 November.
Loveland, I. (1992), 'Square Pegs, Round Holes: The "Right" to Council Housing in the Post War Era', *Journal of Law and Society*, Vol. 19, pp. 339–64.
MacGilp, J. (1995), 'Involving Tenants in the Tender Game', *Housing*, October, pp. 33–4.
Mackintosh, M. (1993), 'Economic Behaviour and the Contracting Outcome under the NHS Reforms', *Journal of Accounting, Auditing and Accountability*, Vol. 6, 133.
Parkin, P. (1994), 'Taking a Tough Line on Tenders', *Housing*, July/August, pp. 23–4.
Prior, D., Stewart, J. and Walsh, K. (1995), *Citizenship: Rights, Community and Participation*, Pitman Publishing, London.
Seal, W. and Vincent-Jones, P. (1997), 'Accounting and Trust in the Enabling of Long-Term Relations', *Journal of Accounting, Accountability and Auditing*, Vol. 10, pp. 406–31.
Spray, W. (1992), 'The First Estate Management Board in London', *Local Government Policy Making*, Vol. 19 (2), pp. 3–12.
Steele, A. and Somerville, P. (1994), 'Involving the Tenant in Housing Management', *Municipal Journal*, No. 23, June, pp. 18–9.
Stoker, G. (1996), 'The Struggle to Reform Local Government: 1970–95', *Public Money and Management*, March, pp. 17–22.
Vincent-Jones, P. (1994), 'The Limits of Near-contractual Governance: Local Authority Internal Trading Under CCT', *Journal of Law and Society*, Vol. 21, pp. 214–37.
Vincent-Jones, P. (1997), 'Hybrid Organisation, Contractual Governance and CCT in the Provision of Local Authority Services' in S. Deakin and J. Michie (eds), *Contracts, Cooperation and Competition: Studies in Economics, Management and Law*, Oxford University Press, Oxford.
Vincent-Jones, P. and Harries, A. (1996a), 'Limits of Contract in Internal CCT Transactions: A Comparative Study of Buildings Cleaning and Refuse Collection in Northern Metropolitan' in D. Campbell and P. Vincent-Jones (eds), *Contract and Economic Organisation: Socio-Legal Initiatives*, Dartmouth, Aldershot.
Vincent-Jones, P. and Harries, A. (1996b), 'Conflict and Cooperation in Local Authority Quasi-Markets: The Hybrid Organisation of Internal Contracting Under CCT', *Local Government Studies*, Vol. 22 (4), pp. 187–209.
Walker, R. and Williams, P. (1995), 'Implementing Local Government Reorganisation in the Housing Service: The Case of Wales', *Local Government Studies*, Vol. 21, pp. 483–508.

Walsh, K. and Davis, H. (1993), *Competition and Service: The Impact of the Local Government Act 1998*, HMSO, London.
White, C. (1996), 'Moving Into the Unknown', *Housing*, November, pp. 28–9.

3 Partnership and Conflict: Working Relationships Between Voluntary and Statutory Agencies Providing Services for Homeless People

DR PHILIP TIMMS

Introduction

I wrote this paper as a way of making sense of some of my experiences working as a psychiatrist with the START team. This is a community mental health team for homeless people working across three South London boroughs with high numbers of homeless people. It was set up as part of the Central London Homeless Mentally Ill Initiative (CLHMI) in 1991, is managed by Lewisham and Guy's Mental Health Trust and is part of the National Health Service. The objective of this initiative was to make mental health services available and acceptable to the many homeless people who suffer from severe mental illness but who have historically had little access to such services.

Experience gained from a previous mental health team working in hostels for homeless men (Brent-Smith and Dean, 1989) suggested that contact with clients was more successfully established and maintained by seeing clients on-site in hostels rather than at off-site clinics. Hence, one of the ideas underpinning the new service was that we would go to see people in their own environment, rather than expecting them to come to us at a clinic or hospital premises. We thus found ourselves working mainly in hostels and day-centres, sometimes on the streets, but always in places that were run by voluntary sector agencies or in situations where the only service providers were from the voluntary sector. Although many mainstream mental health services work with voluntary sector agencies, the CLHMI teams were in a unique position in that virtually all their work was done within the voluntary sector.

We were familiar with the difficulties of trying to work with other statutory agencies, which were highlighted in the Clunis report (Ritchie et al., 1994). However, we were surprised by the intensity of the difficulties that bedevilled our relationships with the many voluntary agencies in whose premises we saw most of our patients. Although many of these difficulties became personalized, it was evident that there was more to it than personality clashes. By taking a more detached view, we have been able to see a way ahead towards overcoming these problems, hopefully to the benefit of our clients.

History

Secular, non-medical institutions for the poor provided shelter and care for substantial numbers of people with long-term mental illness, even in the heyday of the asylum. They were accommodated in the parish workhouse by the same arrangements made for the poor who were not suffering from any mental disturbance. Although workhouses were open to both the poor of the parish and the wandering poor, separate arrangements were made for the two groups under the one roof. However, there was usually no separation between the mad and the merely indigent. This is reflected by the observation in 1889 that, outside London, 14 per cent (11,827) of pauper lunatics in England and Wales were accommodated in general workhouses for the poor (Cochrane, 1988). Following the Poor Law Amendment Act of 1834, parish workhouses had become consolidated into larger units or 'Unions', which developed into the large reception centres for homeless people, vividly portrayed by Orwell in the 1930s. Following the National Assistance Act of 1948 these were gradually incorporated into the Welfare State over the next 30 years. They have now been replaced by smaller, higher quality hostels. These are no longer run directly by the DSS, which has contracted out their management to an assortment of voluntary organizations.

In spite of the development of the welfare state, the homeless mentally ill have, unlike most other sectors of the poor, continued to rely on charity for the provision of many of the essentials of life. This may be partially due to the optimistic, some might say Panglossian, view held by successive postwar administrations that homelessness was a personal aberration and that individuals needed merely to be offered the opportunity to lead a more settled way of life. The National Assistance Board described the purpose of reception centres as being 'to make provision whereby persons without a settled way of living may be influenced to lead a more settled way of life'. During the second world war these institutions had been virtually emptied by the war effort and it was hoped that they could be done away with completely. However, peacetime proved less forgiving than wartime – the asylums and reception centres filled up again, in spite of the fact that both types of institution were in the process of being run down.

Moreover, legislation has encouraged statutory services to define the single homeless person as being outside their remit, resources being targeted at families with children. However, single people with multiple needs have inconveniently not disappeared. While direct state provision has withered on the vine, there has been a proliferation of voluntary agencies providing services to the homeless, a large proportion of whom have experienced severe and/or enduring mental health problems. For example, the START team deals with around 30 different voluntary agencies, many operating from several sites (START, 1996). This is not a recent development. In 1969, a psychiatrist and social worker who had found a high prevalence of psychosis in a Salvation Army hostel (Crossley and Denmark, 1969) commented 'It is surely not right to unload onto a voluntary organisation, whose function is not to act as a therapeutic agency, patients who still need community care'. The fact is, these institutions had always housed, fed and looked after substantial numbers of people with severe mental illnesses. Indeed, they still do today. The Royal College of Physicians recent report (Connelly and Crown, 1994) commented that 'direct access hostels should not be expected to provide care for severely mentally ill people'. Whether or not it is an ideal situation, voluntary sector institutions such as these remain the main providers of services for many people with long-term psychiatric illnesses.

One would imagine that the combination of the street-wise flexibility of the voluntary sector (Department of Health, 1993) and the reliability and expertise of the statutory sector would be entirely complementary in meeting the needs of homeless people with multiple problems. Sadly, this has rarely been the case. In fact, the best way of characterizing the relationship between these two sectors is probably hostility and patronage on the one hand, with suspicion and resentment on the other. Not a good starting point for people who are supposed to be working on the same side with broadly the same objectives for the same group of clients/patients. More recently, voluntary agencies have found themselves left out of the process of community care assessment, in spite of their intimate knowledge of their clients (Gorton, 1995). Similar problems have been noted in the US literature and it has been noted that 'the absence of an effective inter-agency network may render ... work (with the homeless mentally ill) ineffective' (Goldfinger and Chafetz, 1984).

Laying the issues of resources aside, I believe that the reasons underlying these difficulties have much to do with the very different organizational structures of the voluntary and statutory sectors. These repay some examination using simple notions of organizational theory. Morgan (1997) has used a number of different metaphors to understand organizations. One of these involves regarding organizations as organisms that are adapted to a particular environment, demanding specific tasks for survival. These tasks impose upon the organization different structures. Although there is a whole range of organizational types generated by this way of thinking, they can all be viewed as existing somewhere along a continuum, with 'organic' organizations at one extreme, 'mechanistic' organizations at the other, each operating to survive in very different environments. Table 3.1 summarizes the characteristics of these two extremes. Neither type of organization is good or bad in itself. The crucial question is whether it is properly adapted to meet the demands that will be made of it.

Classically, health services have been long-established, large organizations with fairly rigid ways of doing things. They have been dominated by the nursing and medical hierarchies, although recently these have been joined by psychologists, occupational therapists and other professional groups. These hierarchies are stable, separate and explicit. The functions of each level of each hierarchy have been clear and communications tend to be vertical, up and down the hierarchy. For instance, junior doctors are answerable to more senior doctors, junior nurses are answerable to more senior nurses. The majority of communications take place within the nursing and medical hierarchies, not between them, although both sets of workers have the same objective; the welfare of the patient. This independence of functioning, a tendency not to communicate between different professional groups and lack of any over-arching authority or arbiter between these groups has been a headache for many health service managers. Each profession takes a fierce pride in its own competence and is reluctant to accept supervision or dictats from outsiders. There is a tendency to see things from the perspective of the interests of one's own professional group rather than from the view of the whole service. On the other hand, professionalism can produce dividends in terms of the standards set within each profession and the felt obligation of its members to adhere to them. Historically, most changes in the pattern of demand have been relatively slow. The emphasis for professionals has been on the acquisition and use of skills that will be relevant for a lifetime of use, assuming a relatively unchanging pattern of demand. Even when changes have occurred, they have often been driven by developments arising from within the professions rather

Table 3.1 Organizational types

Mechanistic (Statutory sector)		Organic (Voluntary sector)
	Environment	
Stable		Highly unpredictable
	Nature of task	
Efficient production of a standard service		Searching for new tasks/opportunities
	Organization of work	
Jobs clearly defined in terms of tasks		Jobs usually defined by individuals ad hoc
	Nature of authority	
Hierarchy clearly defined Seniority important		Authority changes with the nature of the current task
	Communications	
Pattern is usually specified by rules and regulations		Free and informal
Usually vertical		As often horizontal as vertical
	Staff commitment	
Commitment to a particular job rather than to any overall organizational task		Full commitment to the overall organizational task
Uncertainty uncommon		Uncertainty common

Source: adapted from Morgan, 1997

than by changes in demand from the users of the service. For example, the closure of asylum beds began as a result of advances in drug and social therapies in the mid-1950s, a decade ahead of either the public demand for this to happen or for any political will to be expressed. Funding has usually been relatively stable from year to year, allowing for long-term planning, and staff have traditionally been secure in their jobs. So, established mainstream health services have tended to conform to the 'mechanistic' organizational model. In fact, Griffiths characterizes most health services as being a good examples of 'professional bureaucracies', relatively inflexible but suited to the execution of complex tasks in relatively stable conditions.

By contrast, most voluntary sector agencies have been relatively small and youthful, with little in the way of operational dogma. They have come into being in direct response to a demand, or set of demands, from the world external to the organization. Consequently, they are used to changing their procedures quickly in response to changing conditions. This characteristic has been fostered by the regular review of their activities imposed by their funding cycle, which has usually been yearly. Although this ensures sensitivity to the demands of funders, it has made it difficult to plan for the long term. Professional hierarchies are absent because, on the whole, those employed have not had professional backgrounds. Tasks have not been defined by professions, but instead have tended to be constructed pragmatically, according to current demand and the personnel available, changing as the need arises. Likewise, the nature of communication has not been defined by professional jargon or confined by professional boundaries, but takes place as the need arises between the personnel concerned. Protocols and procedures have often been lacking, the success of the enterprise resting on the workers' energy, enthusiasm and ability to learn quickly. Workers' awareness of the overall mission of the organization is unclouded by professional agendas. Staff have often been insecure in their jobs, not knowing whether the following year's funding will be sufficient, and it is arguably only their continuing sense of mission that allows such organizations to survive. Rather than doing the same thing from year to year, voluntary sector agencies have tended to be active in searching out new opportunities. So, voluntary services have tended to conform more to the 'organic' organizational model.

This notion of NHS services as being 'mechanistic' and voluntary agencies being 'organic' is, of course, an oversimplification. These two theoretical categories will not describe perfectly the characteristics of all existing organizations in the two sectors. The divide has become more blurred over the last 10 years. The voluntary sector has grown in both size and professional sophistication, the National Health Service has become increasingly fragmented into competing trusts. However, I feel the mechanistic/organic categories do describe the positions from which the two sectors have developed.

Another major and important difference has been in the type of people involved in these very different organizations. To work in the health sector generally demands a rigorous selection process followed by years of not always appropriate training before you get anywhere near a service user. So, workers tend to be older than in the voluntary sector, to have invested a huge amount in their training, and to see their careers as developing within the NHS. On the other hand, in the voluntary sector it is not unusual for untrained volunteers to be helping very needy people with little or no training. They tend to be younger than workers in the health service and to have invested relatively little in the organization they have joined. They will often see the job as useful experience before moving on to a career or further training elsewhere. On the whole, turnover of workers is relatively high. Moreover, there has been far greater use of ex-users in the voluntary sector, particularly in drug and alcohol agencies. It has been argued that, for all these reasons, the sense of mission is more easily preserved in the voluntary sector.

Table 3.2 Staffing

Statutory sector	**Voluntary sector**
'Mature'	Young
Training +	Training -
Experience +	Experience -
Low turnover	High turnover
Volunteers -	Volunteers +
Ex-users -	Ex-users +
Career development +	Career development -
Mission -	Mission +

Other Problems

Added to the difference in organizational structure and staffing, there will inevitably be differences in organizational values. These often revolve around the central issue of self-determination versus dependence or control. For instance, a housing association may well hold the view that we are all responsible for all our actions at all times. A psychiatric service will tend to believe that this does not hold when someone is in the throes of a psychotic breakdown. So when a person in a delusional state behaves noisily and disturbs his neighbours, there may be a disagreement as to whether he should be evicted or admitted to hospital for treatment and the situation reviewed.

There is sometimes the assumption amongst voluntary agencies that, because statutory services have statutory obligations, they can somehow conjure up a service on demand. Of course, in these days of cash-strapped services, this just is not true, if it ever was. Looking down the other end of the telescope, statutory services often assume that voluntary sector hostels are all like the old Salvation Army dormitory hostels and will take all-comers, however drunk or disturbed or violent they may be. Hence the bad practice of patients being discharged from acute psychiatric wards to direct-access hostels without any information being sent to the hostel.

The common lack of any kind of joint planning means that housing associations may set up a project with perhaps 15 spaces for people with mental illness and high levels of need without ever discussing this with local health services. They are then surprised when they get a frosty reception from the local psychiatric service which perceives that a small asylum has been set up in its area without any discussion about the demands that it might place on services. A mainstream mental health team may employ street outreach workers, without any discussion with the three or four non-medical outreach teams that already exist and thereby increase the already considerable chaos on the streets. The irritation thus generated tends to obscure the reality, which is that such a facility might be as much a resource as a demand. Consultation is the key to solving these issues. It is perhaps not as common as it should be because organizations have often seen the only satisfactory conclusion as one which gives them everything they want, rather than accepting a mutually-satisfactory compromise which withholds total victory.

So, there are at least two very different kinds of organization trying to work cooperatively with a client group that has traditionally found it difficult to find a voice. This matters because of the expectations that each sector has of the other. Each tends to assume that the other will have many of the same admirable characteristics as itself. For example, statutory services have often been amazed by the poor documentation and note-keeping of voluntary services. Voluntary services, by contrast, cannot understand the apparent procrastination and sluggishness of statutory services. Overall, each finds it hard to understand the nature and structure of the other's service and there is relatively little experience of joint working or planning. Each responds to the disappointments it experiences from the other by imposing on it a negative stereotype.

Points of Convergence

Certainly in terms of health provision, the statutory sector is becoming increasingly subject to restrictions with which the voluntary sector has worked for years. The purchaser-provider split has established Health Authorities as the funding agencies, independent of the hospital and community trusts who actually provide the services. These independent agencies are cash-strapped and want to get value for money from their providers. They have consequently subjected providers to regular scrutiny, and a one year cycle of funding and refunding. The lack of agreed outcome and quality standards has made it difficult to make commissioning decisions on strictly rational grounds, and decisions can often appear capricious to those on the receiving end. Although health providers remain relatively large, voluntary sector agencies have also increased in size. St Mungo's is one of the longest-established voluntary sector homelessness agencies. It started in 1969, with a single house in Battersea, and now has a turnover of more than £15 million per year (St Mungo's, 1997). There has been a parallel development of professionalism, with an increasing emphasis on specifying procedures and maintaining standards. Many have moved away from the emphasis on volunteers, increasingly employing qualified staff in more hierarchical structures. The health service has tried to de-emphasize the traditional power of hospital consultants and to work, at least in clinical teams, with less authoritarian, flatter hierarchies.

Voluntary agencies have always, in effect, competed for funding from a limited range of funding agencies. Health providers, in contrast, have historically assumed continuing funding with relatively little scrutiny. The advent of the internal market and competition between health trusts means that health providers are having increasingly to think in different terms. It remains to be seen how far this will be modified by the new administration. This has certainly meant that health providers have experienced some of the insecurity experienced by voluntary agencies every year as they have to renegotiate their funding, increasingly from Health Authorities that are also funding voluntary sector agencies. In some areas, activities that used to be the preserve of the Health Service are now provided exclusively by voluntary agencies; in North Southwark residential alcohol detoxification is provided by a voluntary agency, Drink Crisis Centre, with no inpatient de-tox services available from the local health provider. Moreover, the new CPA arrangements contain the possibility that the lead agency in caring for individuals might be a voluntary agency, with all the statutory responsibilities that this implies. Within the Health Service, some variants of multi-disciplinary working have emphasized the blurring of professional roles and the importance of interdisciplinary communication. This is particularly so in the case-management model of service for people with severe mental illness who may find it difficult to engage with more than one or two people. A single key worker is responsible for coordinating the necessary services for the client and may be called upon to provide some of those services themselves. For instance, a nurse may find himself helping a client with his or her benefit claims. This is referred to by the optimistic as multi-skilling, by the pessimistic as de-skilling! Either way, it is rather more like the more flexible ways of working that have been common in the voluntary sector.

Ways Ahead – Organizational

Working more closely with other agencies is one of the great cliches of our age. It sounds so easy and yet is so often found to be so difficult, often for the reasons described above. It has been commented on in virtually every enquiry into homicides by people with mental illness and was a central finding of the Clunis report (Ritchie et al., 1994). However, exhortation apart, little seems to have been written about how to implement this. The first step in improving the situation must be for statutory agencies to acknowledge the contribution that has been made by the voluntary sector over the last 50 years. It provides for those who, while they may live at the margins of society, may well be seen as needing its help the most. It may be galling for highly-trained professionals to admit it, but the day-to-day care and support of many of their clients is in the hands of people with little or no training in mental health issues. That is the reality and it must be recognized. There then follows the tricky process of finding ways of working together.

Starting at the top, joint funding of services may create a firm foundation for collaboration but is, as yet, unusual. The HHELP health team for homeless people in East London is an elaborate example of multiple health and social care agencies jointly funding a specialist service (Appendix A, Connelly and Crown, 1994). This has proved effective in ensuring joint working, but time-consuming to maintain. Joint planning has generated many committees but all too few genuinely collaborative enterprises. The difficulty may be that an impossible unanimity is often striven for, rather than a less-ambitious pragmatic adjustment where the interests of the different parties coincide. At a lower level, it can be helpful for statutory agencies to involve representatives from the voluntary sector in the process of appointing new staff.

One of the first explicit references to the voluntary sector in a government document (Griffiths, 1988) set out the need for clear agreements to be made between statutory and voluntary agencies. The START team has set in train a process of establishing service-level agreements with the majority of its client agencies (START, 1997). This makes clear to each agency what they can expect from the other and establishes expectations that are realistic on both sides. It also provides a benchmark by which performance can be compared, facilitating the process of regular feedback. This happens at a six-monthly meeting between the START team leader and the manager of each voluntary project concerned. For example, a time-limit is set within which the START team must respond to referrals from the voluntary agency. This is clear, negotiable and susceptible to straightforward audit.

Ways Ahead – Training

START Team's Training Programme for Voluntary Sector Homelessness Organisations (Glover, 1997)

The notion of training in mental health issues for voluntary sector workers is not new, at least in theory. It was suggested in the late 1960s as one of a range of solutions to the high levels of psychiatric morbidity in the old DHSS reception centres (Edwards et al., 1968, Lodge Patch, 1971), although never implemented. More recently, impetus was gained from the publication of the Newby report (Davies et al., 1995) which highlighted the importance of training for voluntary sector staff. The Mental Health Foundation report 'Creating Community Care' (Mental Health Foundation, 1994) recommended that *all* agencies dealing with the general public should ensure that their staff have received appropriate training in mental health issues. Bearing in mind that a high proportion of the people who use homelessness facilities are suffering from major mental illness, it would make sense to consider the work on family interventions in schizophrenia (Kuipers et al., 1992). This educational and problem-solving work has been demonstrated to significantly reduce the risk of relapse of the family member suffering from schizophrenia (Leff et al., 1985). Staff in voluntary agencies often find themselves functioning as *de facto* family members and might well find this kind of intervention helpful. It would help them to increase their understanding of the psychotic experiences of their residents, to find practical ways of coping with strange or difficult behaviours, and to know when to call for help. However, until recently, no mental health training of any sort has been regularly available to the voluntary sector.

The START team had been offering mental health services to homeless people since 1991. In terms of the mechanistic/organic continuum discussed above, it was in the position of being organizationally a traditional mental health service, although taking on some of the characteristics of a more organic organization. From the outset, START nurses, doctors and social workers had offered training to local voluntary agencies working with homeless people, but always on a fairly ad hoc basis. As the team became more widely known, referrals increased to the point where it was difficult to justify activities not directly related to patient care. Moreover, several shortcomings were identified in the original START training programme. Most of the team members had received no training in teaching methods and so the standard of the sessions was variable. The content of the sessions often reflected the knowledge and enthusiasms of the team members rather than what the voluntary staff really needed to know. Sessions were usually held in the place of work, which was usually uncomfortable, noisy or prone to interruption. Up to eight team members might be involved in a single day's training and there was no one with the responsibility for coordinating an increasingly complex process. It became evident that the size of the enterprise (17 START team clinical workers dealing with nearly 30 voluntary agencies), meant that dedicated time and money would need to be assigned to training if it was to be anything more than a token exercise. So, a part-time trainer and an external training consultant were employed to establish the feasibility of a more structured approach to training.

From April to July 1996 they carried out a thorough consultation, carrying out semi-structured interviews with 20 different client agencies. For each agency this identified the primary commissioner of training, current access to training opportunities and the different roles and responsibilities of workers. A number of themes came out of this exercise. Courses needed to be centred clearly within the context of homelessness, to be practical, to cover the areas recommended by the Newby report and to incorporate the interaction of mental illness with other areas of need such as alcohol and substance abuse. On the whole, agencies preferred that courses should be tailored to the specific agency, rather than being open to a range of agencies.

In the spring and summer of 1996, all START team workers attended a basic 'training the trainers' course provided by Lewisham and Guy's Mental Health Trust, so they would be properly equipped to participate in the training programme. In addition, a limited amount of money was allocated to buying-in outside trainers, who were asked to prepare materials that could be used by START for future training sessions.

From September 1996 to March 1997 a number of initiatives were established. A programme of new courses was constructed that was open to applications from all agencies (see Appendix) and a mixture of in-house and multi-agency courses were run. A monthly open afternoon and presentation was set up at the START office, offering a chance for new staff in the voluntary sector to become familiar with the way the START team worked. Between September 1996 and March 1997, 32 training events took place – nine two-day courses, nine one-day courses and 18 other sessions – involving 384 voluntary sector staff.

The feedback received from trainees was extremely positive, although they felt that there should be more role-play and case studies, greater service-user involvement, a greater emphasis on practical skills and more material concerning personality disorders. There was little interest in following a programme of sessions unless they were part of a formal training qualification such as an NVQ. Trainers remarked upon the fact that the mixed-agency, open-access sessions seemed to produce a much better learning environment and that using several disciplines in the training helped trainees to understand better what could be offered by mainstream services. It was also noted that there was a group of more experienced voluntary sector workers who would have benefited from more advanced training modules.

In March 1997, a questionnaire was sent to managers of staff who had attended the training over the previous six months. Analysis of their responses suggested that the introductory course needed to be run on a regular basis to allow new staff to attend as part of their induction programme. They valued the way that the training targeted their agency's needs but, in spite of the trainers' positive experiences of multi-agency sessions, many agency managers still preferred in-house training. They agreed that more advanced sessions were needed for more experienced staff. Following this evaluation a training plan was developed for the next 12 months. The programme now consists of 10 open access courses, including one for more experienced staff. Local social services and mainstream health providers are now involved in delivering these packages of training. The training is subject to regular feedback from both course participants and the managers of the agencies involved. The programme has developed by using workers and trainers from outside the START team where necessary, but we still make sure that team members are involved because of the credibility they have established with the client agencies through their day to day contact.

It cost £10,000 to employ an outside consultant and to establish the basic programme. With oncosts, the team has had to find £25,000 per year to fund a worker four days per week to maintain and develop the training programme.

Conclusion

Although the START team has employed all the above-mentioned ways of improving working relationships with voluntary agencies, the single most effective intervention in this process has been the training programme. One can speculate about why it seems to have been so successful. A major reason would seem to be that it is meeting a need that has been deeply felt, if not always articulated, by the agencies concerned. This is perhaps not surprising, bearing in mind the fact that they had been working for years as the untrained, unacknowledged carers for large numbers of people with severe mental illness.

The initial consultancy was vital in terms of involving our client agencies in the process and spreading the sense of ownership for the programme. It also made it more likely that we would deliver what they needed rather than what we felt was appropriate. Although outside trainers are used, many trainers are members of the START team. They, like the trainees, are actively working with homeless people and this gives the sessions a credibility they might not have if delivered by trainers with no experience of the homeless milieu. The training acknowledges voluntary workers as partners in the process who already have considerable skills in helping people with profound mental health problems. In an ideal world where ownership was truly shared, the training programme would be jointly funded by START and its client agencies, but voluntary sector finances do not at present allow this. A further development might be for a consortium of voluntary agencies to offer training in homelessness issues to local health, housing and social service departments.

As the voluntary sector becomes increasingly involved in community care, relationships between it and statutory services become increasingly important. Although this training project has taken place in a service dealing with homeless people, the principles developed are more widely applicable and not limited to the voluntary/statutory divide. For example, similar programmes could be established between different types of statutory agency with shared tasks, for example Local Authority housing departments and Mental Health Trusts.

Bibliography

Brent-Smith, H. and Dean, R. (1990), *Plugging the gaps*, Lewisham and North Southwark Health Authority, London.

Cochrane, C. (1988), 'Humane, Economical and Medically Wise: the LCC as Administrators of Victorian Lunacy Policy' in W. F. Bynum, R. Porter and M. Shepherd (eds), *The Anatomy of Madness, Vol III The Asylum and its Psychiatry*, Routledge, London.

Connelly, J. and Crown, J. (1994), *Homelessness and Ill Health*, Royal College of Physicians, London.

Crossley, B. and Denmark, J.C. (1969), 'Community Care – a Study of the Psychiatric Morbidity of a Salvation Army Hostel', *British Journal of Sociology*, Vol. 20, pp. 443-9.

Davies N., Lingham, R., Prior, C. and Sims, A. (1995), *Report of the inquiry into the circumstances leading to the death of Jonathan Newby*, Oxfordshire Health Authority, Oxford.

Department of Health (1993), *Working together for Better Health*, Department of Health, London.

Edwards, G., Williamson, V., Hawker, A., Hensman, C. and Postsyan, S. (1968), 'Census of a Reception Centre', *British Journal of Psychiatry*, Vol. 114, pp. 1031-9.

Goldfinger, S.M. and Chafetz, L. (1984), 'Developing a Better Service Delivery System for the Homeless Mentally Ill', in R.H. Lamb (ed.), *The Homeless Mentally Ill*, American Psychiatric Association, Washington DC.

Glover, K. (1997), *Training Staff to Work Effectively with Homeless People who have Mental Health Problems*, START team, Lewisham and Guy's Mental Health Trust, London.

Gorton, S. (1995), *Not Getting Through – the Impact of Community Care Legislation on Homeless People with Mental Health Problems*, Health Action for Homeless People, London.

Griffiths, R. (1988), *Community Care: Agenda for Action*, HMSO, London.

Kuipers, L., Leff, J. and Lam, D. (1992), *Family Work for Schizophrenia – a Practical Guide*, Gaskell, London.

Leff, J.P., Kuipers, L. and Berkowitz, R. (1985), 'A Controlled Trial of Social Intervention in the Families of Schizophrenic Patients: Two-year Follow-up', *British Journal of Psychiatry*, Vol. 146, pp. 594-600.

Lodge Patch, I. (1971), 'Homeless Men in London: I. Demographic Findings in a Lodging House Sample', *British Journal of Psychiatry*, Vol. 118, pp. 313-7.

Mental Health Foundation (1994), *Creating Community Care*, Mental Health Foundation, London.

Morgan, G. (1997), *Images of Organisation*, Sage, Thousand Oaks.

Ritchie, J.H., Dick, D. and Lingham, R. (1994), *The Report of the Inquiry into the Care and Treatment of Christopher Clunis*, HMSO, London.

START Annual Report (1997), Lewisham and Guy's Mental Health Trust, London.

St Mungo's Yearbook (1997), St Mungo Community Housing Association, London.

Appendix

START Training Prospectus for 1997/1998

Introductory Course:

1 Understanding and Recognising Mental Health Problems
A 2 day course to equip hostel and day-centre staff with a basic knowledge of mental health problems and their treatments. It will enable staff to recognise signs and symptoms of serious mental illness and when to call for help.

Intermediate Courses:

2 Talking Sense – Making Interaction Useful
A 1 day course to enable staff to communicate effectively with people with serious mental health problems. It also offers strategies to manage behaviours that cause anxiety in hostels and day centres.

3 Getting the Best out of the System
A 1 day course to equip hostel and day centre workers with a sound working knowledge of the mental health system so that they can appropriately refer to and use mental health services.

4 Managing Care and Support
A 1 day course presenting a number of formal and informal systems of care, discussing key issues in managing the care of people with serious mental health problems.

5 Young People
A 1 day course to equip staff with a knowledge of the mental health problems particularly affecting young people and what services are available to meet these needs.

Advanced Courses:

6 Alcohol, Drugs and Mental Health
A 1 day course to equip staff with a knowledge of the relationship between alcohol and drug use and mental health problems and the interventions that may be helpful with people who have multiple problems.

7 Challenging Behaviour – Personality Disorder, Madness or Myth?
A 1 day course which explores how people with challenging behaviours may be diagnosed as suffering from personality disorders and the range of effective interventions.

4 Better A Public Tenant Than A Private Borrower Be: The Possession Process and The Threat of Eviction

CAROLINE HUNTER AND JUDY NIXON

Introduction

Owner-occupation has been promoted as the 'normal' or 'natural' tenure of choice by governments in this country for over 30 years. Conservative governments have, for many years, set home ownership at the centre of their housing policy. While the Labour party may not have placed such a great emphasis on home ownership, nonetheless it has adopted the view that 'most families want to own their own homes' (Labour Party, 1997, p. 25). As Kemeny (1981, p. 11) points out:

> ... the almost mystical reverence for home-ownership' is nicely reflected in the eulogy of home-ownership presented in an otherwise dry British Government White Paper on housing (United Kingdom, 1971, p. 4):
>
>> Home ownership is the most rewarding form of house tenure. It satisfies a deep and natural desire on the part of the householder to have independent control of the home that shelters him and his family. It gives him the greatest possible security against the loss of his home; and particularly against price changes that may threaten his ability to keep it.

This view of home-ownership has been characterized by Kemeny (1981, p. 11) as a 'myth'. Yet it is one which has been successfully perpetuated during the 1980s with home-ownership continuing to rise, partly as a result of the promotion of the 'right to buy' council dwellings. Thus between 1979 and 1995 home ownership in England and Wales rose from 56 per cent to 68 per cent of households (DoE, 1995b, p. 13).

Over the last ten years, however, the myth has become increasingly difficult to sustain, as mortgage arrears and repossession rates have soared. Notwithstanding this, the Government, in 1995, felt able almost to repeat the view from 1971 (DoE, 1995b, p. 12):

> A high level of home ownership, alongside a healthy rented market, is good for the country and good for the individual. 80% of people favour home ownership over other forms of tenure. They value independence and control over their own home.

Although the difficulties of the recession and in the housing market were acknowledged in the White Paper, 'they need to be set alongside the long term advantages of home ownership'.

We still do not have an economic or housing system which is tenure neutral (i.e., where the choices between owning and renting are not distorted by economic or other factors); hence the preference for home ownership still emerges. We are not able in the space of this chapter to enter into the debate as to the underlying reasons for this preference (see Saunders, 1990; Cole and Furbey, 1994; Malpass, 1996; Forrest and Murie, 1994; Murie, 1991). What we have sought to do is explore the element of the myth that home ownership provides greater security than renting. Furthermore, we consider whether the reality for those who encounter difficulty in maintaining payments for housing is in fact tenure neutral. Saunders (1990, p. 119) argues that the advantages of owner-occupation are 'grounded in the rights of private property', but might not the fact that they are 'private' also provide disadvantages in maintaining those rights?

Drawing on findings from a recent empirical study into housing debt (which evaluated the changing management of mortgage and rent possession cases in the county court and the impact of different forms of representation, including the absence of any form of representation or participation by defendants on the outcomes of cases (Nixon et al., 1996)[1]) we start by describing the distinct ways in which borrowers' and tenants' possession hearings are dealt with by the legal system. We then examine the impact of tenure on the distribution of the outcomes of such hearings, focusing on the complex interrelationship between the different ways in which tenants and borrowers in debt are treated within the legal system and the outcomes of judicial possession action.

The study showed that following possession action borrowers were twice as likely as tenants to be at risk of enforced eviction (see Table 4.1). Our analysis of the reasons why borrowers were more vulnerable to losing their homes focuses on: first, the wider determinants affecting the different suppliers and consumers of housing; and, second, the individual statutory and regulatory framework within which judicial discretion is exercised. The chapter concludes by raising a number of questions concerning the impact of the recent convergence of lenders' and landlords' use of the judicial process, as social landlords change their management methods as a response to the increased commodification of public sector housing management.

Housing Debt, Possession Actions and the Risk of Eviction

There is now a substantial body of work into housing related debt.[2] In many respects the findings from these studies show a high degree of tenure neutrality in so far as the reported causes of arrears for both owner occupiers and tenants are remarkably similar. The evidence reveals that for the vast majority of households, housing debt is a serious problem which most commonly forms part of a complex web of multiple debt. In most cases we found there was rarely a single or simple reason for the arrears. While our interviews with debtors showed that over time individuals are likely to experience a variety of reasons for being in arrears of payments, both owner occupiers and tenants identified the same range of factors as being the main causes of the arrears, namely:

- disruption/loss of secure employment;
- changes in domestic arrangements leading to an increase in expenditure or a loss of income;
- failure of the benefit safety net;
- financial over-commitment.

The similarity of the experience of debt for households, regardless of tenure was very striking. Once debt had accrued households were drawn into a dynamic rather than static process, with the risk of individuals losing their home dependent on whether the debt was reducing or, more commonly, increasing.

Given the fundamental similarities in the stated causes of and experience of debt, a tenure neutral system would lead both to similar treatment of, and outcomes for, those experiencing debt. However, the study findings illustrate the tensions apparent in the relationship between the different ways in which rental and mortgage cases are dealt with and the long term risk of a household being evicted. The risk of becoming homeless following possession action was found to be dependent on a complex range of factors. The key findings from the study show:

1 the extent to which individuals played an active part in the legal process had a direct bearing on the outcomes for both tenants and borrowers, with more advantageous outcomes being achieved when borrowers and tenants actively participated in court hearings or were represented and conversely lack of active participation appeared to lead to a higher proportion of outright orders being made, leaving defendants at a greater risk of enforced eviction;

2 however, the way in which the courts manage housing debt cases differs according to tenure. Mortgage actions are heard privately in judges' chambers providing borrowers with an opportunity to discuss their financial and personal circumstances in confidence. In contrast rented actions are heard publicly, in 'open' court with no privacy and with as many as 104 cases listed for one session. Thus, if tenants are to participate in such hearings they are required to sit in court listening to other cases while they wait for their turn to be heard. Not surprisingly, most tenants found this system of open hearings humiliating and degrading;

3 we found significant differences in borrowers' and tenants' rates of participation in the court process, with borrowers more likely to attend the hearing in person than tenants. Over half of all the borrowers were actively involved in the process as compared to less than a third of tenants;

4 in light of the positive relationship between defendant participation and outcomes combined with the knowledge that fewer tenants participated in the process as compared to borrowers, it could be anticipated that there would be a propensity for tenants to fare worse than borrowers in terms of outcomes to the possession process. This was not the case however. Indeed, borrowers as compared to tenants were more than twice as likely to have outright possession orders made against them and were five times more likely to have had possession warrants enforced. Figure 4.1 provides details of the outcomes of cases according tenure.

The explanation for these apparently contradictory findings lies in the lack of tenure neutrality in determining the complex relationships between

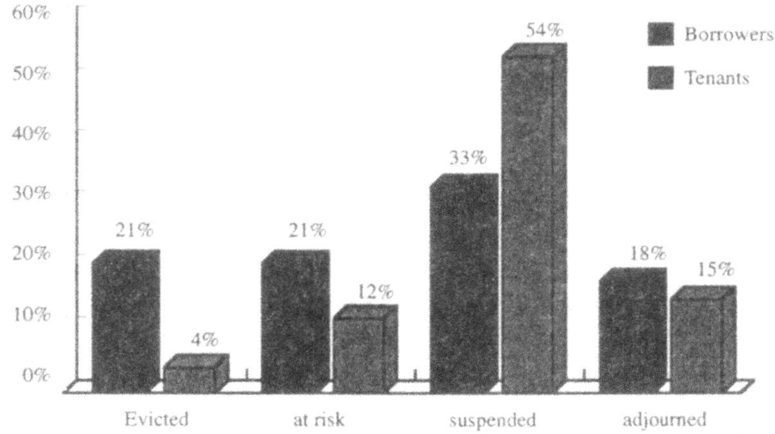

Figure 4.1 Comparison of tenants' and borrowers' 'long term'[3] outcomes[4]

the differing levels of debt for tenants and owner occupiers, the range of arrears management strategies adopted by lenders and landlords, and on the judicial framework and with the exercise of judicial discretion by individual judges. Further analysis of these factors has been facilitated by the work of Stewart (1996) in charting the impact of the changing structures of accountability between suppliers and consumers of housing and the implications for changing legal regulation.

An examination of the application of the law to borrowers' and tenants' possession actions and the resulting differences in outcomes suggests there are in fact three main reasons for the differences in tenants' and borrowers' outcomes (see Table 4.1):

- the differing levels of debt found amongst borrowers and tenants;
- the differing arrears management strategies adopted by lenders and landlords resulting in different types of orders being sought from the court;
- the impact of the application of the law and the statutory framework within which judicial discretion is exercised.

Each of these factors is now examined in turn.

Levels of Debt and the Availability of Financial Assistance

The level of debt, the time-scale over which the debt accrued along with an assessment of the most effective method of recovery of the debt, were all found to be key factors influencing landlords' and lenders' decision to issue possession summons. In the study the levels of debt were measured by reference to the number of missed weekly rent or monthly mortgage repayments to which the arrears were equivalent. Account was also taken of the actual amount of money owed. It is acknowledged that neither of these methods of measurement take into account the dynamic nature of debt accumulation. For the majority of households arrears will have built up over a far longer period of time period than is reflected by the average number of weeks or months of outstanding payments. For example, some households in the survey had been struggling with a rising tide of debt for over ten years.

The level of debt was found to be a significant factor in determining outcomes. The majority of borrowers owed lenders substantial amounts of money with average arrears of £4,224, the equivalent of just over one year's missed payments. In common with previous studies we found that once borrowers have developed long term arrears they are unlikely to ever clear them: 'amongst borrowers with serious arrears approximately three quarters have very little likelihood of repaying what they owe' (Ford, 1995, p. 3).

In comparison to the average amount owed by owner occupiers at the time of the first court hearing, landlords generally issued possession summons when the arrears were relatively low. Tenant average arrears were £750 with the average number of missed payments less than the equivalent of four months' rental payments. A number of factors were found to help explain why borrowers arrears were so much higher than those found amongst tenants. First, the actual amount of monthly mortgage repayments were far higher than weekly rental payments and thus it could be argued that owners' propensity to debt was greater than that of tenants. Second, there were noted differences in the type of assistance for housing costs that was available to owner occupiers and tenants.

Eligibility for help with rental payments depends on a number of factors including income, the number of dependants, rent levels, etc., but can be as high as 100 per cent of rent due. For borrowers on the other hand, the maximum Income Support assistance will only cover the interest payments on the outstanding loan and, indeed, recent changes in Income Support regulations have resulted in the withdrawal of even this limited assistance to borrowers during the first nine months of a new claim (see the amendments made to the

Table 4.1 Factors determining tenants' and borrowers' outcomes in possession hearings

Levels of debt at the time of the first court hearing

	Borrowers	**Tenants**
Average arrears	£4,224	£750
Average number of missed payments the debt is equivalent to	13 months	15 weeks
Availability of assistance with housing costs	maximum assistance partial with interest payments only	maximum of 100% assistance for low income households

Plaintiffs' arrears management strategies

	Borrowers	**Tenants**
Type of organization	Financial institutions	Social housing organizations
Sphere of operation	The market place	Public service/welfare provision
Principal aim of arrears management	To protect the interests of investors by obtaining repayment of the debt within a specified time period or repossess the property to realize the debt	To sustain tenancies to those in housing need and to ensure that current repayments are maintained with an amount paid off the arrears

The judicial process and the impact of judicial discretion

	Borrowers	**Tenants**
Nature of relationship	Private determined by business ethic	Quasi-market / public sector ethos
	Market forces underpinned by the exchange value of the dwelling	Contractual regulation underpinned by assessment of housing need and the use value of the dwelling
	Protection of commercial interests	Protection of the use value
Type of hearing	Private in chambers	Public in 'open' court
Long term outcomes	Just under half evicted or at acute risk of eviction	Less than a quarter evicted or at acute risk of eviction

Income Support (General) Regulations 1987 by S.I. 1995 No. 1613). Failure of the benefit system to provide a safety net for households on very low incomes was cited by a number of respondents as being a major contributory cause of their arrears. In particular, problems with the benefit system were experienced by borrowers whose pattern of employment fluctuated and who were repeatedly entering, leaving and re-entering the labour market. As Dan explained:

> I tried paying bits off here and there but it was slowly getting bigger and bigger and then I was eventually made redundant ... and that was the end of that and I was unemployed for a while and then I got this job that I was just made redundant from again, and the arrears got bigger and bigger and everything seemed to snowball. And of course when you've been unemployed even though they're paying some of the interest off your debt, it's still growing and growing ...

Not only does the availability of assistance influence the level of debt, it also affected the attitude of judges to the claim for possession. Almost without exception interviews with district judges confirmed that the type of financial assistance available to households was relevant in determining the type of order made. In December 1991, most lenders entered into a voluntary agreement not to take judicial possession action where borrowers were in receipt of Income Support and interest payments were paid directly to lenders. More recently there appears to have been some change in lenders' approach to interest direct payments, and where the payments do not meet 100 per cent of the monthly sum required, lenders have commenced judicial action to obtain possession (Nixon et al., 1996). Judges had a variety of views of the importance of direct payments. One judge stated: 'Income Support for mortgage interest has had a significant impact on the way the courts tend to exercise their discretion, although it is arguable whether or not it should.' Another judge commented: 'Interest payments direct from DSS? Very significant, 10 out of 10 for importance.' This particular judge explained that in such cases he invariably granted a suspended possession order on the condition that current instalments were paid with nothing further to pay off the arrears until the case was reviewed in 6–12 months. Other judges stated they gave less regard to defendants' sources of income and took the view that if less than 100 per cent of interest due was paid, an outright possession order would be considered.

A more uniform approach taken by judges was noted in relation to tenants in receipt of Housing Benefit. A safeguard accepted by virtually all the judges in our sample was that in cases where tenants were dependent on Income Support the repayment of arrears from their benefit should not exceed the amount that DSS was prepared to deduct directly from their benefit. There was also a general agreement about the type of problems perceived to be associated with benefits (e.g., delayed payments, non-dependent deductions and overpayment of benefit), and all said they would either consider adjourning cases in order for benefit problems to be resolved or make a suspended order on minimal repayment terms.

To sum up, for both borrowers and tenants there is a positive relationship between the level of debt and the type of order made by the court. Generally, the higher the levels of debt, the more likely an outright possession order will be granted. This association in part provides an explanation as to why borrowers, with higher levels of debt, had a greater propensity to being evicted as a result of possession action. More detailed analysis of the court data, however, revealed that other factors such as the plaintiffs' objectives in taking judicial action combined with the form of participation by defendants and the use of judicial discretion also play an important role in determining the risk of a household losing their home.

Plaintiffs' Arrears Management Strategies

The formal possession process can be used to meet a range of different objectives in an arrears management strategy. As well as being used to obtain actual possession of a dwelling the process can be used to establish contact with a household or to formalize existing repayment agreements or even to settle disputes over the reasons for and/or the amount of the debt. Depending on the objective of the plaintiff the courts will be asked to consider granting different types of orders. We now examine the impact of the differing economic and political framework within which lenders and social landlords operate and their influence on the type of order likely to be sought.

The Type of Organization and Sphere of Operation

The first point to be made is that all organizations established to lend money for house purchase are in essence financial institutions operating in the market place with responsibilities to their shareholders or investors to secure their investment and minimize losses. As Murphy (1994, p. 195) points out, operating within this framework lenders' approach to arrears automatically results in them viewing debt primarily as a product of forces beyond their control which are most effectively minimized by seeking immediate repossession of the property:

> For building societies operating under the discipline of the financial system, arrears may be tolerated as a short term aberration in a household's repayment history but not as a long term problem (Murphy, 1994, p. 196).

Stewart provides further insight into the reasons why building societies have experienced difficulty in dealing with the rapid increase in arrears by reference to their historic role principally as money lenders rather than housing advisors or debt counsellors (Stewart, 1996, p. 59). In this context it is not surprising that lenders have appeared to find it difficult to reconcile the interests of their investors with the development of arrears management which is sympathetic to the borrower. Even when such systems have been developed there is a continuing emphasis on maintaining regular payments or moving rapidly to enforced repossession (Ford, 1994).

In contrast, social landlords are essentially non profit, housing organizations rather than financial institutions 'which aim to meet housing needs while private sector landlords are profit oriented businesses which cater for "effective demands" in the market place rather than for "needs"' (DoE, 1993, p. 14). The emphasis on a needs driven service is reflected in the aims of housing management which have been summarized by the National Federation of Housing Associations (NFHA, 1987) as being:

> about providing good quality housing and services to those who have been in housing need and about maximizing the useful life of limited stock ... One basic aim is to ensure that housing services go to those in greatest need.

With the focus on providing housing for those in greatest need, social landlords have not traditionally been so ready as lenders to commence legal action for nonpayment of rent and have viewed issuing a summons for possession as a last resort in an arrears management strategy. As one housing officer explained in a study into housing management performance: 'Taking a tenant to court is an admission of housing management failure and an eviction or voluntary termination of a tenancy with large arrears rarely leads to the recovery of those arrears' (DoE, 1989, p. 59; see also DoE, 1994, p. 8).

In examining the range of motives underlying landlords' and lenders' decision to commence legal proceedings it is possible to trace the importance of the different organizational frameworks within which lenders and landlords operate. Once in court lenders and landlords tend to be seeking quite different orders because of the type of organization they represent and their sphere of operation. Lenders are seeking to protect their investment, while landlords are seeking to maintain the tenant in his home and recover something off the arrears. This attitude of plaintiffs, however, cannot explain entirely the differences in outcomes, but rather is a reflection of the fundamental differences in the nature of the relationship between borrowers and lenders on the one hand and tenants and landlords on the other, which also finds expression in the legal structures and the attitudes of the judiciary.

The Judicial Process

Nature of the Relationship

The nature of the relationship between the different parties is both reflected in and determined by legal structures. Comparison of the structural and legal frameworks operating for owner occupiers and tenants highlights the different historical roots of the two tenure groups. Property rights can be constructed in a number of ways, one simple dichotomy can be drawn between commercial/exchange value of the property and the use value. For lenders their primary interest is in the commercial/exchange value of their property rights; borrowers may be concerned as to commercial property rights, but their dominant interest will be in maintaining the use value, i.e., a home. For tenants (save for the right to buy) the rights granted through the tenancy are primarily of a use value. Social landlords have primarily been seeking, within certain constraints, to provide use value rights, although as we shall discuss below, this position may now be changing, as such landlords increasingly operate in a commercial and contractual structure.

The Borrower/Lender Relationship

Stewart (1996, p. 49) argues that the standard building society mortgage agreement constructs a relationship in which the mortgagor is potentially at severe legal disadvantage:

> There has been very little consideration by the courts of this arrangement because the relationship between the mortgagor and the building society is a product of the position which the societies have held in the wider financial world.

Inherent to the judicial regulation of property transactions is the assumption that there are two equal parties to the commercial transaction. Such an assumption is called into question by the recent dramatic increase in repossessions, which reflects the current reality of an increasing number of economically vulnerable households unable to support the burden of ownership. This mismatch between the theoretical framework and the day-to-day economic reality has resulted in a tension in the way that property owners are perceived within the legal system:

> with changing social and economic circumstances the courts are attempting to adapt concepts which allow for the development of new property rights, the extent to which this occurs depends to a considerable extent on the exercise of judicial discretion (Stewart, 1996, p. 31).

The exercise of that discretion can only take place against the background of the legal framework. The common law construct of the mortgage, with the mortgagee entitled to possession 'from the moment the ink is dry' has been subject to very little judicial or statutory interference. It was not until 1970 that the first statutory controls on repossession were introduced, the courts having rejected any jurisdiction to do so in *British Citizens Permanent Building Society v Caunt* [1962] Ch. 883. The provisions of the Administration of Justice Act 1970, s. 36 and the Administration of Justice Act 1973, s. 8 provide a discretion to the court in a mortgage possession action to adjourn or suspend the action if the borrower can demonstrate that they can repay the arrears *'within a reasonable period of time'*. This is the single matter which is relevant to the court in exercising its discretion whether to adjourn or suspend an application for possession. Thus the focus is entirely on whether the borrower can pay the contractual sums due, whether now or within a reasonable period.

Protection of the Commercial Interest of the Lender

Analysis of the way in which judges exercise their discretion provides evidence of the dominance of market forces and the primary importance of the exchange value of the dwelling. The evidence from the study (Nixon et al., 1996, p. 48) and from others (DoE, 1995a) suggests that there has been an increasing use of suspended orders for mortgagees, although still at a much lower rate than for tenants. This, it might be suggested, is a recognition by lenders and judges that the use value of borrowers' homes should be protected. The comments of judges suggest, however, that it is more a reflection of the economic reality of a depressed market and, in particular, the emergence of negative equity. Thus one judge commented: 'I have the impression that lenders, mortgagees, are increasingly aware that it doesn't actually necessarily pay them to get a possession order ...', suggesting that the change comes from the demands made on the courts by lenders. The demands of the outside market are also reflected in this comment:

> Again commercial and more importantly estate agents who don't want to completely wreck the market for their estate agency ... usually the last thing they want is the house to sell or trying to sell the house.

So the changing pattern of orders can to some extent be explained by the outside pressure from lenders. But almost inevitably such demands become internalized, and part of the dominant thinking, whether pressed by lenders or not. A clear awareness of the primacy of economic interests in mortgage actions was exhibited by many of the judges. For example:

> I think most of the good building societies know they don't want another house on their books they just want some payment. We know that if we serve possession in twenty eight days, that the house may sit on the market for two years before anyone even goes to look at it. So what's the point?

Thus, although there has been a move towards a greater use of suspended possession orders in mortgage cases, this move is not primarily generated by the law seeking to protect the use value of the home to the borrower. Indeed one judge was clear that in some cases it would, in his view, be preferable if defendants recognized the inevitability of possession.

> They would probably be better biting the bullet now ... he is really much better ... going to rented accommodation which he can get the DSS to pay the rent rather than to struggle and end up by having a lot more debt and indeed the building society having a shortfall so their investors lose.

Rather, the approach of judges that has been urged upon them by lenders and which has been internalized in the application of discretion, is one which recognizes that the role of the judge is to defend the commercial property rights of the lender. This is not to say that some judges have not been motivated by a sympathy for, and desire to protect mortgagors, indeed that was evident in some of the comments made by them (see also Ford, 1997). Rather it is that the predominant ideological framework within which judicial discretion is exercised is premised on the commercial value of the dwelling, and this comes into focus when compared to decisions taken in relation to tenants. The importance of this commercial approach is summed up, maybe at its most extreme, by the following comment:

> ... it is a matter of commercial decision, lenders are beyond my powers and I have taken the view that the powers given in mortgage cases are limited as they are because otherwise we are going to make all the building societies go bankrupt.

Tenant/Landlord Relationship

Turning to the social rented sector, which is dominated by local authority landlords, there are significant and major differences in the framework within which property relationships are expressed. As Stewart (1996) points out, local authority landlords are a creation of the state and an embodiment of the state responsibility for the welfare of its citizens. She also argues that public sector housing has been constructed legally through both the regulatory sphere and through judges' interpretation of individual tenants' rights and the responsibilities of public landlords. This position can be seen in the development of the legal framework for public sector tenants. Prior to 1980 neither local authority nor housing association tenants had any meaningful individual property rights. None were granted by statute and the courts were not willing to interfere with the administrative decisions of local authorities as to whether and when to evict tenants (see e.g. *Bristol City Council v Clark* [1975] 3 All ER 136). This might be characterized as the regulatory approach.

This position changed with the introduction of the Housing Act 1980, giving secure tenancies to local authority and housing association tenants. The relevant statutory provisions are now to be found in the Housing Act 1985.[5] This requires that once the arrears have been proved, the court must be satisfied that *it is reasonable* to make an order for possession, before such an order can be made. Guidance in determining what factors the judge must take into account when considering reasonableness is very broad and includes: 'all relevant circumstances as they exist at the date of the hearing ... giving weight as he thinks right to the various factors in the situation' (per Lord Greene M.R. in *Cumming v Danson* [1942] 2 All ER 653 at p. 655).

In effect there are two legal approaches to the possession process: one that it is a purely administrative task that should be left to the landlord; the second of statutory regulation, but which gives a huge discretion to the judge. Notwithstanding the introduction of the Housing Act rights as long ago as 1980, both approaches were to some extent evident in the way judges viewed their task.

Trust in the Landlords

In relation to the first approach this manifested itself in the trust put in the local authorities. One judge was quite clear that he could rely on what the authority requested to determine the nature of the order:

> ... as an awful lot of defendants don't turn up in local authority cases one would have a problem of what the right order should be, if it wasn't for the fact that the arrears officers will tell you and they're fair and they're reliable.

Another judge commented that he had been dealing with the same officer for 18 years and the officer 'knew what he could get away with'. So for some judges, the process is not much more than administrative, i.e. rubber-stamping the request of the landlord. The view of the process as purely administrative was also reflected in some tenants' comments about the hearing: 'It went against everybody before I got up. The judgments went against them, they knew they were going to get a judgment no matter what. It was all loaded in [the authority's] favour.'

Thus the outcomes achieved in relation to tenants may in part be a reflection of the process whereby social landlords are generally seeking to keep tenants in their homes, and asking for suspended orders, and the judges are simply facilitating this outcome. Thus it is a reflection of the type and sphere of operation of the landlord.

Protection of the Use Value of the Dwelling

It is also clear that judges take a very different view of the rights which have to be protected in cases against tenants from those involving borrowers. Unlike mortgage cases, where the application of judicial discretion is viewed as a balancing act requiring judges to weigh up the interests of both lenders and their investors, and borrowers, in rented actions local authorities (as landlords) are not viewed as having any rights which require protecting:

> I'm not looking at any number of years to pay off the arrears of tenants, I never have done actually, I look to see what can he realistically afford. ... The council will say, well we accept in this case a suspended order of the rent plus two pound thirty a week and I say well with the arrears at this level you know this lady's going to live until she's a hundred and sixty before she's paid them all, you realize that .... They write it off, they expect to write it off.

Indeed, given local authority responsibility towards the homeless, some judges actually viewed it as in the interests of the authority to maintain their tenants in their homes:

> Local authority cases, not many people actually turn up on local authority cases, far less, but on the whole it doesn't make a great deal of difference, for this reason, the local authorities are not private mortgagees, sort of out for every penny in a sense and they've got the re-housing if they turn them out, the local authority's got the re-housing responsibility anyway, so they behave responsibly.

It was clear that for many of the district judges the primacy of the use value of the dwelling and the protection of the defendant featured more highly as a priority in rented actions as compared to mortgage actions. For those judges who did not view the process as simply administering the landlord's list, there was a concern expressed for protecting the tenant. On more than one occasion judges mentioned practices by landlords which they considered to be unfair on tenants and from which tenants needed protection, for example requesting high repayment terms. One judge commented on his relationship with landlords in the following terms:

> If you [the landlord] come with too high an order and the person isn't here to tell me that they can afford to pay that, I'm going to assume that they can't, so bring them if you've got an agreement like that and then we can all work together, if you don't bring them, I think that your rent collector has screwed them down to something and what is the point because if they cannot pay the original rent what chance have they of paying that plus so much more?

Clearly, here tenants were considered to be in need of protection from the landlord trying to recover the debt at a rate greater than the tenant could afford. This was in marked contrast to the position of borrowers set out above, where the starting point was repayment to the lender within a reasonable period.

Much greater stress was placed on the need to keep tenants in their homes and the consequences should this not happen. This concern with sustaining tenancies is also reflected in the recent review of access to justice undertaken by Lord Woolf. In discussing rent arrears he states: 'Judges, recognizing that possession may not really be in the interests of either party often seek to give the tenant a last chance to pay by granting a suspended possession order' (Woolf, 1996, para. 20, p. 202). The importance of the consequences of granting an outright possession order in rented actions was also reflected in judges' concerns about the welfare of the family and the consequences for children:

> One thing I find that tenants don't realize because no one explains it to them is that if they get themselves evicted through non payment of rent that the likely consequences is that their children will be taken into care.

Contrast this with the view taken (albeit by a different judge) in relation to a mortgage case:

> It is all to do with money, we are talking again only about mortgage cases – it is all to do with money. It is irrelevant to me why they got into problems, what is relevant is what is going to happen in the future, can they get out of their problems? Marital status is only of interest about what they need to live whether the wife is working, children are also important because of what it costs them out of their salary to keep them. So it is all to do with money ...

Judicial Discretion: Attitudes to Borrowers and Tenants

Housing possession actions involve a substantial exercise of judicial discretion as to the relative weight to give a range of factors when applying the substantive law. A judge in deciding whether to make an outright or suspended possession order must be guided by the statutory provisions, which in part require an assessment of the future capacity and competence of the defendant. Such an assessment appeared to be informed by a range of factors including judges' perceptions of the socio-economic standing of defendants. Thus, whilst judges' use of discretion and approach to defendants reflects the implicit dominance of either commercial/exchange value or use value of the dwelling, the use of discretion also appeared to reflect judges' personal views of the two tenure groups. When asked why fewer tenants than borrowers attended hearings one judge responded:

> I think one is dealing with a totally different sector of the community. Those who had mortgages were certainly at one time better off than at the time they obviously came to court. Whereas local authority tenants in particular I don't think have ever been quite so well off. They are very often illiterate or don't understand English and they are unaware of what is involved. Whereas the mortgagees have a better understanding and are able to obtain advice and assistance better than tenants.

Another felt greater attendance amongst borrowers was a reflection of the financial interest that the borrower has in the property:

> Mortgagors tend to attend because it's a sort of person who's owned their own

> house, bear in mind, at one stage, so they've tried to be, I won't say entrepreneurial, but they've had a financial interest ... I am particularly sympathetic to them in the sense they mustn't be dealt with as though they were criminals.

In dealing with tenants a much greater deal of paternalism was exhibited: 'Mind I won't stand any nonsense, I'll say to the tenants you let me down, I'll put you out ... they pay; it's the head master's study you see.' Such paternalism did not go unnoticed by tenants, some of whom found the judge's approach to be impersonal, patronizing and even arrogant. As Linda commented:

> Well he made you feel so small. I was just looking at him thinking you're no better than me just because you're sat up there. I know it's his job but he didn't even glance at me. It was humiliating actually. I wouldn't go again.

Thus it appeared that there was a tendency for judges' approach to defendants to be coloured by their perceptions of the social class and background of the defendant. Borrowers were perceived to be better educated, and more able to protect the financial interest they have vested in the property and therefore less in need of protection from the judiciary. Tenants on the other hand were perceived as vulnerable, unable to protect themselves, and to be treated like children.

Type of Hearing and Use of Open and Closed Courts

We have sought to set out above the different values which the law is seeking to protect as a way of explaining the differences in outcomes in possession cases. It may also provide some explanation of the different court processes which apply to borrowers and tenants. For borrowers, because of the county court rules, the hearing is in 'chambers', i.e., in the judge's office with no members of the public allowed into the room. Tenants on the other hand are effectively put through a ritual of public humiliation should they chose to attend the hearing.

Tenancy possession cases are listed in large blocks, with all the cases listed for the same time. Because tenants are concerned about missing their 'turn', all defendants and indeed landlords' representatives are usually sat in court as the case is called on. Interviews with tenants showed that they clearly considered the system to be degrading and embarrassing as their personal and financial affairs were aired in public.

Judges were reluctant to move to a chambers system for tenancy cases, since it would make it impossible to get through them at the required rate: reflecting an essentially administrative process. Others were sensitive to the concerns expressed by tenants:

> I find it absolutely appalling that very intimate and private matters, as finances are to most people, particularly if they have to admit they have been sacked ... [are discussed]. To have to do to that in a large court room, with an array of people ... with a judge sat up fully wigged, is ... overpowering to most people.

While some judges were concerned that justice should be seen to be done in the case of tenants, none expressed a similar concern in the case of borrowers. It seems to be accepted that what is concerned here is a private matter, which is not of public interest. The distinction in the treatment of the two tenures was, however, recognized as 'indefensible' by nearly all those who made submissions to the Woolf enquiry (Woolf, 1996, para. 36, p. 207) and he concluded (para. 37) that on balance all possession proceedings should take place in chambers, although there should be no overall ban on public attendance.

Moves Towards a Converging Approach?

Stewart (1996) argues that since 1980 occupiers of council housing have been reconstructed from tenants in need of decent housing through tenants with rights to tenants with choices in a social market. The '90s, she concludes, can be characterized as the era of public citizenship: 'we now see the transformation of tenants into consumers of public commodities' (p. 174). This process she argues is, however, fraught with contradictions, namely at the same time as the rhetoric of council tenants as individual consumers operating within the social market is emphasized, the actual choices open to tenants have been reduced through the process of residualization, as public housing becomes the tenure of last resort (see Murie, 1997). The contractualization of the relations of local government is exemplified by the introduction of CCT.

> The public landlord is required to manage the consequences of the economic and social residualisation of the council sector in a context where the emphasis is on the local authority as housing facilitator and purchaser of housing services (p. 185).

During the 1980s, as local authorities' development role has been reduced, the emphasis has shifted to local authorities as managers of services and as landlords operating within a similar legal framework to private sector landlords. 'The form of relationship between landlord and tenant has changed substantially from one based on public administration to one encapsulated in a contract' (p. 186). The history and development of council housing, argues Stewart, have provided council housing with a number of distinctive characteristics, for example notions of affordability maintained through rate subsidy and rent pooling, allocation on the basis of need rather than ability to pay and political accountability.

It was the last Conservative government's aim to blur this distinction:

> We aim to encourage a wider range of private landlords into the sector, alongside existing housing associations, and to expand the programme of voluntary transfers of council housing with tenants' consent to new landlords (DoE, 1995b, p. 26).

Within the profession there are opposing views on the role of local authority landlords. The contractual role is emphasized by some in an attempt to eliminate social objectives from housing management, and promote the role of local authorities as enablers (see Hunter and Selman, 1996). This view maintains that the local authority function should be concerned solely with property management functions and in this respect little different from private landlords. The opposing view recognizes that the social welfare role is very much part of the landlord role (CIOH, 1993; Clapham, 1987).

Changes over the last thirty years point towards a growing convergence between the public and private sectors with the growing commodification of public sector housing moving away from the basis of provision as a right of citizenship towards the provision 'to consumers of a public commodity purchased through a contract with rent as a consideration' (Stewart, 1996, p. 122). There does not yet seem to be any recognition of this changing role of social landlords, and local authorities in particular, amongst the judiciary. It has not gone unnoticed, however, amongst tenants: 'They try to run the council as a business now, which is great, but they have got to try and accept some kind of social responsibility somewhere down the line.'

Thus it is increasingly likely that authorities and their managing agents, with strict targets for rent arrears, will not be willing to accept court orders which will not see the arrears paid within the lifetime of the tenant. Nor will they wish to continue to house tenants who are going to have ongoing problems of meeting their rental commitments. It seems likely that the judicial process will be under increasing demand to recognize the new reality of a commodified social housing sector, where the maintenance of the use value of the home is not the dominant property right being sought to be protected by both landlord and tenant.

From the other side there is already some evidence that the judicial system is recognizing the changing nature of the owner-occupied sector. In the recent decision of *Cheltenham & Gloucester Building Society v Norgan* [1996] 1 All ER 449, the Court of Appeal have recognized that how much the borrower can afford to pay both now and in the future is a relevant consideration to determining what constitutes a 'reasonable period' to repay the arrears, and that the starting point for determining the period should be the remaining period of the mortgage term. This must, though, still be weighed against whether it is reasonable to expect the lender to recoup the arrears of interest over the whole of the original term, within a shorter period, or even within a longer period, by extending the repayment period. One judge recognized that: 'Academically we have far greater discretion in tenancy cases. Given the right information I think we are able to do as much in mortgage possession cases as we can in tenancy cases ....'

At the moment, the greater chance of loss of the home for owner-occupiers in debt can be alleviated by a move into housing in the social rented sector. If the risk of loss of the home becomes equally as great for those in financial difficulties in the social rented sector, where will those whose financial circumstances inevitably lead to the likelihood of debt be able to secure a home? If there is to be continued divergence should not those on the margins of owner-occupation be made aware of the risk before they purchase a home?

Notes

1 The study (Nixon et al., 1996) was based on a detailed survey of 490 housing cases heard in ten courts, five of which had court based advice schemes and five of which did not. In addition a national telephone survey was undertaken to establish listing practices and the extent of the provision of court based advice schemes. The survey data was subsequently augmented by in-depth case study interviews with a sample of 26 defendants and six district judges operating in six of the ten sample courts.

2 Nixon et al. (1996) builds on the findings of the following earlier studies into rental or mortgage default: DoE, 1989, 1994; Audit Commission, 1984; Duncan and Kirby, 1983; Ford 1988,1994,1995; Gentle, Dorling and Comford, 1994; Davis and Dhooge, 1993.

3 The possession process is dynamic with outcomes changing over time. Long term outcomes were measured by tracing cases over a minimum of six months. It is recognized that in some cases even these outcomes are not final outcomes and could change over time.

4 'Evicted' refers to all cases where warrants for possession had been executed: 'at risk' refers to cases where warrants had been issued but had not been executed and cases with a 28 day possession order outstanding; 'suspended' refers to cases with a suspended possession order on file; 'adjourned' refers to cases which had been adjourned.

5 For housing association tenancies granted after 15 January, 1989 the governing statute is the Housing Act 1988. Although a mandatory ground for possession for arrears is contained in the 1988 Act, none of the landlords in the study used it; all were relying on the discretionary grounds.

Bibliography

CIOH (1993), *More than Bricks and Mortar: Housing is fundamental to social welfare*, Chartered Institute of Housing, Coventry.

Cole, I. and Furbey, R. (1994), *The Eclipse of Council Housing*, Routledge, London.

Clapham, D. (1987), 'Trends in Housing Management' in D. Clapham and J. English (eds), *Public Housing Current Trends and Future Developments*, Croom Helm, London.

Davis, R. and Dhooge, Y. (1993), *Living with Mortgage Arrears*, Council of Mortgage Lenders, London.

DoE (1989), *Taking Tenants to Court*, HMSO, London.

DoE (1993), *Managing Social Housing*, York Centre for Housing Policy, HMSO, London.

DoE (1994), *Rent Arrears in Local Authorities and Housing Associations*, HMSO, London.

DoE (1995a), *Mortgage Arrears and Possession: Perspectives from Borrowers, Lenders and the Courts*, HMSO, London.

DoE (1995b), *Our Future Homes*, Cm 2901, HMSO, London.

Ford, J. (1993), 'Mortgage Possession', *Housing Studies*, Vol. 8, No. 4, pp. 227–40.

Ford, J. (1994), *Problematic Home Ownership: the Management, Experience and Consequences of Arrears and Possessions in a Depressed Housing Market*, Loughborough University, Loughborough.

Ford, J. (1995), *Which way Out? Borrowers and Long-term Mortgage Arrears*, Shelter, London.

Ford, J. (1997), 'Mortgage Arrears, Mortgage Possession and Homelessness' in R. Burrows, N. Pleace and D. Quilgars (eds), *Homelessness and Social Policy*, Routledge, London.

Forrest, R. and Murie, A. (1994), 'Home Ownership in Recession', *Housing Studies*, Vol. 9, No. 1, pp. 55–74.

Forrest, R., Murie, A. and Williams, P. (1990), *Home Ownership: Differentiation and Fragmentation*, Unwin Hyman, London.

Hunter, C. and Selman, A. (1996), *Compulsory Competitive Tendering of Housing Management*, Lemos & Crane, London.

Kemeny, J. (1981), *The Myth of Home Ownership*, Routledge, London.

Labour Party (1997), *New Labour, Because Britain Deserves Better*, London.

Malpass, P. (1996), 'Unravelling of Housing Policy in Britain', *Housing Studies*, Vol. 11, No. 3, pp. 459–70.

Malpass, P. and Murie, A. (1994), *Housing Policy and Practice*, Macmillan, Basingstoke.

Murie, A. (1991), 'Divisions of Home Ownership: Housing Tenure and Social Change', *Environment Planning*, pp. 349–70.

Murie, A. (1997), 'Beyond State Housing' in P. Williams (ed.), *Directions in Housing Policy: Towards Sustainable Housing Policies for the U.K.*, Paul Chapman, London.

Murphy, L. (1994), 'The Downside of Home Ownership: Housing Change and Mortgage Arrears in the Republic of Ireland', *Housing Studies*, Vol. 9, No. 2, pp. 183–98.
NFHA (1987), *Standards for Housing Management*, NFHA, London.
Nixon, J., Smith, Y., Wishart, B. and Hunter, C. (1996), *Housing Cases in the County Courts*, Policy Press, Bristol.
Saunders, P. (1990), *A Nation of Home Owners*, Unwin Hyman, London.
Stewart, A. (1996), *Rethinking Housing Law*, Sweet & Maxwell, London.
United Kingdom (White Paper) (1971), *Fair Deal for Housing*, Cm. 4728, HMSO, London.
Woolf, H. (1996), *Access to Justice*, Final Report to the Lord Chancellor on the civil justice system in England and Wales, HMSO, London.

5 The Sorting of the Forks from the Spades: an Unnecessary Distraction in Housing Law?

HELEN CARR[1]

Introduction

The legal distinction between a lease and a licence focuses on whether an occupier gains a property or a personal interest in the residence. In doing so, it fails to address the diverse needs of consumers (both providers and occupiers) in the housing market, who are ill served by a legal principle based on outdated notions of property. For example, a provider of accommodation may not wish to grant a lease because that is inconsistent with their role or purpose, not because they do not wish to grant a property right. Further, an occupier of short term, move-on accommodation may not want to take on the more legalized obligations of a lease.

This essay considers two examples in which the lease/licence distinction is unhelpful despite lawyers' attempts to bend the facts of the agreements into the prevailing lease/licence construct. I want to examine a new legal approach based on consumerist rather than property principles. The first stage of the argument is to examine the current background of letting arrangements. Of particular importance to this discussion are the security of tenure policies in the private rented sector. This suggests a contrast with the position of the occupier in the public sector. Next, it is necessary to analyse the relevance of the lease/licence distinction in the context of the needs of residential occupiers. It is suggested that the debate has been detrimental to the interests of tenants because the law has concentrated upon a specious recognition that tenants have property rights; thus, it has obscured the weakness of their real social and economic position. It is concluded that a consumerist perspective should be adopted as a future method of progression in this sector.

Background

Bright and Gilbert summarize the current legal basis of leases as follows: 'The modern tenancy relationship reflects the contractual agreement between landlord and tenant, the property nature of the lease and public regulation of leases' (Bright and Gilbert, 1995). Tenancy agreements were treated as mere contractual (and, therefore, personal) agreements until the twelfth century when the current concept of tenancies granting exclusive possession (and, therefore, property) emerged. Thus, the leading case makes the following claim for the tenancy arrangement:

> The tenant possessing exclusive possession is able to exercise the rights of an owner of land, which is in the real sense his land albeit temporarily and subject to certain restrictions. A tenant armed with exclusive possession can keep out strangers and keep out the landlord unless the landlord is exercising limited rights reserved to him by the tenancy agreement to enter and view and repair (*Street v Mountford* [1985] 2 All ER 289, 292, *per* Lord Templeman).

Complexities have arisen during the twentieth century partly because of the conflict between the political concern to protect tenants from exploitation by landlords and the need to ensure that landlords retain meaningful property rights. The former argument has force because there is a mismatch between supply and demand to the extent that the inequality inherent in the relationship is exacerbated (see Partington, 1993, p. 128). The latter argument gains force because it has been argued that the huge decline in market share of private residential tenancies has been caused by, inter alia, an effective loss of the owner's rights due to security legislation (there is a huge literature here, but see Crook and Kemp, 1996; DoE, 1987).

The basic form of holding property as an occupier has remained a tenancy but at different times the value to the tenant has varied according to the values inherent in the security of tenure legislation. Different statutory solutions have been enacted during the century to address the needs of tenants and landlords with varying degrees of success, balancing the tenant's need for security of tenure (the tenant's right not to be evicted without due processes of law) with the right of the landlord to regain the property.[2] Additionally, a balance needs to be drawn between the tenant's desire for rent to be affordable and the landlord's desire to maximize the rate of return. It has been suggested that the different legislative principles enacted whenever there has been a change of government has contributed to the decline because landlords can never be sure which way the wind will blow (Kemp, 1993). The result has certainly been that 'layers of legislative complexity have been piled on layers of legislative complexity' (Partington, 1993, p. 128).

Features of the Legal Debate

Whether an agreement is a lease or not is highly significant because the creation of leases creates property rights for the occupier and it *also* triggers the mechanisms of statutory protection. By way of contrast, where an agreement creates a licence, then a purely personal interest is created which, for the most part, does not attract statutory intervention.[3] Value judgments have been superimposed upon this discourse to the effect that the rule is that leases were good and licences bad – this was particularly true amongst the advocates of occupiers' rights. Indeed, so strong was the articulation of this view that Lord Donaldson MR was prompted to comment that 'it is not a crime nor is it contrary to public policy for a property owner to licence occupiers to occupy a property on terms which do not give rise to a tenancy' (*Aslan v Murphy* [1989] 3 All ER 130, 135).

At the same time, lawyers for landlords and residential occupiers have each tried to maximize the position of their respective clients by fine debate over the lease/licence distinction. Two legal positions can be identified in this debate. First, the stated intentions of the parties in entering into the agreement with regard to the granting of property rights should be regarded as paramount. Thus, in *Murray Bull & Co. Ltd. v Murray* [1952] 1 All ER 1079, McNair J said 'it was clear that their common intention was that the defendant should ... be granted a mere personal privilege with no interest in the land'. On this view, once the intention of the parties has been identified, then this is the determining factor in deciding whether the agreement creates a lease. This argument might be explained in terms of the sanctity accorded by the law to the bargain created by the parties; as such, it met the exigencies of the situation, although it did fuel a black market in residential licences as landlords attempted to avoid the security provisions in this way (see Street, 1985; Kemp, 1992, p. 64).

On the other hand, the second position discounted the label put on the agreement by the parties by constructing the totality of the tenancy agreement and then considering whether it grants the requisite rights to qualify as a tenancy or not. The binding decision in *Street v Mountford* represented a significant watershed in reaffirming the importance of exclusive possession for a term at a rent as the defining feature of a tenancy. In other words, the intention of the parties, as expressed in labels, is irrelevant. The only relevant matter is whether the agreement itself grants exclusive possession for a term at a rent (cf. *Ashburn Anstalt v Arnold* [1988] 2 All ER 147) and not what the parties call the agreement. Lord Templeman clearly made this point:

> If the agreement satisfied all the requirements of a tenancy, then the agreement produced a tenancy and the parties cannot alter the effect of the agreement by insisting that they only created a licence. The manufacture of a five pronged implement for manual digging results in a fork even if the manufacturer, unfamiliar with the English language, insists that he intended to make and has made a spade.

Thus, the current position is that determining the 'real bargain' between the parties is the central issue. *Street* came against the background of landlords reacting to the increasing burden imposed upon them in the Rent Acts by attempting to create licences. *Street*, on the other hand, disavowed this position. Some landlords who did not choose to exit from the business of letting attempted to avoid these adverse consequences by the use of devices, pretences and shams. It was commonplace within the private rented sector to attempt to avoid the legislation, for instance by supposedly providing services to the occupier (the best method of avoiding the grant of exclusive possession). Thus, the provision of phantom breakfasts; or mysterious locked rooms to which the landlord insisted he had 24 hour a day access; or never exercised rights of the landlord to introduce new occupiers to the property. What *Street* did was to provide 'authority for a new doctrine of pretence that enables courts to override contractually agreed terms where they have been inserted solely to avoid the application of the Rent Acts' (Bright, 1991).

The Development of Private Sector Statutory Regimes

The Revolution in Private Sector Tenancies

From 1915–80 there was a gradual, albeit uneven, increase in security of tenure and other rights of the private rented tenant attached to leases so that the Rent Act 1977 expressed in statutory terms the closest approximation to owner-occupation for the tenant. That Act gave strong rights to rent control by restricting the landlord to achieving only a fair rent, based on certain principles. Furthermore, the tenant could not be evicted without clear notice and the eviction could only be carried out on limited grounds which had to be proved in court. Finally, judges were given an overriding discretion to refuse the landlord possession if they felt it was not reasonable to make such an order. The benefit of the tenancy could also pass on the tenant's death to that person's spouse; a further succession was permitted where members of the family were living in the home after the death of the spouse.

In other words, just like the owner-occupier, the Rent Act protected tenant could be sure that there was provision for a long term home for the whole family which would continue, in most circumstances, to be affordable. The Rent Act tenancy provided what was a home in the emotional and social sense as well as the physical entity since its long term potential allowed for the development of family and community networks. It recognized that 'for many people, housing has a very important psychological and social significance. It is the place from which they create the basis for their social lives and their working lives' (Partington, 1993, p. 126).

However, by the time the Housing Act 1996 came into force, the accumulation of 16 years of legislation had resulted in the drastic reduction of succession rights, security of tenure and rent control. Reforms were motivated by the unpopularity of the Rent Acts with landlords and the then government's preoccupation with free market ideals and legislative laissez faire. In particular, there was a belief that deregulation was necessary to revive the private rental market which could then take a much more important role in the provision of accommodation (see DoE, 1987, pp. 9–12):

> Independent landlords of various kinds using private sector resources ought to have a significant part to play in providing satisfactory rented housing for those who need it. The private sector should be particularly well placed to respond flexibly and swiftly to different local needs and to provide a variety of accommodation readily available in different places for short or long let so as to assist mobility especially for job movers (para. 3.3).

The Housing Act 1980 had already begun this process with the creation of protected shorthold tenancies for a year, but these were considered procedurally complex (although landlords did try to use them). The crunch, however, came in the Housing Act 1988. Rents became market rents, mediated in a very limited sense by Rent Officers, succession could only take place once (to the tenant's spouse), and there were expanded grounds upon which the landlord could regain possession of the property (particularly with regard to rent arrears) with no overriding discretion for the judge. Far more significant, though, was the new notion of the 'assured shorthold tenancy' which provided an additional mandatory ground of possession simply by the landlord giving the tenant two months' notice that possession is required. Such tenancies have quickly become the most popular method of letting residential property (see Morgan, 1996, p. 453).

The Housing Act 1996 Act went even further than this in order to protect the *landlord's* interest. The Act was prefaced by the following comments in a Consultation Paper (DoE, 1995):

> The precise procedures required to create a valid shorthold tenancy are still not widely understood. ... Even where landlords are aware of the procedures, they may still accidentally create full assured tenancies through inexperience, and inadvertently find themselves with a long term tenant (para. 2.7).

> For a private landlord, the majority of whom only have a very small number of properties, having a tenant who does not pay the rent can be financially very difficult (especially for example if there is a mortgage loan to pay) (para. 2.14).

The 1996 Act, thus, further simplified assured shorthold tenancies to relieve the landlord of the burden of giving the tenant notice that the tenancy is to be an assured shorthold tenancy as well as removing the requirement for an initial fixed term of at least six months. The less tangible conceptual belief that a home is more than a roof over one's head has become secondary to the market in the attempt to woo landlords (particularly large commercial organizations) back. Eighteen years of Conservative legislation have seen the reaffirmation of the contractual perspective, with seemingly little emphasis placed upon the inequalities in the relationship and the commensurate ability of the landlord to demand almost anything.

Street v Mountford: the Reality

The decision in *Street v Mountford,* on the face of it enhancing tenants' rights because it was seen by the housing world as a repudiation of sham licences, paradoxically was sandwiched between the Housing Act 1980 and the Housing Act 1988. Whilst the housing world believed it would be an important tool in protecting tenants' rights, at the same time the government was dismantling those rights and radically changing to a market-based system. At a time of rising rents and rising property values landlords wanted to put their property to more profitable use than was possible under the Rent Acts. The deployment of their economic resources in accordance with market criteria 'would not have been possible without changes in the law'. Vincent-Jones, therefore, argued that 'the decision in *Street v Mountford* is likely to be rapidly neutralized by legislation undermining security of tenure attaching to the status of tenant' (Vincent-Jones, 1987).

The Current Framework of Social Housing

The Conservative government elected in 1979 did not envisage a future for council housing, making apparent its tenure preference for owner occupation as the key to extending capitalism and its own mandate. Much of the statutory framework developed from 1979 was consequently concerned with providing the necessary variety of 'exit' routes from public housing (together with a more general attack on municipal socialism: see Loughlin, 1996). Statutory force was given to mechanisms such as the right to buy, tenants' choice, housing action trusts and large scale voluntary transfers (just some such examples involving either individual or mass privatization: see Forrest and Murie, 1991). At the same time, the Housing Act 1980 did however provide tenancy rights for local authority tenants (for the first time – although this does not appear to have been effective immediately: Loveland, 1992) as well as introducing statutory security of tenure within that sector. This appears anomalous, although it has recently been suggested that 'the secure tenancy was primarily enacted as the government needed a defined class of person to exercise the Right to Buy' (Smith and George, 1997). In any event, individualized rights were part of the Thatcherite ethos.

An important contrast is immediately provided between the developments in the public sector and the contemporaneous policies within the private rented sector. Whilst the latter operated to grant private sector landlords maximum control over their property, the local authority landlord had its power commensurably reduced (through the increase of both individual rights of tenants, for instance giving the right for tenants to have lodgers without permission, and collective rights, such as the right to be consulted about future housing strategies). Whilst by and large tenants were not attracted to the rental alternatives presented to them, the right to buy and strict funding limits served to deplete local authority stock. The pressure put upon local authorities through the statutory duty to house the homeless and allocate properties to those on the waiting list transformed the sector from its traditional role of housing the 'respectable working class' to that of being forced to target its increasingly scarce resources to those in greatest housing need (Loveland, 1995).

Housing associations, 'the third arm' of the provision of rental housing, emerged from a relative backwater during this same period. 'Labour's stance was to support the associations as an alternative to the private rented sector while the Conservatives saw them as an alternative to the local authorities' (Hughes and Lowe, 1995, p. 35). The legal status of the housing association tenant has varied with the prevailing political philosophy. When the Rent Acts were supreme, during the previous Labour governments' office, housing associations were seen as quasi-public providers of housing and thus were within the secure tenancy regime of the Rent Act. The passage of the Housing Act 1988 operated to transfer the housing association tenant from the public sector to the private sector and thus into the assured tenancy and market rent regime (see, further, Stewart, 1996, ch. 5).

The re-creation of housing associations as 'Registered Social Landlords' in the 1996 Act, who would compete with other potential housing companies for public and private funds, continued the experiment with the provision of social housing in the private sector. Yet the private sector is not a convincing framework for the housing association landlord, because of its inevitably close relationship with Local Authorities, its different funding arrangements as well as the diverse nature of its tenants. As Cowan suggests, commenting on arrangements by housing associations to house the homeless, 'the transaction is better seen as being one composite transaction between the local authority, the Housing Association and the homeless person' and thus as far removed from the private sector as could be (Cowan, 1992). It is important to note that the market regime does not operate to its limits within the sector as assured, rather than assured shorthold, tenancy agreements are the norm (a practice exhorted upon them by the overseeing regulatory and funding body: the Housing Corporation).

The lease/licence distinction is equally significant within the social rented sector as the statutory regimes are constructed in a way which is either identical to the private rented sector (housing associations) or using the concept of exclusive possession as its basis (local authorities). The debate has largely ended in the private rental sector as a result of the declining value of security of tenure and therefore the end of the motivation of the landlord to create sham licences (see Vincent-Jones, above). However, it continues with some venom in the other parts of this sector. Nevertheless, the position adopted by case law can be suggested to be of little relevance here. As Hill (1996, p. 213) points out, '[i]n *Street v Mountford* the statement in the agreement between the parties that the occupier was a licensee rather than a tenant was not motivated by a desire to ensure that the occupier's interest would not be binding on any subsequent purchaser of the land: it was an attempt to avoid the statutory controls contained in the Rent Acts'. The social landlord is not similarly motivated against granting of property interests in the same way. Rather, its *intentions*, often to reduce the rights given to its residential occupiers, may be entirely *consistent with its aims* in providing social housing.

Two Practical Examples

It is instructive at this point to consider the legal realities through consideration of the difficulties faced by two similar, socially motivated housing projects.

Our first client was a housing association specializing in the provision of accommodation for the non-statutorily homeless, particularly single vulnerable men. It provided accommodation for a group who are vulnerable because of alcohol and drug abuse, violence and petty criminality. There were strict terms and conditions in the agreements which its workers, using their knowledge and expertise, believed were appropriate for the project to succeed in its aim of providing a long term stable and secure environment for the residents. The Housing Corporation, its funder, put the client under pressure to grant leases to new residents, presumably motivated by the view that leases are good and licences bad. The association accepted with reluctance that it could no longer evict peremptorily and issued assured shorthold tenancy agreements but with the same strong rules to protect the association from possible major misdemeanours by the occupiers.

Then it had to go to court to evict in two cases heard by different judges. One judge said, in effect, 'I don't know why you have gone through all of this, this agreement is quite clearly a licence'. Another judge said of an attempt to evict an occupier, Mr A, whose agreement predated the tenancy policy and was therefore a licence, 'Well if you have an agreement with Mr B on the same terms and conditions as the one with Mr A but Mr B's agreement is called a tenancy then Mr A's agreement whatever you call it must by definition be a tenancy'. At a stroke the second judge's decision made tenants of all the occupiers, unless and until another judge decides to follow the reasoning of the first judge.

Next, one lawyer looked at their tenancy agreement and advised 'Some of these terms are totally inconsistent with the concept of tenancy – for instance, the requirement that the occupier is constantly in residence. If there are terms within the agreement which are inconsistent with the grant of a tenancy they are unenforceable.' Another lawyer advised, 'No! The very presence of those terms prevents the agreement being the lease that you have purported to grant'. The organization threw up its hands in despair. They tried to do their best by their residents and keep their funder happy, but they could not be clear about the legal consequences of their actions, despite being careful to seek good legal advice.

The second client was a similar organization. It ran a 150 bed hostel for a similar group of young men. It solved the problem in a much more typical way, with an agreement which called itself a licence and stated several times in large letters 'the occupier shall not receive exclusive possession'. For instance, it was suggested in general terms and conditions:

> 'It is hereby agreed and declared that this Licence Agreement creates a licence only and it is the intention of each part hereof that NO tenancy shall be hereby created.' Condition 9 stated 'for the avoidance of doubt it is hereby agreed and declared that possession, management and control of the Bedroom and the Hostel remains vested in the Licensor who will retain keys to the Bedroom and who in case of emergency or valid reason has an absolute right of entry therein at all times exercisable by the Licensor, its servants or agents either with or without other persons'.

Condition 11 said 'the landlord agrees: to allow the Licensee to occupy the Premises and receive the services detailed in the Agreement. It does not give the Licensee an interest in the Premises nor does it grant a tenancy.' Just in case there was any doubt in the mind of the person signing the agreement, the document ended with the following phrase in block capitals:

> I, THE LICENSEE HAVE READ OVER THIS LICENCE AGREEMENT. I ACKNOWLEDGE THAT THIS LICENCE AGREEMENT CONSTITUTES THE WHOLE OF THE ONLY AGREEMENT BETWEEN THE LICENSOR AND MYSELF IN RELATION TO THE BEDROOM AND THE HOSTEL. I UNDERSTAND THAT THIS LICENCE IS GRANTED ON THE BASIS THAT I DO NOT HAVE EXCLUSIVE POSSESSION OF THE BEDROOM AS AGAINST THE LICENSOR.

The nature of the agreement with communal eating arrangements, daily cleaning of rooms (except at weekends when residents are expected to tidy up after themselves) and the prohibition of visitors between the hours of 11.00 pm and 9.00 am made it likely that this agreement was exactly what it said it was. However, this was not because of what it says it is but because of the terms within it *reserving control* over the occupier's rights to the accommodation. The reason it makes the points so obsessively is a direct result of the complexity of the legal discourse and the inconsistency of judicial decision-making. Judicial instincts are to prefer the individual cause to the collective. Those instincts are valuable in preventing oppression of the individual but the organizers of social housing believe that they might blind the judge to the overall value of the landlord's purpose (if this is, in fact, relevant).

What both of these examples illustrate is that the law is failing to serve one of its primary purposes: clarity. In addition, they illustrate that the debate around the lease/licence distinction fails to address their needs in the provision of housing. So, when Cowan argues that 'it is absolutely essential that there should be a flexible system of housing management, aided (not hindered) by the application of legal principles' (Cowan 1993), he is arguing that the law should facilitate the *purpose* of the organization in providing affordable accommodation. The law is not only failing to facilitate the achievement of worthwhile purpose, but also its intervention can be argued to be counterproductive.

A Brief Diversion – the Judicial Relevance of 'Purpose'

Whilst *Street* seemed to discount anything other than the tenancy agreement, there have been recent movements in case law suggesting that purpose can be relevant (although, once again, this is uncertain and used irregularly). The beginning of this line was in *Antoniades v Villiers* [1990] 1 AC 417. In that case, four independent agreements were signed by the occupiers of the four bedroomed premises, none of whom was entitled to exclusive occupation of any part of it. The courts decided that there was no artificiality in the contracts but 'a sensible and realistic arrangement to provide accommodation for a shifting population of individuals who were genuinely prepared to share the flat with others introduced from time to time who would, at least initially be strangers to them'. By referring to the purpose of the arrangement the court was able to be confident that the lack of exclusive possession essential to create a tenancy was an absence that genuinely reflected the nature of the bargain.

In *Westminster C.C. v Clarke* [1992] 1 All ER 695, a case not dissimilar from the facts of the practical examples outlined above, the House of Lords gave crucial relevance to the purpose of the landlord's. Clarke lived in a self-contained bedsitting room with kitchen facilities and a locking door, which was owned and managed by Westminster. On moving into the hostel, an agreement was signed called a licence to occupy. The agreement included the following term:

1. This Licence does not give you and is not intended to give you any of the

> rights or to impose upon you any of the obligations of a tenant nor does it give you the right of exclusive occupation of any particular accommodation or room which may be allotted to you or which you may be allowed to use nor does it create the relationship of landlord and tenant. The accommodation allotted to you may be changed from time to time without notice as the council directs and you may be required to share such accommodation with any other person as required by the Council.

In the Court of Appeal, the difficulties faced by the landlord in the provision of this type of accommodation to fulfil their homelessness functions were regarded as irrelevant.

> It is not suggested the terms of the licence to occupy which the defendant signed and accepted were in any way sham. They set up a framework which the Council considered appropriate for the discharge of their statutory duty to provide accommodation for homeless person with priority needs. ... but the problems of the Council as a local authority in discharging those duties and the reasonableness of the framework they have set up are irrelevant to the question we have to consider.

That analysis was a direct application of the *Street* doctrine: exclusive possession for a term at a rent were the criteria. The only clause which prevented the agreement providing security of tenure was the mobility clause which prevented the grant of exclusive possession – a clause analogous to the clauses in the second practical example.

However, Lord Templeman (who had earlier been entirely responsible for the *Street* doctrine) in the House of Lords considered the problem from another angle entirely. His analysis insisted upon an examination of the accommodation's purpose. So, he argued that: 'From the point of view of the Council the grant of exclusive possession would be inconsistent with the purposes for which the council provided the accommodation at Cambridge Street.' Furthermore:

> In reaching the conclusion [that exclusive possession had not been granted] I take into account the object of the Council namely the provision of temporary accommodation for vulnerable homeless persons, the necessity for the Council to retain possession of all the rooms in order to make and administer arrangements for the suitable accommodation of all the occupiers and the need for the Council to retain possession of all the rooms not only in the interest of the Council as the owners of the terrace but also for the purpose of providing for the occupier supervision and assistance.

This was justified by restricting the decision to the very special circumstances of the case (cf. Cowan, 1992, who points out that 'this factual matrix must be replicated country-wide').

Apparently, in nine cases out of ten the intentions of the parties are not going to be relevant. In those cases, however, where a definite accommodating purpose is served by the arrangement and exclusive possession is not granted to the occupier (because of the degree of control retained by the landlord), then an examination of the purpose should be undertaken in order to check the validity of the arrangement and whether the non-transfer of the property interest is genuine. That examination of purpose inevitably involves social policy considerations.[4] Sometimes it is clear which values a judge will choose to support to the extent that there is some consistency in marginal decisions, but the subjective nature of the judicial decision-making causes a lack of clarity. As has been suggested: 'The more convincing explanation of the outcomes is that the court will strain to find that there is no tenancy when it would be unfair on the owner to confer statutory protection on the occupant' (Bright and Gilbert, 1995), even though such an interpretative technique has been expressly disavowed by the judiciary (see further, Hill, 1996). It also distracts attention from what could be a constructive debate about what rights (if any) it might have been appropriate to give to Clarke, irrespective of any property rights.

Back to the Practical Examples

Consideration of the restrictions on occupiers' behaviour which our first client, the housing association, felt obliged to insert into the agreement (regardless of whether it thought it was granting a lease or a licence) indicates the significance of the contractual terms. For instance, the association believed it was necessary to state that it would undertake:

> Not to interrupt or interfere with the tenant's right peacefully to occupy the premises except where access is required because the health, safety or welfare of the tenant or other tenants, staff, visitors or neighbours is thought to be at risk.

Additionally and perhaps more significantly, the tenant came under an obligation 'to inform the association if the tenant plans to be absent from the premises for more that 7 days'. Further:

> If the premises are without the agreement of the Association left unoccupied for a continuous period in excess of 2 weeks the association may re-enter the premises and thereupon the tenancy created by this agreement will determine but without prejudice to any other rights and remedies of the association.

These are important erosions of the rights that a residential occupier might reasonably expect to have simply arising from the contract of occupation. Even exclusive possession itself might be a right that a reasonable landlord might agree would be appropriate to grant, as it entails a strong premium on privacy, but the landlord must be careful not to grant a property interest. So, the focus on the lease/licence (and therefore property/personal) distinction prevents any such consideration given to this discourse. Instead the debate revolves around whether the terms are consistent with the proprietary nature of the arrangement. A court could take either of two views dependent upon its assessment of the true nature of the bargain. On the one hand, it might strike out those clauses which are inconsistent with exclusive possession. On the other, it could take the view that these terms prevent the agreement being one which grants exclusive possession and therefore, whatever the agreement calls itself, it is a licence. If the second view is correct then the housing association is left with a problem. It sees only limited difficulties for itself in providing accommodation on the basis of assured shorthold tenancies supported by these additional terms. However, it would find running its type of project practically impossible without clear rules limiting the behaviour of its occupiers.

A further example of the linguistic perfidy forced upon landlords was that of requiring assured shortholds to specify a fixed term of a minimum of six months. Even though this is no longer a requirement, a period of six months after commencement must elapse before a possession order can automatically be granted. Nevertheless, Turner writes: ‘There is one advantage for all concerned as I see it after the commencement of … the Housing Act 1996. We can all get back to telling the truth about what we are doing and what we mean and there are positive advantages in doing so’ (Turner, 1997, p. 24). If there are advantages in being clear that a periodic tenancy is being granted as opposed to a fixed term tenancy, what advantages could be obtained from a clear statement of the reality of the bargain between the landlord and the occupier? The primary advantage would be a clear recognition of the inequality of their relative bargaining positions and a recognition that our obligations towards the occupier needs a clearer protection than that currently provided. There is a need for clearly written documentation that means what it says so that each side understands its obligations and provides for certain minimum standards for property. Obsession with property rights stops us from achieving this.

Conclusion

My argument has been that the lack of progress in furthering the rights of the residential occupier has been hampered by the property basis of the tenancy (Stewart, 1996, p. 93). This property bias ignores the *social* relationship between landlord and tenant which must be part of the residential lettings equation. The protection provided by leases in the private residential sector proved ephemeral in the face of the Conservative onslaught since 1980 to the extent that they have now been substantially eroded. In 1987, the government argued: 'Once a tenant has a market rent tenancy and is occupying a property as his or her home it is right that he or she should have a reasonable degree of security of tenure' (DoE, 1987, para. 3.10). Yet, by 1996, the automatic assured shorthold virtually guaranteed that no new letting would get the benefit of anything more than notional security of tenure. In the face of such a shifting view of what the value of the tenancy should be to the tenant, it seems foolish to rely on protection provided by outdated notions of property.

The Protection from Eviction Act 1977, which can be seen as a piece of 'consumer' (as opposed to tenure-based) legislation, indicates one way forward. It is accepted that it is hardly a statutory model of clarity since its complex language and structure reflects the history of the recent development of housing law. This is symptomatic of the legislature's habit of building upon old statutes rather than new statements of the law. Nonetheless, protection under the statute is not provided on the basis of proprietorial interests (to lessees) but on which type of occupier is deemed by the statute appropriate to receive protection. The Act therefore protects residential occupiers, but excludes (inter alia) those with residential landlords who no longer have the benefit of a contract. One may not agree with the political priorities of that legislation (for example, by arguing that people who live in their landlord's homes are more in need of protection than others). However, the Act at least represents an acknowledgement that it is the vulnerability of the residential occupier to harassment (cf. Nelken, 1983). *That* should be the focus of the law rather than a concentration on appropriate protective mechanisms dependent on the property base of your occupancy.

The most logical development of this argument is the requirement to provide clear contractual obligations. The concept of residential occupation being best protected through the operation of consumer standards in contracts is growing, as a result of judicial intervention, in the United States of America. There, landlords have for some time been subject to an implied contractual term that warrants the habitability of accommodation to the occupier. In *Javins v First National Realty Corporation* 428 F.2d 1071 (DCCir.), Skelly Wright J argued that: 'In order to reach results more in accordance with the legitimate expectations of the parties and the standards of the community, courts have been gradually introducing more modern precepts of contract law in interpreting leases ....' Extrajudicially, the judge gave his opinion of the subconscious rationales affecting his decision as follows:

> ... I was indeed influenced by the fact that, during the nationwide racial turmoil of the sixties and the unrest caused by the injustice of racially selective service in Vietnam, most of the tenants in Washington D.C. slums were poor and black and most of the landlords were rich and white. ... I didn't like what I saw, and I did what I could to ameliorate, if not eliminate, the injustice involved in the way many of the poor were required to live in the nation's capital.
>
> I offer no apology for not following more closely the legal precedents which had cooperated in creating the conditions that I found unjust (letter to Rabin, 1984, p. 549).

One can argue that similar conditions persist in the UK in 1997, despite the existence of protection on the basis of property rights (see, for example, Law Commission, 1996, in relation to the state and condition of property; Forrest and Murie, 1991, ch. 4, where it is suggested that those occupying public sector housing are the most marginalized and excluded by society; for evidence of direct and indirect discrimination despite the existence of the Race Relations Act, see Ginsburg, 1992 (where experience is summarized), as well as DoE, 1994 (racial harassment and appropriate mechanisms to overcome it)). Thus, a movement towards the consumerist approach can reap benefits.

In the UK, Stewart (1996, p. 268) says of the public sector that:

> Arguably, contractual arrangements are replacing direct statutory entitlements based on legally differentiated providers. These contracts are overlaid with a variety of regulatory mechanisms which seem to be more consistent with market provision, such as codes of conduct, either self-imposed or imposed by the regulators. Occupants differentiated by sector are being reconstructed as consumers of housing.

One potentially potent example of this type of tool, which a consumer oriented approach would provide to scrutinize terms of leases, is now available in the Unfair Terms in Consumer Contract Regulations 1994 (SI No 3159). The regulations are similar to the Unfair Contract Terms Act 1977 but, as Holbrook points out, 'unlike UCTA they probably apply to contracts relating to land and have a wider scope than exclusions of liability' (Holbrook, 1997, p. 24; see further Whitehouse's chapter in this volume and Whitehouse, 1998). Such European initiatives giving consumer-based protection may begin to have an impact and perhaps the occupier, identified as a consumer, will be more successfully protected than the occupier, identified as tenant, although there could be dangers if the law fails to recognize the peculiar vulnerabilities and lack of homogeneity that characterize the residential occupier (see, also, Partington, 1993).

What is needed is a private rented sector with a supply of decent affordable housing catering for a wide range of potential occupiers. It is a bold move to say that those occupiers receive little value from being endowed with property interests, but automatic assured shorthold tenancies indicate how ephemeral such property interests can be. The Conservative reforms of the private rented sector were passed with little objection except from housing lawyers, arguably because the arcane nature of the tenancy concept which was being redefined meant little to the general public. A deregulating government would find it more difficult to remove rights established in law on an agreed set of consumer principles, transparent to all and without the overlay of changing legislation or the underlay of ancient land law.

Notes

1 The author is grateful to David Cowan for his comments and suggestions.

2 In the past, it has certainly been the case that the landlord's interest has been better protected, which has led to the success of unsavoury characters like Peter Rachman, etc. This has, in fact, had an indelible effect on landlord and tenant law: see Kemp, 1992; for a leading sociological study in this area, see Nelken, 1983.

3 The exception to this rule is that agreements which grant exclusive possession do attract security of tenure in the public sector: s. 79(4), Housing Act 1985; that being the precise issue in *Westminster C.C. v Clarke*, discussed below.

4 Thus, it is accepted that ho(s)tels serve a useful recognized social purpose in accommodating people day to day and so, even if a resident enters into an agreement with the intention of staying for a significant length of time, the agreement will be construed as a licence as in *Brillouet v Landless* (1996) 28 HLR 836. Old people's homes which let single rooms with exclusive occupation but which do not have the facilities to care for the elderly if they become in need of constant care and attention are let on licences (*Abbeyfield Harpenden Society v Woods* [1968] 1 All ER 52).

Bibliography

Arden, A. and Hunter, C. (1989), *Housing Act 1988*, Sweet & Maxwell, London.

Bright, S. (1991), 'Beyond Sham and into Pretence', *Oxford Journal of Legal Studies*, Vol. 11, pp. 36–145.

Bright, S. and Gilbert, G. (1995), *Landlord and Tenant Law: The Nature of Tenancy*, Clarendon Press, Oxford.

Cowan, D. (1992), 'A Public Dimension to a Private Problem', *Conveyancer*, pp. 285–92.

Cowan, D. (1993), 'Lease/Licence Distinction: Changing Emphases?', *Conveyancer*, pp. 157–68.

Crook, A. and Kemp, P. (1996), 'The Revival of Private Rented Housing', *Housing Studies*, Vol. 11, pp. 51–68.

DoE (1987), *Housing: The Government's Proposals*, HMSO, London, Cmnd 214.

DoE (1994), *Racial Incidents in Council Housing: The Local Authority Response*, HMSO, London.

DoE (1995), *The Legislative Framework for Private Renting – Consultation Paper Linked to the Housing White Paper 'Our Future Homes'*, DoE, London.

Forrest, R. and Murie, A. (1991), *Selling the Welfare State*, Routledge, London.

Ginsburg, N. (1992), 'Racism and Housing: Concepts and Reality' in P. Braham, A. Rattansi, and R. Skellington, *Racism and Antiracism: Inequalities, Opportunities and Policies*, Sage, London.

Hill, J. (1996), 'Intention and the Creation of Proprietary Rights: are Leases Different?', *Legal Studies*, Vol. 16, pp. 200–16.

Holbrook, J. (1995), 'Unfair Terms in Housing Contracts', *Legal Action*, August, pp. 24–5.

Hughes, D. and Lowe, S. (1995), *Social Housing Law and Policy*, Butterworths, London.

Kemp, P. (1992), 'The Ghost of Rachman' in C. Grant (ed.), *Built to Last*, Roof, London.

Kemp, P. (1993), 'Rebuilding the Private Rented Sector?' in P. Malpass and R. Means (eds), *Implementing Housing Policy*, Open University Press, Buckingham.

Law Commission (1996), *Landlord and Tenant: Responsibility for State and Condition of Property*, HMSO, London, Law Com. No. 238.

Loughlin, M. (1996), *Legality and Locality*, Oxford University Press, Oxford.

Loveland, I. (1992), 'Square Pegs, Round Holes: the "Right" to Council Housing in the Post-war Era', *Journal of Law and Society*, Vol. 19, pp. 339–64.

Morgan, J. (1996), 'The Casualisation of Housing', *Journal of Social Welfare and Family Law*, Vol. 18, pp. 445–61.

Nelken, D. (1983), *The Limits of the Legal Process*, Academic Press, London.

Partington, M. (1993), 'Citizenship and Housing' in R. Blackburn (ed.), *Rights of Citizenship*, Mansell, London.

Rabin, E. (1984), 'The Revolution in Residential Landlord-Tenant Law: Causes and Consequences', *Cornell Law Review*, Vol. 69, pp. 517–605.

Smith, N. and George, G. (1997), 'Introductory Tenancies: a Nuisance too Far?', *Journal of Social Welfare and Family Law*, Vol. 19, pp. 307–20.

Stewart, A. (1996), *Rethinking Housing law*, Sweet & Maxwell, London.

Street, R. (1985), 'Coach and Horses Trip Cancelled?: Rent Act Avoidance after Street v. Mountford', *Conveyancer*, pp. 328–36.

Turner, M. (1997), 'Private Rented Housing: a Return to Reality?', *Solicitors Journal*, 4 July 1997, p. 35.

Vincent-Jones, P. (1987), 'Exclusive Possession and Exclusive Control of Private Rented Housing: a Socio-legal Critique of the Lease-Licence Distinction', *Journal of Law and Society*, Vol. 14, pp. 445–58.
Whitehouse, L. (1998), 'The Home Owner: Citizen or Consumer?' in S. Bright and J. Dewar (eds), *Land Law: Themes and Perspectives*, Oxford University Press, Oxford.

6 The Impact of Consumerism on the Home Owner

LISA WHITEHOUSE

Introduction

A consistent objective of the Conservative governments, during the period 1979–97, was to redefine the role of the state in the provision of 'public' goods and services. The minimalist role they envisaged for the state led to the implementation of privatization initiatives which promoted the market system as the guardian of choice, competition and accountability, themes apparent within the Citizen's Charter (1991). If the market failed to ensure that these elements were in operation, or abused its role, the state, it was claimed, would redress the imbalance through direct regulation. The individual was therefore assured, through the rhetoric of consumerism, that the authority granted to the private sector for the provision of these goods and services would be regulated, either by market forces or by the state, so as to avoid its abuse. This paper questions whether those assurances have been satisfied within the context of home ownership.

It was clear throughout the period 1979–97 that the Conservative governments were committed to increasing the number of home owners within England and Wales, an objective which had also been apparent in the policies of their predecessors. For the Conservatives, however, increasing home ownership was not perceived as an end itself but formed part of a wider ideological objective. Their aim was to create a housing system in which households no longer looked to the state for the provision of their housing, but purchased that 'commodity' within the private home ownership market. Their success in this respect was assisted to a large degree by the increased availability of mortgage finance, providing households, who previously may not have considered home ownership as an affordable option, with access to this sector.

The transference of a greater degree of authority for the provision of housing to the mortgage market, achieved through the introduction of policy initiatives such as the council tenants 'right to buy', created a new and more powerful role for mortgagees. They became the 'gatekeepers' of the owner occupied sector, determining who would and who would not be allowed to enter and remain within home ownership. The rhetoric of consumerism promoted by the Conservative governments claimed that in exercising these decisions, mortgagees would be made accountable to their mortgagors through the introduction of a number of regulatory measures. An examination of these measures, undertaken in the first section of this paper, indicates that the Conservative governments placed a heavy reliance on the regulatory efficiency of market forces, introducing a scheme of self-regulation only after repossessions rose dramatically during the early 1990s. The only form of direct legal regulation evident within the mortgage relationship concerns the legal process of possession and section 36 of the Administration of Justice Act 1970 (AJA 1970) which the Conservative's retained in its original form.

The second part of this chapter examines, through the analysis of qualitative data obtained as result of a primary research study involving lenders and district judges, the extent to which the regulatory framework introduced by the Conservative governments, which still operates today, achieves a balance between the interests of the mortgagee and the mortgagor. The findings indicate that mortgagees enjoy a degree of power in excess of that afforded to the mortgagor, placing the mortgagor at a severe disadvantage within the repossession process. Unlike other recent studies (Whitehouse, 1997; Nixon, Hunter, Smith and Wishart, 1996; Ford, Kempson and Wilson, 1995), however, this chapter contends that the vulnerability of the mortgagor derives not from the legal process itself, but from a complete failure by central government to regulate the activities of mortgagees.

The paper concludes by suggesting that the benefits usually associated with consumerism have not materialized for the home owner. The National Consumer Council (1996, p. ii) state that they focus on seven key consumer tests, namely, '... access, choice, safety, information, equity, redress and representation'. Apart from safety, the mortgage relationship and the repossession process fail them all. In a housing system dominated by home ownership, with 42 per cent of all dwellings currently subject to an outstanding mortgage debt (Social Trends, 1997, p. 4), it is essential that effective regulation is introduced so as achieve a balance between the interests of the mortgagor and mortgagee.

Methodology

The qualitative data presented in the chapter was obtained during a series of semi-structured interviews involving representatives of 13 lenders, six district judges and a representative of the CML. Due to the economic and political sensitivity of repossession, the respondents requested, and have been granted, anonymity. The aim of the fieldwork was to obtain information regarding the practical implementation of the legal process of repossession. This necessarily implied that respondents would be providing information which related to their personal experiences of the repossession process. In order to ensure that the information obtained during the fieldwork provided a valid account of the repossession process, it was necessary to ensure that the respondents constituted a 'representative' sample within each category.

In deciding which district judges to contact, time and financial constraints necessitated contact with local judges, therefore 13 district judges located in Hull and Yorkshire were contacted. In order to achieve a comparison with other areas, four district judges located in Birmingham and London were also approached. The lack of representation within other areas was not considered to be significant as the aim of the research was to gain the personal views of the district judges on the legal framework which applies equally to all areas of England. It was also considered that if the views of the district judges in Birmingham and London differed significantly from those located in the North because of the difference in location, other district judges from different areas would be contacted. These additional contacts proved unnecessary.

Due to the fact that mortgage provision operates within a market context, certain lenders hold a relatively large proportion of the total number of mortgages. By contacting only a handful of mortgagees, it is possible to obtain information regarding repossession policies which covers over 50 per cent of all mortgagors (lenders' annual reports provide information on their share of the mortgage market). In choosing which lenders to contact, the aim was to obtain information from those who held relatively large shares of the mortgage market, therefore emphasis was placed on the larger building societies and banks. However, in order to discover whether repossession policies differed according to the market share held by the lender a sample of medium and small sized lenders were also contacted.

Analytical Approach

The qualitative data collected as a result of primary research concerns the views of those who participate in the repossession process regarding the practical implementation of the relevant legal provisions. It must be noted that personal perspectives on the legal process may be inaccurate for a number of reasons, including, for example, a lack of knowledge regarding the legal framework. In order to avoid such inaccuracies the process of 'triangulation' (Denzin, 1978) has been adopted. This involves the use of multiple sources of information to verify a single statement made during the primary research programme. Therefore, through the secondary analysis of information gained from the semi-structured interviews, library sources, organization reports, and statistical data, it has been possible to validate the qualitative data used in this paper.

Regulating the Mortgage Relationship – the Consumerist Model

The housing system in England and Wales has undergone dramatic changes in the last century. The most obvious change relates to the pattern of housing preferences, with home ownership having increased from only ten per cent of all dwellings in England and Wales in 1914 to 68 per cent in 1997 (Malpass and Murie, 1994 p. 13, Table 1.1; Social Trends, 1997, p. 4). The causes underlying these changes are numerous (see Balchin, 1995; Kemeny, 1981; Malpass and Murie, 1994); the individual's choice of housing may be influenced by a number of factors including relative cost, the need for mobility, and family circumstances. The range of housing types which constitute the choices available to the individual, however, are determined to a significant extent by the housing policies of central government. As Balchin (1995, p. 6) notes, '[a]lthough a large number of factors determine household tenurial preferences, government policy has undoubtedly had a significant impact on tenure choice over the past three-quarters of a century and particularly since 1979'.

The promotion of an increase in home ownership has been a recurrent theme in the housing policies of successive governments throughout this century. The period during 1979–97, however, witnessed a new approach within housing policy. The commitment to increasing the number of home owners within England and Wales remained but support for the public rented sector did not. The introduction of the council tenants 'right to buy' in the Housing Act 1980 combined with a reduction in the financial support provided by central government resulted in the 'residualization' of the public rented sector (Malpass and Murie, 1994). The reduction in the quantity and quality of local authority accommodation created a perception that it was no longer the responsibility of the state to provide housing but the responsibility of individual households to obtain that commodity for themselves. As Lewis (1996, p. 3) notes:

> Changes in the perceptions and practices of government have moved almost unilinearly; they have been 'anti-state', they have favoured individualism, have extolled market solutions and, significantly, self-expression, even if the preferred language has been self-help.

The principal choices available to households therefore became home ownership or private renting. The fact that the majority 'chose' to enter into home ownership was due, to a large extent, to the housing policies of central government (Malpass and Murie, 1994, p. 14). The Conservative governments held a clear and explicit preference for home ownership, as indicated by Michael Heseltine, the then Secretary of State for the Environment (HC Debate, Vol. 65, Col. 1445, 1980):

> There is in this country a deeply engrained desire for home ownership ... It reflects the wishes of the people, ensures the wide spread of wealth through society, encourages a personal desire to improve and modernize one's home, enables people to accrue wealth for their children, and stimulates the attitudes of independence and self-reliance that are the bed-rock of a free society.

Their bias towards home ownership, it may be argued, derived from their ambition to impose a consumerist model on the housing system. Unlike the other forms of housing available to households, home ownership would provide households with a commodity which they could choose to retain, in the hope that its value would increase, or exchange and use the money derived from that sale to purchase a different dwelling. The millions of transactions which would take place within the owner occupied sector would allow the forces of demand and supply to determine price, quality and allocation of housing. The role of the state would be merely to supervise this market, thereby ensuring that it operated effectively.

The major difficulty faced by the Conservative governments in their attempts to increase the number of home owners was that the majority of households in England and Wales did not have the funds necessary to purchase accommodation. The answer to this problem came in the form of an increased use of mortgage finance. This method of funding the purchase of accommodation had been available to households for decades, but the relative cost, availability of cheaper accommodation in the form of local authority housing, and stringent lending criteria meant that the majority of households were unwilling or unable to utilize it. There was also an inherent contradiction in using mortgage finance as the means of achieving an increase in home ownership. By virtue of the English law of mortgage, mortgagees are granted an inherent right to possession (see *Four-Maids Ltd v Dudley Marshall (Properties) Ltd* [1957] Ch 317 at 320 per Harman J). They could, therefore, withdraw the status of home owner from their customers whenever they wished, without reference to the courts. The decision by mortgagees to undertake large numbers of repossessions might potentially defeat the Conservative governments' aim of increasing and maintaining high levels of home ownership.

These obstacles to the increased use of mortgage finance were removed by the 'deregulation' of the mortgage market in the early 1980s. Building societies, the traditional mortgage lenders, were to be joined by other institutional lenders, including in particular the banks, in the provision of mortgage finance. The introduction of increased competition within a market which had once been dominated by the building societies, led to calls for the reform of the legal framework regulating the activities of the societies. Prior to 1986, building societies were regulated by legislation enacted over 100 years previously in the Building Societies Act 1874 (this Act was consolidated in the Building Societies Act 1962). They were concerned that the 'new' mortgagees would have an unfair advantage because of their ability to offer services other than mortgage finance and restricted forms of saving accounts. In response to the calls for change, the Conservative government introduced the Building Societies Act 1986 (BSA 1986). The main objective of the BSA 1986 was summarized by the then Economic Secretary to the Treasury, Mr Ian Stewart (HC Debate, Vol. 89, Col. 592, 1985):

> In today's fast-changing markets, societies need to be able to offer a wide range of facilities to an increasingly sophisticated public if they are to continue to compete effectively ... I believe that, by allowing the societies more scope, we will not only enable them to develop their business but will bring extra healthy competition into housing and finance.

The BSA 1986 increased the scope of services which building societies could provide thereby introducing a 'level playing field' in the new competitive mortgage market. The government's determination to introduce effective competition within this market served a number of purposes. In the first instance, it ensured the increased availability of mortgage finance, thereby enabling a wider range of households the opportunity of entering into home ownership.

With mortgagees competing for business, they were willing to offer higher percentage mortgages on the basis of less stringent requirements regarding the status of the mortgagor. As Malpass and Murie (1994, p. 101) state:

> Following this legislation [the BSA 1986] there was a pronounced shift from mortgage rationing towards lending on demand and loans related to a high proportion of property value. Lenders competed for custom by being willing to lend more.

Second, it provided a justification for the withdrawal of government support from the housing system. The increased availability of mortgage finance made the reliance on state funded services unnecessary. Households could enter into home ownership and pay monthly instalments, as though they were renting, but would have the added advantage of owning their own home. Any fears regarding the substitution of the state for the commercial lenders were assuaged by reference to the regulatory efficiency of competition. Where there was competition, it was claimed, there would be choice, and choice would ensure that mortgagees operated in a manner consistent with the demands of consumers. As Lewis (1996, p. 11) notes:

> If markets are efficient in maximising people's wants, then they are justified because expressing wants and having them delivered is a choosing exercise. And choice as freedom is at the heart of the human condition.

The opportunity to enter the owner occupied sector was therefore made available to the majority of households, but it was still necessary to encourage them to take advantage of it. Unlike renting, home ownership would involve households undertaking the largest single debt that they were ever likely to encounter. The Conservative governments sought to assist households with their decision. The most obvious encouragement given to households to enter into home ownership, and consequentially to undertake the burden of mortgage finance, was the provision of fiscal incentives for home owners, as opposed to private, state and quasi-public tenants. The main source of assistance was provided in the form of Mortgage Interest Relief at Source (MIRAS) which, during the 1980s, increased by over 50 per cent in real terms (Pearce and Wilcox, 1991, p. 9). As Kemeny (1981, p. 72) notes:

> The most obvious measures designed to encourage home-ownership are clearly ones which increase subsidies or selectively reduce taxation on home-owners with the explicit purpose of making home-ownership both more relatively

attractive and accessible to more households, and this is the best-researched and most widely understood meaning of how governments encourage home-ownership.

Coupled with these fiscal privileges was the promotion of home ownership as the form of housing which could provide the greatest degree of security and financial benefit. John Stanley MP (1980, p. 6) the then Minister for Housing and Construction, on the question as to why home ownership was one of the government's top priorities, stated that '[i]t provides a measure of independence, choice and financial benefit that for most people, cannot be achieved to the same degree by renting'. The security afforded to the home owner derived, it was claimed, from their status as consumer, combining choice and competition with direct legal regulation in the form of section 36 AJA 1970. The ability to repossess would be available to mortgagees but, where that decision was taken, the home owner would receive a degree of protection by virtue of section 36 AJA 1970. This provides district judges with the discretion to suspend a possession order on specified payment terms or to adjourn the hearing if:

> ... it appears to the court that in the event of its exercising the power the mortgagor is likely to be able within a reasonable period to pay any sums due under the mortgage or to remedy a default consisting of a breach of any other obligation arising under or by virtue of the mortgage ...

Mortgagors would therefore, in most cases, be granted an opportunity to clear their arrears and thereby avoid repossession. The doubts which households might have had regarding the use of mortgage finance in meeting their housing needs were, therefore, dispelled by the rhetoric of consumerism. As a result, the number of dwellings within the home ownership sector increased by ten per cent during the 1980s (Wilcox, 1994, p. 111). The Conservative governments had achieved a number of their objectives, including increasing the number of home owners in England and Wales and replacing the role once played by the state in the provision of housing with the private sector. The extent to which the Conservative governments had achieved their 'consumerist ideal', however, came under question in the early 1990s when repossessions reached unprecedented levels.

The causes of this housing 'crisis' have been sufficiently detailed elsewhere (Ford, Kempson and Wilcox, 1995) for the purposes of this chapter, the important factor relates to the measures which were introduced in response to the rising number of repossessions. They included:

1 the consideration of proposals designed to implement a 'mortgage rescue' scheme, under which mortgagors could transfer to shared ownership or tenant status, thereby potentially becoming eligible for Housing Benefit;

2 the enactment of the Social Security (Mortgage Interest Payments) Act 1992 which provided for the payment of Income Support for mortgage interest direct to the lender, rather than to the claimant as was the case previously; in return, lenders agreed that they would not repossess where full Income Support payments were being received;

3 the publication of the Council of Mortgage Lenders (CML) *Statement of Practice* in July 1992 encouraging its members to adopt more efficient methods of communication with their borrowers and more flexible arrangements for assisting them in clearing their arrears.

The point to note about these initiatives is that they did not involve the direct regulation of the activities of mortgagees. It would appear that the government remained committed to their belief in the regulatory efficiency of the consumerist model which they had sought to introduce into the housing system. They were, therefore, reluctant to intervene directly in the 'free' operation of the mortgage market, preferring instead to rely on self-regulation in the form of the CML *Statement of Practice*.

The extent to which mortgagees have responded to the consumerist values promoted by the Conservative governments is indicated by their attempts to simplify the contractual terms of the mortgage. The rhetoric of consumerism demands that effective choice can only exist where there is sufficient information regarding the goods and services on offer. As Lewis (1996, p. 7) notes, '[i]t needs to be underlined that accessible information is a precondition for choice to be effectively exercised'. In response to this demand for information, some mortgagees have introduced 'plain English' into their mortgage contracts. A term taken from one lender's set of mortgage conditions indicates the new 'user-friendly' approach,

> You must repay the Amounts Secured by the end of the Term. You must pay the Monthly Payment by direct debit on the Monthly Date. If you make the Monthly Payment by any other method, We will charge You an administration fee. We may change the amount of Your Monthly Payment or this administration fee at any time. We will tell You about any changes.

The element of protection afforded to consumers through the simplification of the mortgage contract was further enhanced by the Unfair Terms in Consumer Contracts Regulations 1994 (SI 1994 No. 3159), which came into force on 1 July 1995. Unlike the Unfair Contract Terms Act 1977, the 1994 Regulations do apply to contracts concerning land (DTI, 1995, pp. 7–8). Under these Regulations, any 'unfair' term in a contract concluded between a seller or supplier and a consumer, where the said term has not been individually negotiated (para. 3(1)), shall not be binding on the consumer (para. 5(1)). The Regulations (para. 4(1)) define an 'unfair term' as '... any term which contrary to the requirement of good faith causes a significant imbalance in the parties' rights and obligations under the contract to the detriment of the consumer'. The Regulations (Sch. 2) provide guidance on the assessment of 'good faith', stating that regard shall be had in particular to: the strength of the bargaining positions of the parties; whether the consumer had an inducement to agree to the term; whether the goods or services were sold or supplied to the special order of the consumer; and the extent to which the seller or supplier has dealt fairly and equitably with the consumer.

With the new arrears management procedures implemented by many mortgagees and the apparent protection mortgagors were receiving within their contractual relationship, the Conservative governments considered it appropriate to continue the increasing withdrawal of the state from the housing system. Their new line of approach was to reduce the level of indirect financial support provided to home owners. Having achieved their aim of creating a housing system dominated by home ownership, it was no longer necessary to provide significant fiscal incentives. The level of MIRAS was therefore gradually reduced over a number of years falling from its peak in 1989/90 of £6,900 million to £4,300 million in 1993/94 (Wilcox, 1993 p. 165, Table 84). More significant, in relation to less financially stable households, were the changes made to the payment of Income Support for mortgage interest under the Social Security (Income Support and Claims and Payments) Amendment Regulations 1995 (SI 1994 No. 3159).

Under these new rules, borrowers who took out their mortgage before 2 October 1995 and who claim Income Support after that date, do not receive mortgage interest payments for the first eight weeks of their claim; for the next 18 weeks, they receive half of the amount otherwise payable; full payments are then made. Those who entered into a mortgage after 2 October 1995 do not receive any mortgage interest payments for the first 39 weeks of their claim; after that time they receive full payments. The Conservative government's aim in introducing these reforms was to further privatize the housing system by making individual households responsible for insuring themselves against future financial difficulties, rather than relying on state support (Ford, 1995). As Stewart (1996, p. 23) notes, '... increasing home ownership has been at the heart of Conservative policy of transferring social responsibilities to the market'.

The legacy of 18 years of Conservative rule is a housing system radically different to that which they inherited in 1979. The residualization of the public rented sector combined with the promotion of home ownership as the tenure to be preferred resulted in a 15 per cent increase in the number of home owners between 1979 and 1997 (Social Trends, 1997, p. 4). The measures they introduced in pursuit of a 'consumerist ideal' have created a home ownership market which operates free from substantial state intervention. The elements of choice and competition, combined with self-regulation and section 36 AJA 1970, were, however, designed to ensure that repossessions remained relatively low. The following section examines whether this consumerist ideal has been achieved in practice.

The Repossession Process – Does Consumerism Work?

The deregulation of the mortgage market was undertaken in order to ensure that competition operated between different mortgagees and it would appear, at face value, that it achieved this objective. The range of lenders and mortgage products available to the consumer appears to be wide with, for example, the choice of a repayment or endowment mortgage at a fixed or variable rate with a bank or building society. A closer examination of the mortgage market, however, reveals that effective choice is denied to most mortgagors. The 'price' and methods of repayment may differ between different mortgagees but the fundamental terms of the mortgage contract do not.

In practice, mortgagees offer standard terms which are similar throughout the mortgage market. Potential mortgagors are therefore obliged to accept these terms if they wish to obtain mortgage finance. As one mortgagee notes, '[w]e computer generate the mortgage deed and mortgage offer, because it's computer generated the offer has standard special conditions and it is very much like bolting them on, and to the extent of giving free standing conditions it is very rare'. The inability of mortgagors to negotiate the terms of their mortgage contract provides mortgagees with the opportunity of imposing terms which favour them. Terms incorporated into these standard contracts include, for example, making the mortgagor liable for much of the cost involved in the mortgage transaction. The fact that these terms are put into 'plain English' merely ensures that the mortgagor is absolutely clear about what the rights of the mortgagee are.

The ability of mortgagees to construct the terms of the standard mortgage contract allows them to be selective in terms of the information they provide to prospective mortgagors. As regards repossession, the inherent right to possession granted to mortgagees by virtue of the English law of mortgage enables them to undertake possession 'before the ink is dry on the mortgage contract'. Mortgagees recognize, however, that the aim of the modern mortgage transaction is to allow the mortgagor to occupy the property. It is common therefore to find mortgage terms which state that the right to possession will not be exercised until default by the mortgagor. What the contract does not state, however, is how or when this process will be initiated. In failing to provide such information, mortgagees are reserving for themselves the ability to exercise an unstructured and unaccountable discretion as regards repossession. The nature of accountability requires that where decisions are made which affect the interests of individuals, information regarding how those decisions were taken should be made available to the individual in question. As Lewis (1996, p. 24) notes, '[i]t is inherent ... in the nature of choice that those in authority should render an account to those who chose them in the first place'.

Accountability also implies that sanctions should be imposed where the decision-making processes, adopted by those in authority, fail to meet the required standards. The only standards within the repossession process are those set out in the CML *Statement of Practice.* This encourages its members to seek repossession only as a last resort and only following the breakdown of a 'forbearance arrangement'. These arrangements offer mortgagors the ability to clear their arrears through a number of methods, including 'freezing' the arrears for a defined period or lengthening the term of the loan. Mortgagees are not, however, under any obligation to adhere to the guidelines set out in the *Statement of Practice*. It has no legal force and the CML cannot impose any sanctions on those who do not follow it. As a representative of the CML stated, '[w]e hope that they do but in detail many wouldn't because they are generalised recommendations and the reality of mortgagees is that they have a different approach and an obvious difference is the speed with which they take repossession'.

The ability of mortgagees to operate unaccountable decision-making processes as regards repossession obscures the difference in approach adopted by different mortgagees towards the repossession issue. In practice, the majority of mortgagees do adhere to the CML guidelines but primary evidence suggests that there are some who do not. As the following statement by a mortgagee indicates, they operate an 'automatic' system of arrears management:

> There are a number of trigger points – three months arrears with a minimum of £1000 arrears, solicitor will send letter before action and that usually gets customer to respond; no payments goes back to solicitor and order is sought.

These mortgagees will seek a repossession order as a matter of course immediately upon the mortgagor falling three months in arrears, regardless of whether there is a forbearance arrangement in place. Other lenders, however, operate a discretionary system deciding each case on its merits and viewing legal proceedings as a last resort. As one lender notes:

> If they continue to default they will be asked to come in for a counselling session. If they don't reply telephone calls will be made. If it's wilful intent or a no-hoper of a case then those factors come in. We don't lightly take repossession proceedings. I have some cases with huge arrears and we still haven't taken possession.

The lack of accountability and inconsistency in the repossession policies adopted by mortgagees produces a repossession process in which mortgagors in similar circumstances are not treated in similar ways. It also places mortgagors at a severe disadvantage within the mortgage relationship for the reason that mortgagees may seek a possession order whenever they wish without recourse to any enforceable standards and impose all costs on the mortgagor. It may be argued, however, that their discretion is limited by the supervisory role undertaken by district judges within the legal process of repossession. This process has been promoted as the means by which the commercial aspects of the mortgage transaction are overridden by the aims of social justice. In *Centrax Trustees Ltd v Ross* [1979] 2 All ER 952 Goulding J believed that 'Parliament has attempted to give legislative shelter to a wide class of owner-occupiers ... in what may be called social legislation'.

Research previously undertaken into the legal process of repossession (Whitehouse, 1997; Nixon, Hunter, Smith and Wishart, 1996; Ford, Kempson and Wilson, 1995) has indicated that the mortgagor is at a severe disadvantage due to the manner in which district judges exercise their discretion under section 36 AJA 1970. The chapter by Hunter and Nixon in this collection indicates that district judges afford the economic interests of the mortgagee a disproportionate degree of protection. This is due in part to the wording of section 36 AJA 1970 which implies that the only question which has to be considered is whether the mortgagor has the financial status necessary to clear their arrears within a reasonable period whilst maintaining their normal monthly payments. As one district judge made clear in describing the aims of section 36 AJA 1970:

> In layman's language I suppose it is to ensure as far as possible, in respect of the roof over their head, that you keep them in that property as long as you are satisfied that at the end of the day the lender is going to get their money back.

District judges are therefore limited in their ability to exercise their discretion within the repossession process by the terms of reference established by section 36 AJA 1970. As one district judge indicated, '[w]e are restricted by the amount of income which the borrowers have got'. This chapter contends, however, that the ultimate decision regarding repossession lies not with district judges, but with the mortgagee and it is the failure to regulate this discretion which places mortgagors at a severe disadvantage within the repossession process.

Due to the mortgagee's inherent right to possession, the district judge is obliged to grant them an order for possession. The order may be suspended on specified payment terms or for 28 days to allow the mortgagor time to find alternative accommodation or pay the entire mortgage debt. As one district judge notes, '[i]f the borrower doesn't turn up isn't paying his mortgage and the arrears are simply worsening I have no jurisdiction to make anything other than a possession order'.

Having obtained the possession order, whether it is suspended or not, the mortgagee is then allowed to determine a course of action which they consider to be appropriate. If the order is for outright possession, they can choose to ignore it and come to an arrangement with the mortgagor knowing that if the mortgagor fails to comply with that arrangement, they can then implement the possession order. As one lender notes:

> The powers of district judges are not as wide as people think. If they do make an order then they should make it on payments which cover the arrears within a reasonable period. In some cases the borrowers simply cannot afford to pay a sum which is sufficient to pay off the arrears within a reasonable time. We've got round that by asking the judge to make an order suspended for 28 days and we make an arrangement outside the court.

If the order is suspended on payment terms, the mortgagee cannot take possession provided the mortgagor continues to comply with those terms. The ability of the mortgagor to meet this criteria will be dependent to a large extent on the length of suspension granted by the district judge. A mortgagor who owes £1,000 will obviously find it easier to clear those arrears over five years rather than two. The definition of the 'reasonable period' under section 36 AJA 1970 has, however, become one the most contentious issues within the repossession process. The Court of Appeal in *Cheltenham & Gloucester Building Society v Norgan* [1996] 1 All ER 449 has suggested that the starting point for determining that concept should be the remaining term of the mortgage. District judges, however, feel unable to implement this recommendation due to the increasing costs which mortgagors will have to sustain whilst they remain in arrears.

> I suppose depending on what the parties problems have been one has to say that if one goes beyond the period of six years one has to ask whether you are doing them any favours. You can't forget that although you are making orders in respect of what has got to be paid off the arrears, you have got to think of what the incidence of interest is going to be.

The reasonable period is therefore likely to remain relatively short. District judges did, however, suggest that they would be willing to go beyond the usual period, which on average amounts to three years, if the lender agreed. The influence of the mortgagee within the repossession process therefore extends to determining the exercise of discretion by district judges. As one judge made clear, '[w]ith the lender's consent I made an order for fourteen years'.

In some cases, however, the length of suspension is irrelevant for the reason that the mortgagee can alter those terms as they wish in favour of the mortgagor. As one lender notes, '[i]f we get a court order for two years and the borrower can't cope then we will try and stretch it over four years'. In circumstances where the mortgagor fails to meet the terms set out by the court under a suspended possession order, the mortgagee has the discretion to continue allowing the mortgagor to make payments or to seek possession. As one lender states, '[i]f it is suspended on terms the mere fact that the borrower did not pay that does not bring the order into effect immediately, it is the choice of the society'. If they choose to take possession following the breach of a suspended possession order, they will usually seek a warrant for eviction from the County Court. As with the original order, the district judge has the discretion to suspend the warrant but only if the mortgagor requests such action.

The power afforded to mortgagees within the repossession therefore appears to be unlimited. In the cases illustrated above, however, the power to override the decision of the court was generally exercised in favour of the mortgagor, allowing them more time or reducing the payments specified by the court. This does not, however, provide a justification for the exercise of this degree of influence for there is evidence that it can be used to the disadvantage of the mortgagor. In some cases, lenders were utilizing the legal process of possession as debt recovery service, ensuring, through the threat of repossession, that mortgagors met the terms of any 'forbearance arrangement'. As one lender notes, '[t]he repossession process is just a process we can utilise to ensure that the mortgagor recognises the responsibility he has got' .Using the process in this manner can, however, have a significant impact on the ability of the mortgagor to avoid repossession due to the fact that they will be liable for all costs involved. A mortgagor will find it more difficult to convince the court that they have the funds necessary to clear their arrears when they have also to pay the costs of the court hearing. The National Association of Citizens Advice Bureaux (1993, p. 15) make their opposition to this policy clear when they state that:

> In the view of the CAB Service it is not an appropriate use of the courts to seek a suspended possession order merely to formalise an agreement to repay arrears, which the borrower has kept. There is presently no disincentive to the lender to use the courts in this way, since any costs incurred can be passed on to the borrower.

This policy is particularly damaging to the interests of the mortgagor where the mortgagee involves them in a number of hearings. If a mortgagor does fail to meet the terms of a suspended possession order, the lender may seek a warrant for eviction which may be suspended again. This process can continue, involving a number of court hearings costing on average approximately £600 each time. The mortgagor will therefore find it increasingly difficult to avoid repossession each time the case is brought before the court, a factor recognized by district judges who in some instances believe that it is better to grant repossession than to involve the mortgagor in any further costs. As one district judge notes, 'I have to take that into account if the arrears are X pounds they will be X pounds plus £600 each time the case comes back'.

District judges do have the power to award costs against the mortgagee but they may only do so where the case has been brought 'unreasonably' (RSC. Od. 62, r6(2)). Due to the fact that in most cases, the mortgagor will be in breach of their mortgage contract, it is extremely difficult for district judges to determine that the case has been brought 'unreasonably'. As one district judge stated, '[t]he lender has a contractual right to impose costs so it's beyond my jurisdiction'. The reluctance of district judges to take a more interventionist role within the mortgage relationship and instead to rely on the principle of freedom of contract may change following the introduction of the Unfair Terms in Consumer Contracts Regulations 1994. It may be possible to argue that the imposition of court costs in a contract which is not freely negotiated '... causes a significant imbalance in the parties' rights and obligations under the contract to the detriment of the consumer'. It is difficult to state at this point, however, whether these regulations will have any significant impact within the mortgage relationship.

The legal process of possession therefore offers no protection against the excessive power exercised by mortgagees within the mortgage relationship. They can initiate legal proceedings knowing that they have nothing to lose. If the order is granted outright, they can sell the property and reclaim the debt. If it is suspended, they will receive the payments which they contracted for and an amount off the arrears. As this lender made clear:

> There is a tendency to give the benefit of the doubt to the borrower which doesn't overly prejudice us because if they don't pay the sum agreed in the order then we can get our warrant and if they do pay then that is exactly what we want.

In practice, the legal process of possession serves as an administrative process in which the financial status of the mortgagor is assessed. This task could be undertaken by an independent body which might prove to be a cheaper option than referring to the court. It must be noted, however, that the legal process does offer sufficient protection to those mortgagors who do have the funds necessary to meet the payment terms set out in a suspended possession order. For those mortgagors who are in a more vulnerable financial situation, the process serves only to inhibit their chances of avoiding repossession.

The Impact of Consumerism

The policies implemented by the Conservative governments were intended to create a housing system in which a balance was achieved between the interests of consumers and suppliers by virtue of the effective operation of the market system combined with self-regulation and the legal process of possession. The Conservative's reliance on the regulatory efficiency of the concepts of choice and competition have allowed mortgagees a degree of power within the mortgage market which far outweighs that of the mortgagor. It is the lack of choice within the mortgage market which has caused the imbalance in the power relationship between mortgagors and mortgagees, allowing as it does, mortgagees to construct a set of standard mortgage terms which favour them. It may be assumed therefore that by introducing choice, the balance may be restored. As Lewis (1996, p. 12) notes:

> ... the justification for markets is a human rights/choice justification so that where markets impede effective choice then it follows that the constitution is obliged to restore choice and freedom; to regulate markets, especially where competition, and therefore choice, is impeded.

Choice within the mortgage market is impeded by the reluctance on the part of mortgagees to enter into negotiations regarding the terms of their mortgage contract and to publish information relating to their repossession policies. The means by which the current Labour government could ensure that choice is introduced into the mortgage market would, at the very least, require mortgagees to publish their repossession policies. Tinkering with the system will not, however, achieve the changes required to bring about a balance of power within the relationship between mortgagors and mortgagees. It is essential that the state intervenes directly in the contractual stages of the mortgage relationship, ensuring that the prospective mortgagor is allowed a degree of influence within the negotiations, the application of the Unfair Terms in Consumer Contracts Regulations 1994, which have not yet been applied to mortgage contracts, may go some way in achieving this.

The introduction of greater equality in the bargaining strengths of mortgagors and mortgagees will serve to protect the interests of both parties but it is also necessary to look beyond the contractual stages of the mortgage transaction. As Stewart (1996, p. 71) notes, one impact of the consumerist model adopted by the Conservative governments has been to alter the process of grievance redress: 'Home owners are expected to be less reliant on the state, pursuing, as consumers, any complaints they may have against the providers not against the government.' As regards the decision to repossess, mortgagors can only look to a legal process which favours the mortgagee thereby denying them of effective participation in a decision which has significant implications for their welfare. Allowing mortgagees to continue to undertake repossessions completely free of regulation should no longer be tolerated in a housing system which promotes home ownership as a symbol of security and status.

Reforming the legal process of repossession within its current remit, however, will do little to alter the imbalance within the mortgage relationship. Its focus on the ability of the mortgagor to afford their mortgage payments perpetuates a characteristic element of the consumerist approach adopted by the Conservative governments, namely that home ownership should only be available to those who can afford it. The justification put forward for this aspect of consumerism is that the millions of transactions entered into by consumers determine the price and quality of goods and services. The market will therefore offer a range of goods and services which vary in price thereby allowing all consumers, regardless of their financial status, to exercise some degree of choice. The fact that some consumers will have a wider choice than others is merely an outcome of market forces which is beyond the control of central government. As Saunders (1993, p. 63) argues, '[i]n a privatized system of provision based upon the principles of market exchange, access to resources is governed by a different principle, namely, the ability (and willingness) to pay for the good or service demanded'. The emphasis which is now placed on 'affordability', however, is unjustified for the reason that it tends towards exclusion within the housing system.

It is the aspect of affordability which dominates the repossession process. The inherent right to possession granted to mortgagees is in practice deferred until the mortgagor fails to comply with the terms of the mortgage contract. The power exerted by the mortgagees within the mortgage relationship therefore has little significance for those mortgagors who can afford to meet their mortgage payments. For those who cannot, their ability to avoid repossession will be dependent on their financial status. If their financial difficulties are short term, section 36 AJA 1970 will offer them sufficient protection against repossession. If, however, their problems are more long term they may find it extremely difficult to avoid repossession, particularly if their mortgagee considers it appropriate to continually involve them in legal proceedings and consequentially in mounting legal costs.

The ability to remain in home ownership is therefore dependent on the financial status of the home owner; however, having encouraged people to undertake owner-occupation, the majority of which could only do so with the aid of mortgage finance, the Conservative governments have left mortgagors to fend for themselves in times of financial difficulty. In a housing system dominated by home ownership, constituting over 68 per cent of all dwellings in England and Wales (Social Trends, 1977, p. 4), those who cannot afford their mortgage payments are excluded from the benefits which the majority are perceived to enjoy and are relegated to a public rented sector which has come to be viewed as a 'welfare net'.

Conclusions

The policies implemented by the Conservative governments effected fundamental changes within the housing system. The increase in home ownership and the residualization of the public rented sector account for some of the more substantive changes, but a more subtle and perhaps a more fundamental alteration has been achieved in our perceptions of housing. The privatization initiative implemented within the housing system has created a perception that housing is a commodity in the same respect as cars or televisions. Consumers are expected to purchase the commodity which best suits their perceived housing needs based on what they can afford. Housing is not therefore seen as a universal entitlement but as a product which can be purchased by those who can afford it. The fundamental nature of housing, however, demands that it should be available to all. As Beteille (see Lewis, 1996, p. 13) notes:

> ... the principle of universality demands access to certain basic things irrespective of ability or performance. Drinking water, food, shelter, and also elementary education and primary health care should be universally available to all, and in their case questions of merit do not arise.

It is essential therefore that we reappraise our conception of housing and the role of the state in its provision. This will obviously take some time to achieve. Therefore, in the immediate term, it is necessary to ensure that those who have already been encouraged to enter into home ownership by the state, are provided with some degree of protection against the excessive power currently afforded to mortgagees.

Bibliography

Balchin, P. (1995), *Housing Policy: An Introduction*, Routledge, London.

Council of Mortgage Lenders (1992), *Avoiding Possession: Arrears Management in Practice*, Council of Mortgage Lenders, London.

Council of Mortgage Lenders (1995), *Income Support for Mortgage Interest*, Council of Mortgage Lenders, London.

Denzin, N. K. (1978), *The Research Act: A Theoretical Introduction to Sociological Methods*, McGraw-Hill, London.

Department of Trade and Industry (1995), *The Unfair Terms in Consumer Contracts Regulations 1994. Guidance Notes*, DTI, London.
Ford, J. (1995), *Which Way Out?*, Shelter, London.
Ford, J., Kempson, E. and Wilson, M. (1995), *Mortgage Arrears and Possessions; Perspectives from Borrowers, Lenders and the Courts*, HMSO: London.
Ford, J. and Wilcox, S. (1992), *Reducing Mortgage Arrears and Possessions: An Evaluation of the Initiatives*, Joseph Rowntree Foundation: York.
Forrest, R. and Murie, A. (1984), *Right to Buy? Issues of Need, Equity and Polarisation in the Sale of Council Houses*, SAUS: Bristol.
Foster, S. (1990), *No New Homes*, Shelter, London.
Foster, S. (1992), *Mortgage Rescue: What does it add up to?*, Shelter, London.
Kemeny, J. (1981), *The Myth of Home Ownership*, Routledge and Kegan Paul, London.
Lewis, N. (1993), 'Markets, Regulation and Citizenship: A Constitutional Analysis' in R. Brownsword (ed.), *Law and the Public Interest*, Franz Steiner, Stuttgart.
Lewis, N. (1996), *Choice and the Legal Order*, Butterworths, London.
Lewis, N. and Birkinshaw, P. (1993), *When Citizens Complain*, Open University Press, Buckingham.
Lister, R. (1990), *The Exclusive Society*, Child Poverty Action Group, London.
Malpass, P. and Murie, A. (1994), *Housing Policy and Practice*, Macmillan, London.
National Association of Citizens Advice Bureaux (1993), *Dispossessed*, NACAB, London.
National Consumer Council (1996), *A Code of Practice for Home Loans*, NCC, London.
Nixon, J., Smith, Y., Wishart, B. and Hunter, C. (1996), *Housing Cases in County Courts*, The Policy Press, London.
Oliver, D. (1991), *Government in the United Kingdom*, Open University Press, Milton Keynes.
Pearce, B. and Wilcox, S. (1991), *Home-Ownership, Taxation and the Economy*, Joseph Rowntree Foundation, York.
Plant, R. (1991), *Modern Political Thought*, Basil Blackwell, Oxford.
Saunders, P. (1993), 'Citizenship in a Liberal Society' in R. Turner (ed.), *Citizenship and Social Theory*, Sage, London.
Social Trends (1997), HMSO, London.
Stanley, J. (1980), 'Government Policies on Home Ownership in the 1980s' in *Home Ownership in the 1980's*, SHAC, London.
Stewart, A. (1996), *Rethinking Housing Law*, Sweet & Maxwell, London.
Tyler, E.L.G. (1988), *Fisher and Lightwood's Law of Mortgage*, Butterworths, London.
Whitehouse, L. (1997), 'The Right to Possession. The Need for Substantive Reform' in P. Jackson and D. Wilde (eds), *The Reform of Property Law*, Dartmouth, Aldershot.
Whitehouse, L. (1998), 'The Home Owner: Citizen or Consumer?' in *Law and Land: Themes and Perspectives*, Oxford University Press, Oxford.
Wilcox, S. (1993), *Housing Finance Review 1993*, Joseph Rowntree Foundation, York.

7 Tenure Choice and Ethnic Minorities in Scotland: Recent Research and some Legal Conundrums

MARTIN MACEWEN AND HILARY THIRD

Introduction

Prior to the mid-1980s, little was known about Scotland's minority ethnic communities. Their housing, employment and other circumstances were relatively neglected issues in research terms. Since then, the 1991 Census has provided a range of reliable statistical data at the national level. In addition, a number of small, localized studies have been conducted by bodies such as the Commission for Racial Equality and Race Equality Councils (formerly Community Relations Councils), and the Scottish Ethnic Minorities Research Unit (SEMRU). Research has now been undertaken in Scotland on, for example, refugees (MacFarland and Walsh, 1988), racial harassment (Walsh, 1987; MacEwen, 1986), the voluntary sector (MacLeod, 1988), and the Chinese community (Chan, 1983). There are also studies on the size and distribution of the minority ethnic population in Scotland (Scottish Office, 1991), and in particular localities such as Glasgow (Dow, 1995).

Most relevant to this paper are two pieces of national research commissioned by Scottish Homes. These focused specifically on the housing experiences of Scotland's minority ethnic communities (Wainwright et al., 1994; Third et al., 1997). Both pieces of work – particularly the latter – will be referred to extensively herein.

This paper begins by describing the characteristics of Scotland's minority ethnic groups, in terms of who they are and where they live. It will attempt to highlight some of the relevant features of the Scottish housing context which make the 'race and housing' issue different in Scotland than in England. Drawing on new research evidence, the housing experiences, needs and preferences of Scotland's minority ethnic groups are described.

The paper attempts to draw out the legal implications of some of the findings, focusing on the two key issues of racial discrimination in access to housing, and racial harassment. It concludes that Scottish local authorities are failing to meet their legislative duties under Section 71 of the Race Relations Act (1976), in respect of the promotion of 'equality of opportunity'.

Scotland's Minority Ethnic Population

Although it has grown and spread in recent years, Scotland's minority ethnic population is small and predominantly urbanized. Only 1.3 per cent of all Scottish households belong to a minority ethnic group, compared with six per cent in England. The minority ethnic population is not only proportionately, but also numerically small, totalling less than 63,000 adults out of a total population of some five million (1991 Census). The dominant minority ethnic groups in Scotland are those of Indian, Pakistani and Chinese (Hong Kong) origin. In comparative terms, there are few communities of Afro-Caribbean or of Bangladeshi origin. 60 per cent of the minority ethnic population live in the four main cities (Glasgow, Edinburgh, Aberdeen, Dundee). The greatest concentration is within Glasgow, which is home to a third of the total minority ethnic population in Scotland. Nevertheless, ethnic minorities still account for only 3.2 per cent of the City of Glasgow's population. Analysis at smaller area level shows significant 'clusters' within parts of the City; notably, 70 per cent of Glasgow's total minority ethnic population (24 per cent of Scotland's minority ethnic population) live within the geographical boundaries of 11 inner city community-based housing associations. Indeed, in one of these zones, ethnic minorities account for 31 per cent of the local population.

By contrast, the majority of Scotland's 32 local authorities – particularly those covering rural or outlying areas – have almost negligible representation of minority ethnic groups amongst their populations. Indeed, analysis of Census data at postcode sector level revealed that in only 65 of Scotland's 800 postcode sectors do minority ethnic households account for more than one per cent of the total population.

Housing Tenure in Scotland

Scotland's minority ethnic population differs from the white population in several respects which have implications for housing provision. First, it is a relatively youthful population; 34 per cent are minors, compared with only

20 per cent of the white population. This suggests that they are likely to form new households (proportionately) more rapidly. Second, minority ethnic households are on average larger than white households (four persons per household, compared with 2.3 per household respectively). Third, although there is some evidence of upward social mobility amongst ethnic minorities in Scotland, there are higher rates of unemployment generally, and a heavier reliance upon self-employment amongst those in work. The minority ethnic population is under-represented in professional and managerial grades, and in the major growth area of white collar employment (SEMRU, 1994).

For the purposes of this paper, the most important characteristic of minority ethnic groups in Scotland is in relation to housing tenure. The overwhelming majority (66 per cent) are owner occupiers. While this figure is similar to the proportion of English households who are home owners, it is much higher than the figure for white households in Scotland, only 53 per cent of whom have bought (or are buying) their homes (Table 7.1).

Table 7.1 Comparison of tenure structure: Scotland and England, minority ethnic and white households

	Scotland – white households	Scotland – minority ethnic households	England/ Wales – white households	England/ Wales – minority ethnic households
	%	%	%	%
Owner occupied	53	66	70	61
Private sector renting	5	16	7	11
Social rented sector (total)	42	18	23	28

Source: 1991 Census

On the other hand, ethnic minorities are much less likely than white households to be renting in the social housing sector despite the fact that, according to the 1991 Census, they are statistically more likely to be experiencing certain characteristics of 'housing need'. For example, they are more likely to be living in overcrowded conditions, and to be sharing or lacking basic facilities than their white neighbours. This contrast is particularly interesting in the light of the vast differences between Scottish and English tenure structures. In particular, council housing – traditionally more important in Scotland – still accounts for more than a third of all occupied dwellings, compared with less than 20 per cent in England. This makes the under-representation of minority ethnic groups within the social rented sector (as shown in Table 7.1) particularly difficult to explain.

Another important difference is the existence of a strong black housing association movement in England which has no equivalent in Scotland. In England, there are currently some 60 or so associations which have been set up to meet the needs of minority ethnic communities who have traditionally faced racial discrimination, and poorer housing conditions and circumstances than the general population. The achievements of the black housing movement have been significant (Harrison, 1991) in increasing the access of minority ethnic groups to subsidized housing. However, Scottish Homes has resisted following the lead of the Housing Corporation in England. It argues that because of the size and distribution of minority ethnic communities in Scotland, their housing needs are best met through targeted assistance provided by mainstream housing agencies, rather than by the establishment of new, black-led associations.

Ethnic Monitoring in the Social Housing Sector

The first year in which the Census included a question on ethnicity was 1991. Until this point, there was no reliable national statistical information on ethnic minorities in Scotland. Nevertheless, monitoring of ethnic groups in relation to housing applications and allocation, as well as racial harassment in the social housing sector remains poor, despite its fundamental importance in the delivery of a fair and equitable housing service (CRE, 1989). The lack of ethnic monitoring amongst Scottish housing authorities is symptomatic of the lack of priority this issue is afforded at the local level.

Despite the fact that council housing is still the majority tenure in some parts of Scotland, there are no reliable statistics on the ethnic group of new tenants. Additional research was undertaken by SEMRU for this paper and provides comprehensive information in relation to all 32 Scottish local authorities. The SEMRU survey revealed that less than a third of housing departments conducted ethnic monitoring of applicants, and the proportion which monitored allocations or nominations was even lower (19 per cent and nine per cent respectively).

Consequently, few housing authorities were aware of: a) the proportion of applicants who belonged to a minority ethnic groups; b) the total number of annual allocations made to minority ethnic households; or c) the extent to which applications from minority ethnic groups and/or their take-up of tenancies had changed. Furthermore, most nominations to stock managed by Scottish Homes are still not monitored for ethnic group. The failure to undertake ethnic monitoring is an indication of the extent to which the issue of 'race' has been marginalized by the housing management profession. The lack of ethnic monitoring is significant because without it, the housing needs of minority ethnic groups at the local level will continue to be invisible.

The statistical recording of new housing association lets in Scotland (known as SCORE, which is equivalent to CORE in England) now monitors ethnic group. Analysis for the financial year 1995/6 revealed that three per cent of households accommodated described themselves as being of an ethnic origin other than white, compared with a figure of 2.6 per cent the previous year. Although this represents a slight improvement, there is still a long way to go to redress the balance. There were some regional variations in terms of the proportion of new tenants from minority ethnic groups, which reflect regional differences in the ethnicity of the local population. In Edinburgh, Lothian and Borders, for example the figure was 4.1 per cent, and in Glasgow it was 3.5 per cent, compared with only 0.5 per cent in Highlands and Islands.

Statistics published by Scottish Homes show that amongst Scottish housing associations, only 60 per cent monitor the ethnic group of their tenants, and only 54 per cent monitor applicant's ethnic group. A higher proportion said they monitored ethnicity of staff and committee members, but amongst those associations who did, representation of minority ethnic communities on both counts was low (accounting for 0.8 per cent and two per cent respectively – Scottish Homes, 1996). If – as Scottish Homes argues – the housing needs of minority ethnic groups are best met within mainstream housing provision, it would surely be prudent to ensure visible minority ethnic participation in the management of those organizations.

Housing Disadvantage Amongst Scotland's Minority Ethnic Population

A substantial amount of research on 'race' and housing in Scotland has now been carried out, providing substantial evidence that Scotland's visible minority ethnic communities have suffered significant restrictions on their housing choices as a result of direct and indirect discrimination (MacEwen, Murie and Dalton, 1994).

Following publication of the policy statement *Action for Race Equality* (1994) Scottish Homes commissioned a research study to complement data provided by the 1991 Census in respect of minority ethnic groups in Scotland. The study (Wainwright et al., 1994) provided revealing insights into the predominantly negative housing experiences of minority ethnic groups.

Qualitative evidence in relation to perceived and actual discrimination in the social housing sector was compelling, and reinforced the picture presented by other, more localized research.

There were widely held views that local authorities and housing associations as landlords did not fully understand the minority ethnic communities' cultures and experiences. There was also a strong belief that no attempts were made to cater for them in the type or location of housing which was provided and offered. Public sector landlords were often found to be unhelpful and unresponsive, and had done little to overcome linguistic and cultural barriers. As a result, confidence in these organizations, and expectations of a response, was limited.

For many respondents, the processes operated by housing agencies, and the staff employed by them were regarded as overtly racist, and consequently viewed with suspicion and distrust. Perhaps by way of partial explanation, the additional research carried out by SEMRU for this paper found that most Scottish local authorities do not routinely provide frontline members of staff with training on equal opportunities and racial discrimination. This was despite the fact that CRE guidance stresses the importance of training in the implementation of an equal opportunities strategy (CRE, 1989a). Indeed, training was the exception rather than the rule, having been provided to staff by only a quarter of housing authority employers. Another 38 per cent said they were planning to provide such training in the future. This still left eight local authorities which had not, and did not plan to train front line staff on equal opportunities issues.

A number of Scotland's new unitary authorities said they planned to introduce race equality training in the future. However, these overall findings of the current state raise questions about the extent to which local authorities are implementing Section 71 of the Race Relations Act 1976, which sets out a responsibility to promote equality of opportunity between different racial groups. In short, fewer than half of Scotland's 32 new unitary authorities had a credible approach to tackling racial issues in relation to the provision and management of housing in their areas.

It is clear than in Scotland, minority ethnic groups are disproportionately affected by poor housing according to a range of objective indices, and yet continue to be under-represented in needs-oriented subsidized rented housing and over-represented in the owner occupied sector, which many can little afford (Third et al., 1997). One possible explanation for this is that most of the stock under management in Scotland's large social rented sector is mismatched to the needs of the minority ethnic communities (Bowes et al.,

1989). As MacEwen et al.'s literature review of 'race' and housing in Scotland suggests (1994, p. 27):

> The need for larger but reasonably priced accommodation is apparent for large/extended families. While this choice is expressed for such accommodation in the owner occupied sector this reflects, at least in part, lack of suitable local authority and housing association provision and problems associated with access.

Given that in the Scottish context, minority ethnic groups are relative newcomers in their application to social rented housing, they are therefore likely to be relatively disadvantaged in their access to the best of the housing stock. However, most newcomers are not refugees, and so their disadvantage cannot be explained by the application of the Asylum and Immigration Act 1996.

Future developments undertaken by housing associations are likely to be predominantly designed for smaller family units (including lone parent families) and single people, reflecting more general demographic trends. If the needs of minority ethnic groups are not incorporated into the planning process at an early stage, new developments will not meet their housing needs. Therefore, unless effective systems for ethnic monitoring are now introduced and implemented, and the particular housing needs and requirements of minority ethnic groups in certain areas acknowledged, their exclusion from subsidized rented housing is likely to increase.

Furthermore, it may be argued that the loss of council houses through Right to Buy has already affected, and will continue to affect minority ethnic households disproportionately. This is because the stock sold is predominantly family housing rather than accommodation for single people (Scottish Homes, 1996). Minority ethnic households on the other hand are more likely than white households to live in families, than to live alone or with a partner (1991 Census).

Moreover, because of the under-representation of ethnic minorities in the Scottish public sector, their take-up of Right to Buy is low. As such, that group have missed out on an enhanced capital gain through the heavily discounted purchase of council homes. The contrast is particularly notable when one considers that nationally, a third of Scotland's owner occupiers became home owners through the Right to Buy, but the proportion of minority ethnic home owners who had purchased their council homes as sitting tenants is very small. Right to Buy sales in Scotland have not been monitored by ethnic group, so accurate figures are not available.

In the Scottish context, minority ethnic groups have had less opportunity to exercise the Right to Buy, but even if they had, the English experience suggests that they might still fail to benefit. English research suggests that minority ethnic households who do live in council housing are concentrated in the poorer quality stock and as such would be less likely to wish to take advantage of the Right to Buy. This confirms the more general view that black communities miss out on investment in housing in a range of ways (Mullings, 1991).

Implications of Tenure 'Choice'

Evidence from both pieces of Scottish Homes sponsored research into minority ethnic housing (Wainwright et al., 1994; Third et al, 1997) indicate that the distinctive patterns of tenure amongst minority ethnic households in Scotland could reflect these difficulties caused by barriers of access to social rented housing, as much as any positive attraction of home ownership. Indeed, both studies suggested that a significant proportion of minority ethnic households bought because of a perceived lack of suitable rented alternatives. As Figure 7.1 illustrates, more than a quarter became (or remained) home owners because they were unable to exercise their first choice of housing tenure. This was true for only three per cent of white home owners.

The phenomenon of the 'reluctant home owner' amongst the minority ethnic sample is reinforced by the research findings represented in Figure 7.2. This shows that minority ethnic households were much less likely than

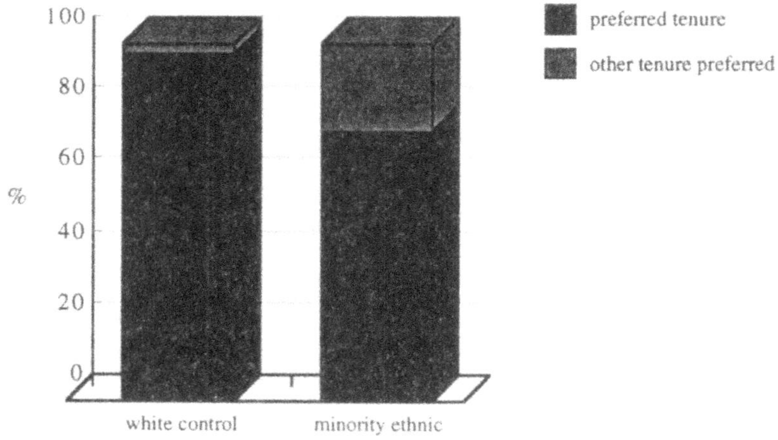

Figure 7.1 Reluctant home owners

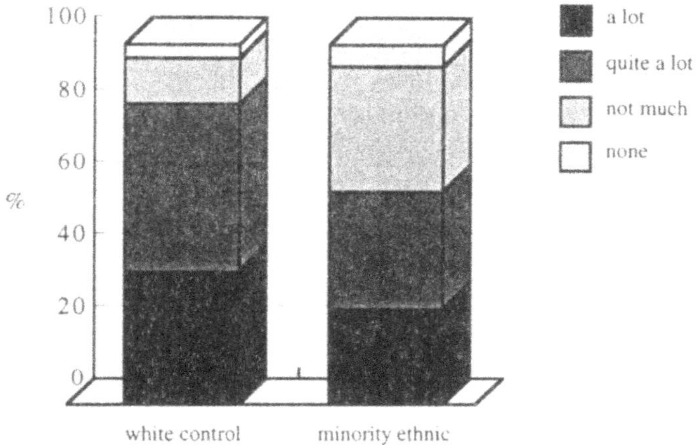

Figure 7.2 Choice about becoming a home owner

their white neighbours to believe they had exercised 'a lot' or 'quite a lot' of choice in the decision to become a home owner.

Amongst those who became home owners because of lack of choice rather than any positive attraction of home ownership, the most popular alternative was renting in the public sector. One in eight minority ethnic home owners said they would have preferred to rent a council house than to buy.

The research identified strong evidence of 'push' rather than 'pull' factors in relation to tenure 'choice' amongst minority ethnic groups in Scotland. This was because for many, housing choices were constrained by actual or perceived lack of access to alternative options. This key finding leads to an overall view that owner occupation can be a very different experience for minority ethnic than for white households. In short, amongst the general population, home ownership may imply affluence and freedom of choice – a measure of their *inclusion* in the norms and expectations of the political, ideological and social climate of the 1990s. This may not be so for households who are forced to buy, largely because of their *exclusion* from a range of other housing options.

Clearly then, owner occupation is not a homogenous tenure, and racial disadvantage in housing cuts across all tenures (Morris and Winn, 1990). Certainly, for many minority ethnic households, owner occupation did not represent an improvement in housing circumstances. Poor conditions were common. For example, minority ethnic owners were more likely than white owners to say they had bought homes in need of major repair or refurbishment, but were less likely to say they planned to undertake the work in the coming year. They were also much less likely to have the money to do so.

Minority ethnic owners were also significantly less satisfied overall with the house they had bought, than their white neighbours. Overcrowding was also commonplace. One in three minority ethnic households was statutorily overcrowded, compared with only one in 14 white households. Despite the fact that they were less satisfied with their homes and with owner occupation as a whole, minority ethnic owners paid more for their homes. Monthly mortgage costs accounted for a greater proportion of lower and less secure incomes than their white owners. Mortgage arrears were also more common amongst minority ethnic owners than their white neighbours.

Racial Harassment

It is not possible to draw an accurate picture of the extent of the problem of racial harassment because there are no reliable data (Home Affairs Committee, 1986, and Home Office, 1986). Indeed, the research carried out for this paper by SEMRU revealed that more than half of Scottish local authorities do not monitor racial attacks and harassment at all. Those which did have monitoring structures in place said that incidents were rarely reported to them. In 1994, a report on racial incidents in council housing (DOE, 1994) stressed the importance of effective policies and strategies for dealing with racial harassment, and required a response from local authorities. However, this did not apply to Scotland, and no equivalent document has been forthcoming North of the border.

In general, those local authorities which had policies and procedures in place had adopted a multi-agency approach to racial attacks and victim support. The multi-agency approach has been commended by a number of government studies (Home Office, 1996) and its value is now widely acknowledged. Although the Home Office guidance on racial incidents does apply to Scotland, the extent to which it has been effectively promoted and implemented by Scottish Office is questionable.

What the available Scottish research suggests is that racial harassment is extensive and increasing. Across Scotland, reported racial incidents have increased dramatically in recent years, almost trebling between 1988 and 1995/6. Furthermore, as the British Crime Survey (Home Office, 1994) suggested, many such incidents are likely to remain unreported. Racial harassment is particularly (but not exclusively) common in areas where there is a concentration of local authority housing (MacEwen et al., 1994). For example, SEMRU research in the late eighties revealed that 43 per cent of minority ethnic tenants in Edinburgh had experienced racial abuse on more than one occasion, but there were significant locational variations. In one peripheral council estate, the figure was 82 per cent (Hancock and MacEwen, 1989).

Although most evidence relates to Edinburgh and Glasgow, research suggests that racial attacks and harassment increase outside the two main cities. SEMRU's research carried out for this paper found, for example, that 23 incidents had been reported to City of Aberdeen Council during 1995 – a not insignificant number, given the relatively small size of the minority ethnic population in Aberdeen.

Despite the growing incidence of racial harassment in Scotland, the SEMRU survey found that most local authorities on the other hand either had no structures in place to monitor racial incidents, or said that none had been reported. The differences between local authority and police statistics illustrate to some extent the failure of the former to monitor racial incidents. This in turn could imply a degree of neglect amongst housing authorities to deal with the issue effectively.

Racial harassment in Scotland has included verbal abuse and threats, racist graffiti on housing and other property, dumping of rubbish, putting excrement through letter boxes, setting fire to property, robbery, vandalism and physical assaults (Walsh, 1987). Recent statistics provided by Scotland's six Race Equality Council's suggest that just under half of the incidents involved verbal abuse. One in seven reported incidents related to physical assault, and around one in five involved damage to property (this figure includes graffiti and arson).

Added to the more general negative views of public sector landlords, there is also a widespread perception – and direct experience – of racial harassment in council housing, which clearly serves as a powerful deterrent to minority ethnic households to this tenure when considering their housing options (Third et al., 1997). There was a dominant concern with living in 'safe' areas. Indeed a good area was often thought to be more important than a good house. However, most minority ethnic households perceived areas where there was a concentration of public sector stock to be unsafe. Furthermore, there is evidence to suggest that in Scotland, as in the rest of the UK, applicants for local authority housing choose location and relocation because of their knowledge or belief about the risks of racial harassment (Bowes et al., 1989; Tibbett, 1987; MacEwen, 1987).

While racial harassment appeared to be most prevalent on council estates, other areas were also perceived as being particularly dangerous, often leading to reluctance – or refusal – to live in these areas. Consistent with other research findings (Walsh, 1987), rates of reporting racial incidents amongst respondents in Wainwright et al.'s (1994) study were low. There was some recognition in the report itself of the difficulties associated with proving that harassment had occurred, which in turn served to deter victims from taking action against perpetrators.

Fear of harassment also limited the choice of houses to buy, since certain areas considered to be unsafe were 'off limits' (Third et al., 1997). This suggests that while house purchase brings with it some freedom of choice in respect of where to live, minority ethnic home owners often buy properties in 'safe' areas at the expense of other factors, such as size, quality and price. Nevertheless, it should not be assumed that home owners are able to escape racial harassment at home; 20 per cent of those interviewed for Third et al.'s study had experienced racial harassment in the area where they had bought their home.

Despite extensive literature on how landlords might deal with perpetrators of racial harassment, and protect tenants (see for example CRE, 1991 Code of Practice in Rented Housing), there is still a clear need for landlords in the social housing sector to review their policies, and to coordinate and implement them more effectively (MacEwen, 1991). Much work has discussed developing multi-agency approaches, as well as pro-active measures to create safer environments and protect residents. However, outside the major Scottish cities the response of housing authorities has been very varied. This demonstrates that a higher priority is required if significant improvements in the life opportunities for minority ethnic communities are to be achieved in the social housing sector. Implementation and monitoring of effective policies on racial harassment and attacks is an essential prerequisite.

Section 71: The Duty of Housing Authorities

A particular obligation was placed on local authorities, now extended to the Housing Corporation, Tai Cymru and Scottish Homes, by virtue of section 71 of the Race Relations Act 1976. That obligation comprises two elements. Those covered must examine arrangements with a view, first, to eliminating unlawful discrimination and, second, to promoting equality of opportunity between different racial groups. The nature of that obligation does not appear to be enforceable by individuals. Although not explicitly provided by the legislation, *implicitly* the Home Secretary may have power to require an authority to comply with this statutory obligation. There is no evidence that this has ever happened. The accusation made by Lord Hailsham at the time of the passage of this section in the House of Lords that it was a mere cosmetic has proved accurate (for discussion see MacEwen, 1985).

Local government reorganization has recently taken place in Scotland and the new 32 unified authorities have just completed their first year. It seemed timely therefore to see what action had been taken to review inherited policies implementing Section 71 of the Act. The SEMRU survey of Scottish local authorities conducted for this paper showed that knowledge of local minority ethnic populations, and ethnic monitoring was more consistent in areas which contained relative concentrations (in Scottish terms) of minority ethnic communities. However, it was notable that most Scottish authorities were unable to say what proportion of their local population was of minority ethnic origin. Given the duties of local authorities under Section 71 and the increasing emphasis on their strategic 'enabling' role, this is a particularly worrying finding. Nevertheless, two-fifths of local authorities said that they had reviewed their arrangements for promoting 'equality of opportunities' in terms of the requirements of the Race Relations Act, and another fifth said they planned to do so.

It is perhaps unsurprising that in general the urban local authorities were more pro-active than some of the rural authorities with relatively small minority ethnic populations. Most of these smaller rural authorities had done little in terms of developing policies on 'race' and continued to interpret their obligations under this section as being add-on options.

It is in the nature of social surveys that the confidentiality of respondents is respected. Consequently, there can be no expectation that individual remedies will be pursued where acts of discrimination come to light. Subject to contrary agreements or understandings, it would be open to the researchers to intimate to affected interviewees that discrimination may have occurred and to advise the interviewee in such circumstances to seek legal advice.

More importantly, the question arises as to the general remedies that may have to be pursued in policy development where patterns of racial disadvantage have emerged, and there is a belief that one or more authorities have contributed to the position. Having established racial disadvantage, however, there can be no assumption that the housing authority concerned will take action nor any assumption that the legal framework will persuade it to take action. For example, a report into the experience of ethnic minorities in the housing allocation system of Edinburgh District Council (Hancock and MacEwen, 1989) identified potentially discriminatory rules which gave priority to those with local ties in certain housing districts. However, the housing authority refused to consider change, having established through their own legal department a point which was not contested by the researchers. The council's argument was that the rules were 'justifiable' on nonracial grounds in supporting established communities.

Scottish Homes 'Action for Race Equality'

This paper began by suggesting that until recently, 'race' and housing issues had been relatively neglected in Scotland. If this is an accepted truth, then Scottish policy in this area has come a long way in a comparatively short time. Scottish Homes now publicly recognizes the under-representation of ethnic minorities in the social housing sector as a serious issue, and acknowledges access difficulties and fear of harassment. The 1994 publication of the policy statement *Action for Race Equality* demonstrates Scottish Homes' commitment – as landlord and regulator – to ensuring fairer access to those groups. Specific measures (including further research) have been recommended and funded. These encompass, for example, monitoring new lets to housing associations and Scottish Homes by ethnic group and providing detailed guidance to associations on how they might improve access for ethnic minorities.

Scottish Homes also intends to monitor the beneficiaries of grant funding to private housing developers, and to launch an integrated information strategy. The aim of the strategy is to ensure that members of minority ethnic communities are aware of – and are able to access – all the housing opportunities available to them.

Finally, Scottish Homes announced in its policy statement on race that it may support the formation of new groups, drawn substantially from the minority ethnic communities, to implement effective housing management practices for both existing and new housing. Their remit would be to improve access of minority ethnic groups to that stock. Nevertheless, Scottish Homes continues to resist the idea of ring-fenced funding for a black housing movement (Scottish Homes, 1994).

The Scottish Office, on the other hand, has failed to match Scottish Homes' lead in relation to the needs of minority ethnic groups. Successive governments have failed to assign sufficient political priority to issues of race relations and racism. As MacEwen (1991, p. 338) points out:

> This is evidenced by the fact that the Scottish Office does not employ one civil servant with an exclusive remit on race relations, has no post designated as that of a race relations adviser, whether shared with other responsibilities or not,

> and has no advisory committee or body whether at political or official level to provide advice, or guidance in implementing Central Government policy.

Furthermore, there is also a question as to how far the Scottish Office has demonstrated any commitment to race relations. Although there was some Scottish representation on the Home Office Racial Attacks Group which produced the 1996 report, there has been little effort to carry forward the recommendations in Scotland. The Scottish Office – in common with the Home Office – has recently published a consultation document on racial harassment, which demonstrates some acknowledgement of the inadequacy of existing measures to protect ethnic minorities against racial harassment. The extent to which this will lead to some positive change has yet to be seen.

Proving Discrimination in the Social Housing Sector

Having outlined the context for and outcomes of recent research in the housing of minority ethnic groups in Scotland and drawn conclusions about consistent patterns of discrimination, this paper now turns to the potential impact of anti-discrimination law in counteracting racial disadvantage.

There are two preliminary considerations in the linkage between racial disadvantage and anti-discrimination law worth emphasizing. First, the discrimination legislation in Britain has a focus on individual complaints and particularized remedies. There is no provision for class action as in the US, no special recognition of collective rights of minorities as in the case of the New Zealand Maori. Neither is there any particular responsibility for counteracting historical disadvantage exemplified by mandatory targets and monitoring in the public sector in Australia, or the employment field in Canada.

The British individuated approach characterizes discrimination as an aberration from normal practice, rather than the everyday product of a racialized society. The conclusion by Lord Scarman in his report of the Brixton disorders (Scarman, 1981) that 'Britain' did not suffer from institutionalized discrimination illustrates an establishment mind-set. This stems from a failure to acknowledge that personal behaviour is a part-product of dominant social norms which in turn reflect stereotypical values about 'other' communities.

Not only is the assumption about nondiscrimination at an institutional level implicit in the legislation, it is also part of the culture and ethos of the courts and tribunals and the legal profession from which they are staffed. Thus the Scottish Law Society itself had 65 members in 1989, none of whom were of minority ethnic origin. The profession has no reference to discrimination in its code of professional practice. It does not issue guidelines in this area. Finally, it does not monitor recruitment to the profession on racial grounds (see MacEwen, 1991).

The legislation does not require the courts to infer a linkage between racial disadvantage and racial discrimination. Consequently, the onus of proof is on the pursuers to demonstrate that the underlying cause of disadvantage is discrimination. Disadvantage may have a complexity of contributory causes such as income, class, education, qualifications, knowledge of the local network etc. This makes the identification of discrimination as a factor problematic. While industrial tribunals have sought to enable inferences of discrimination to be drawn where plausible alternatives have been discounted, the difficulties of proof remain significant.

Given that racial discrimination is a civil rather than a criminal offence, the required standard of proof is the balance of probability. It is a widely accepted fact, however, that the most difficult obstacle for a person alleging discrimination is to prove that he or she is actually the victim of discrimination (SCOLAG, 1988, p. 93). To do so it may be necessary to establish the relevance of demonstrating patterns of discrimination, by reference to statistical data (MacEwen, 1991, p. 17). Generally, such data has been to little avail since, to obtain a remedy, it would have to be established that the litigant was a victim of a specific discriminatory act. On the other hand, in *West Midlands Passage of Transport Executive v Singh* (1988) IRLR 168 the Court of Appeal held that statistical evidence, so far as it established a discernible pattern, might be indicative of discrimination in respect of the specific act alleged.

Where there is evidence to suggest a pattern of discrimination against a racial group, in the absence of a satisfactory explanation to the contrary, the court can hold that it is reasonable to infer discrimination against a member of that group in respect of a specific act. That approach contrasts with the conclusion in *Jalota v IMI (Kynoch)* (1979) ILIR 313 where it was held that statistics had no pro-active value other than with reference to the employer's 'credit' and were consequently inadmissible. In cases of social rented housing, it can be argued, the admissibility and relevance of statistical evidence is important in establishing patterns of racial disadvantage which may be the only evidence of indirect discrimination and constitute a rebuttable assumption that discrimination had taken place in the absence of any contrary evidence. The CRE investigations in Hackney and Liverpool provide examples of where such indirect discrimination clearly took place according to statistical evidence, but no individual had submitted a formal complaint on the basis of their personal circumstances and experiences (CRE 1989; CRE 1984).

In comparison with successful complaints of unlawful discrimination on racial grounds in employment, successful complaints against local housing authorities in access to public housing or the terms and conditions of suitability of let are comparatively few. The following are possibly the more important reasons for this:

1 unlike employment complaints, covered by Part II of the Race Relations Act 1976, which enable complainants to pursue a remedy before industrial tribunals (Section 63 (3)(a)), remedies for housing complaints are only pursued before designated County Courts in England or Sheriff Courts in Scotland (Section 21 and Section 63 (3)(b)). This is also true in respect of complaints in relation to obtaining loans or mortgages (which generally constitute the provision of goods, services or facilities – Section 20). Taking a complaint to the County Court or Sheriff Court is, generally, a more daunting proposition – more expensive, more time-consuming, and more intimidating (see Dhavan, 1988);

2 the process of selection to be placed on a local authority/housing association housing waiting list, and the actual allocation of a house are likely to be less transparent than the process of getting a job. CRE investigations, particularly that into Liverpool City Council Housing Department (CRE, 1989) demonstrate that literally hundreds of acts of direct or indirect discrimination in housing allocations have taken place without challenge; generally, the individual applicant is unaware of the occurrence of discrimination and is not in a position to lodge a complaint (MacEwen, 1991, p. 250);

3 Henderson and Karn (1987) have demonstrated that the perceptions and attitudes of housing staff may be inextricably linked to the process of indirect discrimination as well as direct discrimination. Direct discrimination is likely to stem from the imposition of a rule such as that of providing preference in housing to sons and daughters of existing tenants in the Tower Hamlets authority. While evidently to the significant disadvantage of ethnic minorities, these rules may often be defended by the authority as being justified on other grounds (MacEwen, 1991; Henderson, and Karn, 1987; Smith, 1989);

4 to demonstrate the presence of indirect discrimination, it is necessary to

establish that the authority has imposed a condition or requirement which although not based on racial grounds itself, results in less favourable treatment by reference to racial grounds. In employment cases it has been held that the application of guidelines which do not constitute a hard and fast rule and which, therefore, equate with preference do not constitute a condition or requirement (see MacEwen, 1991; CRE, 1991). Allocation procedures in housing necessarily permit some degree of discretion, but the extent to which implicit or racial discrimination can be hidden within discretion, or indeed interpretation of policy, is difficult to spot and harder still to prove;

5 to demonstrate that a rule has an adverse impact on minority ethnic groups, there must be some statistical analysis to demonstrate relative disadvantage or some other evidence satisfying the courts that racial discrimination has occurred.

Therefore, it is hardly surprising that only about seven per cent of complaints referred to CRE since its inception in 1976 have related to housing, despite the fact that housing constitutes a significant benefit or detriment to a family's living circumstances. Section 71 of the Race Relations Act 1976 clearly sets out the obligation of local authorities to eliminate unlawful discrimination and promote equality of opportunity between different racial groups, but differences between this and other parts of the legislation have meant that it is easy for local authorities to evade, and harder for those who are adversely affected as a result of this, to mount legal challenges.

If there is reason to establish that unlawful discrimination may have occurred, then the Commission for Racial Equality may institute a formal investigation into a named authority. In the event that such an enquiry concludes that unlawful discrimination has occurred, then a Nondiscrimination Notice may be issued requiring the authority to take action to comply. The history of the CRE formal investigation is not one of unqualified success (see McCrudden, 1989). The process has been described by Lord Denning as 'a spider's web' and the CRE Staff Commission and legal advisers have developed cumbersome formal investigation machinery to protect the CRE against the possibility of judicial review. In Scotland, there have been no named investigations by the CRE but both research reports and informal inquiries sponsored by the CRE have helped to clarify the Scottish situation with regard to racial harassment and discrimination (see for example Dalton and Daghlian, 1989).

Conclusion

There is now a reliable body of research evidence which provides sufficient weight to form the conclusion that Scotland's minority ethnic communities have suffered very substantial restrictions on their housing choices as a result of direct and indirect discrimination. Fear of racial harassment has also had an important influence on housing choices. In particular, minority ethnic groups have benefited little from subsidized housing in Scotland's large social housing sector, either as tenants, or, latterly, as purchasers under the Right to Buy.

Minority ethnic groups in Scotland are under-represented in the social rented sector, despite the fact that they are disproportionately affected by poor housing, according to objective and subjective measures of housing need. There are a number of plausible explanations for this. For example, there are issues about the size and location (and consequently the suitability) of existing stock. Such issues are not easy to resolve in the short or even the medium-term, especially in the light of severe limitations on local authorities to undertake new building programmes. However, landlords within the social housing sector must accept some responsibility from a housing and estate management perspective for the continuing absence of ethnic minorities in their housing. Tackling racial harassment effectively is a case in point. Ensuring equality of opportunity in relation to access to housing, and across the board, is another key area in which in most – if not all – parts of the country, there is substantial room for improvement.

However, there is a pervading sense – both implicit and explicit amongst Scottish local authorities, and even in the Scottish Office – that the issue of ethnic minorities is peripheral to more central concerns. Indeed, it can be argued from the research evidence presented in this paper that most local authorities are not fulfilling their legal obligations under the 1976 Race Relations legislation. Unfortunately, this is difficult to challenge. It cannot easily be applied to individual cases, and in any event, contravention is difficult to prove, particularly in the absence of hard data on specific examples of inequality of opportunity.

One of the reasons for collecting data on ethnicity is to establish whether such statistical returns demonstrate patterns of disadvantage unexplained by nonracial grounds. The term 'pattern and practice' employed in the US to denote discrimination which has become embedded into behavioural norms reflects a more profound social acceptance that institutional discrimination is a reality. It also acknowledges the necessary implementation of systematic measures by local authorities amongst others to achieve a social shift.

Unfortunately, the evidence from the series of research findings in Scotland not only confirms the significance of racial disadvantage but also the continuing reluctance of authorities to be standard bearers in the reform agenda. Perhaps the new government and the new Scottish parliament will accept and meet this challenge.

Bibliography

Berthaud, R. and Momood, T. (1997), *Ethnic Minorities in Britain: Diversity and Disadvantage. Fourth National Survey of Ethnic Minorities in England and Wales*, Policy Studies Institute, London.

Bowes, A., McCluskey, J. and Sim, D. (1989), *Ethnic Minority Housing Problems in Glasgow: Final Report*, University of Stirling, Stirling.

Chan, E. (1983), *Needs of the Chinese Community in Edinburgh*, Community in Edinburgh, Community Relations Council, Edinburgh.

Commission for Racial Equality (1984), *Race and Council Housing in Hackney*, report of formal investigation, CRE, London.

Commission for Racial Equality (1989), *Racial Discrimination in Liverpool City Council*, report of a formal investigation into the Housing Department, CRE, London.

Commission for Racial Equality (1989a), *Training for Racial Equality in Housing*, London, CRE, London.

Commission for Racial Equality (1989b), *Positive Action and Racial Equality in Housing*, CRE, London.

Commission for Racial Equality (1991), *Code of Practice in Rented Housing*, CRE, London.

Dalton, M. and Daghlian, S. (1989), *Race and Housing in Glasgow: The Role of Housing Associations*, CRE, London.

Davidson, F. (1988), 'This month cases', *SCOLAG*, No. 1, 41 (June).

Department of the Environment (1994), *Racial Incidents in Council Housing*, HMSO, London.

Dow, D. (1995), *Ethnic Minority Housing in Glasgow*, Scottish Homes Glasgow District Office, Development Funding Strategy, Scottish Homes, Glasgow.

Harrison, M. (1991), 'Black-led Asian and Chinese Housing Organisations in the North', *Housing Review*, Vol. 40 (2), pp. 36–8.

Hancock, D. and MacEwen, M. (1989), *Public Housing and Ethnic Minorities in Edinburgh*, CRE/SEMRU Research Report, Edinburgh.

Henderson, J. and Karn, V. (1987), *Race, Class and State Housing*, Gower, Aldershot.

Home Office (1986), *Racial Attacks*, HMSO, London.

MacEwen, M. (1980), 'Ethnic Minorities and Public Housing Services in Scotland' in *Scottish Council for Racial Equality First Annual Report 1979–1980*, SCRE, Edinburgh.

MacEwen, M. (1985), 'Local Authority Duty to Promote Racial Equality', *SCOLAG*, No. 105 (April), pp. 86–8.

MacEwen, M. (1986), *Racial Harassment, Council Housing and The Law*, SEMRU, Edinburgh College of Art/Heriot-Watt University, Edinburgh.

MacEwen, M. (1991), *Housing, Race and Law*, Routledge, London.

MacEwen, M., Dalton, M. and Murie, A. (1994), *'Race' and Housing in Scotland: Literature Review and Bibliography*, Edinburgh College of Art/Heriot-Watt University, Edinburgh.

MacFarland, E. and Walsh, D. (1988), *Refugees in Strathclyde*, SEMRU Research Paper 6, Edinburgh College of Art/Heriot-Watt University, Edinburgh.
MacLeod, L. (1988), *Irrespective of Race, Colour or Creed? Minority Ethnic Groups and the Voluntary Sector in Scotland*, CRE, London.
McCrudden, C. (1989), 'The Commission for Racial Equality: Formal Investigations in the Shadow of Judicial Review' in R. Baldwin and C. McCrudden (eds), *Regulation and Public Law*, Weidenfeld and Nicholson, London.
Miles, R. and Muirhead, L. (1986), 'Racism in Scotland' in E. McCrone (ed.), *Scottish Local Government Year Book 1985*, Paul Harris Publishing, Edinburgh.
Morris, J. and Winn, M. (1990), *Housing and Social Inequality*, Hilary Shipman, London.
Mullings, B. (1991), *The Colour of Money*, Runnymede Trust, London.
Murie, A. (1996), 'Introduction and Overview' in H. Currie and A. Murie (eds), *Housing in Scotland*, Chartered Institute of Housing, Coventry.
Scarman, L. (1981), *The Brixton Disorders 10–12 April 1981*, Cmnd 8427, HMSO, London.
Scottish Ethnic Minorities Research Unit (1994), *Scotland's Ethnic Minority Community 1991. A Census Summary*, Factsheet No. 1, SEMRU, Edinburgh College of Art/Heriot-Watt University, Edinburgh.
Scottish Homes (1994), *Action for Race Equality*, Scottish Homes, Edinburgh.
Scottish Homes (1996), *Housing Association Statistics*, Scottish Homes, Edinburgh.
Scottish Office (1991), *Ethnic Minorities in Scotland*, SCPR, Scottish Office, Edinburgh.
Scottish Office (1996), *Statistical Bulletin HSG/1996/6*, Scottish Office, Edinburgh.
Scottish Office Home Department (1997), *New Offences of Racial Harassment and Racially Motivated Violence: A Consultation Document*, Scottish Office, Edinburgh.
Smith, S. (1989), *The Politics of Race and Residence*, Polity Press, Cambridge.
Third, H., Wainwright, S. and Pawson, H. (1997), *Constraint and Choice for Minority Ethnic Home Owners in Scotland*, Research Report No. 54, Scottish Homes, Edinburgh.
Tibbett, A. (1987), *Racial Harassment and Council Housing – The Remedies Available to Local Authorities*, unpublished BSc dissertation, School of Planning and Housing, Edinburgh College of Art/Heriot-Watt University, Edinburgh.
Wainwright, S., Murie, A. and MacEwen, M. (1994), *The Experience of Households from Minority Ethnic Groups in the Scottish Housing Market*, Research Report No. 29, Scottish Homes, Edinburgh.
Walsh, D. (1987), *Racial Harassment in Glasgow*, SEMRU Research Paper No. 3, Glasgow Caledonian University, Glasgow.

8 Bureaucracy or Death: Safeguarding Lives in Houses in Multiple Occupation

NICHOLAS J. SMITH

The furore about the reduction of duties placed on local housing authorities (LHAs) towards homeless applicants, the introduction of more extensive powers against 'nuisance neighbours', and the extended right to buy option for tenants of registered social landlords in the Housing Act 1996, hereinafter the 1996 Act, have been debated extensively. Protection offered to occupiers of multiply occupied housing tends to be rather lower down the housing agenda, almost at postscript level. It would appear that houses in multiple occupation (HMOs) are worthy of consideration only when tragedies occur. When such catastrophes do occur they are often deadly. At a hotel in Scarborough, in May 1994, a fire commenced on the second floor, leading to the death of a 31-year-old woman, Cath Harrison, and a young child Terri-Anne Jones. In Palmeira Avenue, Hove, in 1992, five occupiers of self-contained flats, a type of HMO, died in a fire. It is not merely fire that kills in multiply occupied housing, carbon monoxide poisoning led to the deaths of two students in Nottingham, killed by a faulty gas boiler reconnected by a landlord after being declared unsafe by British Gas. There are many tragedies in HMOs, Home Office figures for fire deaths between 1988 and 1992 indicate that 849 people died (HO, 1994). According to Everton (1997, p. 61):

> In the view of the fire service HMOs are the most dangerous type of premises in which the public stay or reside on a temporary or semi permanent basis, a view highlighted by the incidence of death and injury such as that sustained in a hostel fire in Scarborough in 1994.

The fire in Scarborough led to, and fed into, a number of reports and consultation papers. A Department of Trade and Industry report (DTI, 1994) reviewed all legislation for which the Home Office and Department of the Environment (DoE) had responsibility, including HMOs, recommending a review of the HMO definition, placing owners of multiply occupied properties under a duty to provide adequate fire precautions, and envisaged a form of certification process for HMOs. The Department of the Environment issued a consultation paper in November 1994 (DoE, 1994) considering the question of licensing HMOs and issued a further document linked to the 1995 Housing White Paper (DoE, 1995). This outlined the DoE view that HMOs should not be compulsorily licensed as this would lead to excessive bureaucracy and costs being placed upon HMO landlords. This highlighted the conundrum between ensuring a vigorous and thriving sector of the housing market catering for, inter alia, a large and growing student market, and the wish not to overburden the owners of properties letting these properties. This should be contrasted to the undoubted risks of living in a HMO, the National Consumer Council (NCC, 1991) finding the hazard of fire in HMOs is ten times greater than singly occupied homes. Additionally, the English House Condition Survey found 'there is little dispute that HMOs represent a significantly higher fire risk than single family homes' (DoE, 1993).

There are many statistics available indicating numbers of deaths, the dangerousness of existing in a HMO, the lack of amenity and poor standards of accommodation within multiply occupied housing. There appears on the other hand to have been little published research into how legislative safety provisions are operated by LHAs within individual districts and boroughs. The only major exception being research undertaken for the Campaign for Bedsit Rights, supported by the Joseph Rowntree Foundation, into local authority practice (Randall, 1993). This chapter will consider practices adopted by local authority environmental health departments to raise standards and safety within HMOs. Research undertaken over the last two years by the author will be drawn upon. The chapter will be structured to initially consider definitional issues relating to multiple occupation, particularly how these issues impact upon authority activity. Policy responses of environmental health departments, with particular attention to recent legislative changes are addressed. A third element of the chapter investigates consultation between fire and environmental health officers, a matter of contention for both professions. How authorities utilize HMO safety provisions are considered. Finally, the question of registering or licensing multiply occupied accommodation is assessed. Before entering into substantive appraisal of LHAs action, however, the legislative definition of a HMO and statutory supervision in this area should be outlined.

What are Houses in Multiple Occupation?

Section 345, Housing Act 1985, hereinafter the 1985 Act, defines a house in multiple occupation to be 'a house which is occupied by persons who do not form a single household'.

The most effective way of analysing the aforementioned definition is to split it into three parts, defining in turn the meaning of a 'house', 'which is occupied by', 'persons who do not form a single household'. A house is not defined within the 1985 Act, other than at section 399 indicating that a house includes a garden and yard. The courts, however, have given a generous interpretation. In *Reed v Hastings Corporation* [1964] 62 LGR 588 Harman LJ established: 'It seems to me that I am entitled to say that "house" means what it obviously is, namely, a place fitted and used and adapted for human habitation.' Thus a house, it would appear, can include converted offices or shops, or even a garage used as accommodation. The phrase 'which is occupied by', has also been viewed generously in case law, Cumming-Bruce LJ in *Silbers v Southwark L.B.C.* (1977) 122 Sol. J 128 found an occupier merely needed to be 'living in' accommodation, there was no need for the occupier to have exclusive possession. Of greatest difficulty for enforcers of HMO safety measures, and landlords, is the issue of a 'single household'. An extended family probably would be regarded as one household and thus outside the ambit of the section 345 definition. In contrast, a rooming house, or temporary shelter for a large and fluctuating population would fall within the definition according to *Simmons v Pizzey* [1979] AC 37. Complications arise with those households falling in between, particularly student accommodation. This was amply illustrated in *Barnes v Sheffield C. C.* (1995) 27 HLR 719, where Sir Thomas Bingham MR indicated there was no overriding factor which would determine if 'persons do not form a single household' rather there are a series of questions which need to be addressed to determine the status of the occupancy as single or multiple. These factors incorporated: whether the occupants knew each other before entering a tenancy agreement; how the property was occupied, taking into account the allocation of cleaning, cooking, and shopping responsibilities; how vacancies were filled and rooms allotted; whether doors had locks; and also the size of the establishment and group of inhabitants (Smith, 1997). Whilst these indicative factors may be of some benefit to environmental health officers (EHOs) who are charged with the responsibility of HMO safety enforcement, it remains troublesome in certain cases to be clear when a house is a multiply occupied for the purposes of the 1985 Act. This issue will be further explored within the main body of research findings.

Legislative Protection Afforded to HMOs

It is important to outline protective provisions in order to fully grasp the complexity of the role played by EHOs and others in affecting safety within the HMO sector. HMOs are safeguarded by a plethora of statutory provision and regulations. The 1985 Act, as amended, however, is the major statutory housing control of multiple occupation. The major thrust of the legislation is to provide LHAs with powers, and occasionally duties, to facilitate the raising of amenity and safety standards within multiply occupied accommodation. HMO housing law is rather complex, laying obligations on local authorities as well as landlords and owners of multiply occupied premises. It is outside the ambit of this piece to provide a comprehensive analysis of legal provision, a brief resume is, however, helpful to enable deeper understanding of the research findings (see Arden, 1997, Ch. 14 for more detailed coverage). Local housing authorities have various mechanisms available to raise safety and amenity standards. Of primary importance is a section 352 1985 Act notice requiring the execution of works to make a HMO fit for the number of occupants residing within the property. Further, an authority may decide to combine its powers under section 352 with those within section 354 and limit the number of occupants in a property. Additionally, the authority under section 365 of the 1985 Act has the power, and under appropriate circumstances a duty (see s. I, 1997, No. 230), to accept an undertaking from the owner of the property or make a closing order against a property where the authority believes there is an inadequate means of escape from fire or inadequate other fire precautions. Moreover, housing authorities have powers to insist upon the central registration of HMOs within their district, under a simple notification scheme or a more complex control scheme.

In addition to the powers and duties placed on authorities duties are placed on owners and managers of HMOs to adhere to Management Regulations (s. I, 1990, No. 830), requiring a HMO manager to observe effective standards of management and to keep existing facilities in good repair. Furthermore, the 1996 Act will introduce, when this part of the Act is implemented, a new duty on persons having control of the HMO or persons managing the property to keep the premises fit for the number of occupants, in that they must take such steps as are reasonably practicable to prevent the need for an authority to issue a section 352 notice.

The Research

The research comprised two main elements. The first component encompassed a structured questionnaire forwarded to 20 directors of environmental health within local authorities throughout the Midlands region of England. Of these 20 areas approached, 14 agreed to participate in the research (70 per cent). The research was restricted to these authorities partly due to the locality of the author for the undertaking of follow up interviews, but also because the research is seen as a pilot project. It may be that further work will be required in this area investigating the national position at a later stage. The questionnaire was designed to ascertain responses from environmental health departments indicating current LHA activity within the multiply occupied field. The main objects of the research were: to determine how authorities were responding to recent legislative changes; to obtain the reasoned views of authorities on registering HMOs; to consider the difficulties presented by certain types of occupation; and to discover whether, and if so how, local authorities were cooperating with other enforcing bodies. The respondents were all environmental health officers engaged within the multiple occupation arena.

The questionnaire was divided into five parts. Part 1 considered the definition of a HMO, with specific questions on the problems caused by the statutory definition, attention was also paid to whether this definition could be improved upon. Part 2 looked at aspects of authority policy, particularly relating to the issue of whether housing or fire authorities should have lead responsibility for fire safety. Part 3 of the questionnaire focused upon liaison between fire and housing authorities, how this operates in practice and the question of joint visits and policies. Part 4 investigated practical aspects of safety enforcement, including the issuing of notices by LHAs, and the question whether the district had an operational registration scheme for HMOs. Part 5 specifically considered the question of licensing or registering HMOs, obtaining views of authorities on this controversial area.

Whilst the numbers of localities was limited they were carefully selected to represent a balance of authorities. Seven urban areas were chosen incorporating part of the West Midlands conurbation, as well as cities within the East Midlands. Five of these areas had a considerable student population within their district. A further seven authorities had more of a mixed/rural complexion. These authorities tended to be based around market towns, with some having a significant rural element within their area. Only one of these areas had a considerable student body. All the urban areas at the time of the survey were controlled by the same political party. The smaller, mixed, districts had a rather more varied political complexion. However, this appears to have made little difference in the practice of these areas.

The second stage of the research is currently ongoing, involving semi-structured interviews with officers of four LHAs, discussing responses to the questionnaires and eliciting further evidence of HMO safety policies and practices within individual areas.

The Findings

This section will be divided into five parts to coincide with those used in the research questionnaires.

Defining a House in Multiple Occupation

The intricacy of defining a HMO 'on the ground' have been alluded to above. The research endeavoured to establish how authorities overcome these problems, focusing on LHA views with regard to potential improvements to the definition, identifying responses to the most important factors in determining a HMO, and considering the aforementioned case of *Barnes v Sheffield C.C.* as well as its effect on authority practice.

Housing authorities were asked to indicate the practical difficulties caused by the section 345 of the 1985 Act definition of a HMO, 'a house is occupied by persons who do not form a single household'. Whilst one authority indicated they had no problems with the definition, largely it appears due to the small number of HMOs in that area, this was not a widely held view. The overwhelming issue amongst others appeared to be the question of what constitutes a 'household', the vagueness of the definition, 'ancient and contradictory' case law, with special difficulties in areas with large student bodies. Three districts identified issues surrounding students who upon entering accommodation may not be acquainted with one another, and having been initially recruited by the landlord to the property. Thus, the legal status of the property may well be that they reside in a HMO, taking into account the factors related in the *Barnes* case above. However, over time they become friends, start to shop, cook and eat together, bring in further acquaintances as others leave and begin to act as a single household. For LHAs, it appears troublesome to determine when individuals begin to live communally and are thus outside HMO regulation. Linked with this, is the length of time taken by authorities in discussions with landlords, the serving of 1985 Act notices and the court process if these notices are ineffective, or the landlord appeals. Two authorities indicated that by the time the end of this process had been reached, individuals living initially 'essentially independent lives', had evolved into people living in a more communal arrangement. A further issue relating to student accommodation is that over the Summer months students leave their rented property. Thus the accommodation becomes unoccupied and no longer a HMO. Student accommodation is consequently, according to one authority, 'in and out of the definition'.

With all of these difficulties, authorities have developed a number of tactics to address the problem of students living in the private rented sector. One urban authority adopted a particularly robust view, issuing a 1985 Act notice and awaiting an appeal if one materializes. At the other end of the spectrum, another urban authority states: 'No shared student houses were ever considered by this authority as HMOs.' Both of these approaches seem to go too far. Some student accommodation will certainly be within the definition, particularly at the outset of a tenancy, equally houses occupied by students will be outside the HMO definition where the occupiers live as a single household. Due to the complexities and difficulties of the definition, however, it is unsurprising that authorities have chosen to adopt such radically differing views. Local authorities may see these choices as the most effective means of case management open to LHAs with finite, and stretched resources. From a legal perspective, the question need to be raised whether an authority should simply 'overlook' case law and continue issuing enforcement notices for households without the definition as judicially interpreted, and fail to issue 1985 Act notices for properties within the definition. Authorities who adopt either of these approaches are laying themselves open to appeals under the 1985 Act or, potentially, challenge under judicial review.

It is not merely student accommodation which is affected by the definition. One mixed/rural authority indicated

> We have experienced difficulties with large houses run by religious organisations. They are a dwelling for quite a large number of people, they argue that they live as a single household. We cannot disagree.

An urban authority also identified difficulty with former factories converted into residential accommodation, stating 'the word 'house' should be replaced by 'building' to cover factories converted into flats and bedsit living accommodation'. The major issues here are whether those inhabiting the building do so as one household, and additionally the question whether a factory conversion can be a 'house'. The author would strongly argue that such a conversion is a house, given the wide definition of this word,for the purposes of section 345 of the 1985 Act, given by the courts.

LHAs were additionally asked to consider the most important factors in determining whether a property is occupied by more than one household and the effect *of Barnes v Sheffield C.C.* on their view. Most areas were fully aware of the criteria in the case and thus able to state that the factors mentioned were the criteria adopted by the authority. However, some districts ventured components of the decision they found the most important. For example, how the property was occupied, whether the occupiers share household responsibilities such as cleaning and cooking, was still regarded by some as a critical factor. A mixed/rural LHA categorically stating 'Lifestyle of the occupants. Do they provide mutually to the well-being of the group?'. One urban authority adopted a questionnaire for tenants of HMOs asking extensive questions about how the property is lived in:

> Who cleans the communal areas of the property? Do you buy food separately, or do you have a joint food budget? Do you keep your own food separately? Do you do your own washing up? Do you tend to spend time socialising in a common living room in the house?

Prosaic as many of these questions are, they are clearly important in determining a HMO. The other criteria of *Barnes* were not forgotten. Other issues raised, within the authority's questionnaire, considered locks and vacancies and whether the occupiers knew other tenants when they moved in. Thus, whilst the occupation of members of the household(s) remains the most significant factor for a number of authorities the nine factors stated by Bingham MR in *Barnes* have had an impact on LHA operations. Further evidence of this appears from answers to specific questions regarding the effect of this case on enforcement. Five authorities indicated the case had made considerable differences to operational activity in the HMO field. One LHA indicated that the number of notices served on shared student houses had decreased considerably, with the number of landlord appeals having proportionately increased. The views of this authority were supported by another which indicated the decision had prevented the upgrading of fire protection in shared housing and they had lost considerable control of this part of the private sector and. The case was 'deregulation by default'. On a more positive note, authorities indicated *Barnes* had made them take greater care in determining whether a house was a HMO, whereas previously little thought had been given to the matter.

Having established uncertainties with the definition, LHAs were asked to identify mechanisms adopted to overcome these issues. Overwhelmingly, internal legal departments were consulted for views on properties of questionable HMO status. Further, matters would be discussed within the EHO enforcement team. When issues could not be resolved internally counsel's opinion would occasionally be sought. One urban authority, however, endeavoured to undertake a more pro-active approach to overcoming, or rather circumventing, the definition. An Owner's Charter has been agreed between participating landlords and the authority within which the landlord agrees the property is a HMO, accepts to undertake certain works required by the authority, and in return receives certain assurances from the council that action will be taken to the benefit of the landlord. One example of this is a guarantee by the authority that housing benefit is paid within a certain period to enable the landlord to be promptly paid by their tenants.

Whilst some authorities were attempting innovative solutions to the definitions uncertainty, the overwhelming majority wished to see the definition amended. Of the 14 authorities questioned, 13 were of the opinion the definition should be amended, with the majority arguing for a widened meaning. Highlighted below are some of the responses received to a questionnaire inquiry in this area, a number of these opinions being supported by more than one authority.

'Reference should be made in the definition to the number of occupiers' This view was adopted by two areas. One authority indicated the definition should be 'wider to include more than five persons'. This has some appeal in that it is somewhat easier to count people than to follow HMO case law. However, there would surely need to be exclusions, with one of the more obvious being property inhabited by a family. Questions, of course, would then arise as to how to define 'family', would there need to be a blood or marital relationship, and what would the position be with regard to extended families.

'Reference to the number of occupiers included and households' A refinement of the above, with an urban authority expressing the opinion that the definition should include 'reference to numbers of occupants should be included i.e. over five persons and two households'. This view retains some of its difficulties indicated above and also maintains the issue of defining the term household, which is the crux of the problem.

'The definition should include an or likely to be occupied provision' The

rationale here is to enable a dwelling temporarily vacant, perhaps due to students returning home in the Summer, to remain HMO during this period. LHAs would be able to continue with enforcement processes even if the property were empty, overcoming stalling techniques of owners of properties. The objection would naturally follow that this provision makes the HMO definition even less clear and would simply encourage further litigation in this area.

'The term house should be replaced by building' This recommendation follows issues surrounding factory conversions mentioned above.

'Local authorities should have powers to enforce fire safety based on risk assessment hazard analysis, without reference to the legal status of the house' This view, or at least the first portion of it, would appear to be gaining credence within central government. The Department of the Environment, Transport and the Regions (DETR) have commissioned research by a company called EnTec to investigate fire safety in particular types of HMOs. A summary report (DETR, 1997) of their findings at the time of writing this chapter has just been published with the full report available in December 1997. The summary report makes a number of recommendations, the thrust of many of these are based upon a risk assessment analysis of types of HMOs. Although the report recommends the retention of the 1985 Act definition, the document states:

> The level of fire precautions, registration requirements etc. should be decided upon the basis of risk assessment. Thus the definition of a building as a HMO is required to prompt a subsequent risk assessment after which further fire precautions, inspection and registration may or may not be deemed necessary.

'The definition should incorporate reference to how the property is occupied in conjunction with the type of people who occupy it' The above EnTec report makes reference to the importance of the type of occupants within a building in relation to fire risk. It states, unsurprisingly, that hostels housing arsonists have a higher risk rating than student houses. Also, the issue of vulnerable occupants is addressed and the ability to remove, for example, elderly and frail occupiers of a HMO in the event of fire. Thus, whilst the definition a HMO may not be amended to specifically incorporate reference to these matters it is clear that current policy may be based upon a more pro-active assessment of risk rather that reliance on the definition of a house as multiply occupied.

Local Housing Authority Policy Responses

This stage of the research focused upon the views of those within local authorities to the question of enforcement of fire safety, particularly whether enforcement should be the role of environmental heath departments or the responsibility of the fire service. Issues were also raised here relating to views of recent legislative changes introduced by the 1996 Act in the areas of: the duty placed on owners and managers; the extension of mandatory fire duties; limitation on the issuing of works notices; and the issuing of a 'minded to' notices.

Fire safety is enforced by fire authorities in a multitude of property types, both of a residential and commercial variety. Much of the enforcement of fire safety is performed under the authority of the Fire Precautions Act 1971. These provisions cover various types of accommodation which can be viewed as HMOs. However, the major fire protection enforcement authority for HMOs are housing authorities. One of the ongoing controversies within the fire safety community is who should have responsibility for enforcement within multiply occupied housing. The arguments for fire officer enforcement are fairly clear cut, fire precautions officers in the fire service have enormous experience in designing and advising upon, for example, a safe escape route if a fire occurs as well as general risk assessment work within premises. The question was therefore posed to EHOs answering the questionnaire: who should have lead responsibility for fire safety within HMOs?

The overwhelming response supported by 12 of the authorities surveyed was that fire safety enforcement in HMOs should remain the responsibility of environmental health staff. This was the view adopted by all urban, larger authorities. The rationale in support of their views focuses on the belief that issues within multiply occupied housing are more extensive than simply fire safety, incorporating a range of matters more suited to EHO rather than fire precaution officer involvement. The general assessment was that other housing issues overlap and interrelate with fire safety. Under the ambit of the 1985 Act, and DoE Circular 12/92 giving advice upon the Act, environmental health officers must also take account of the storage, preparation and cooking of food, including sinks with a satisfactory supply of hot and cold water; EHOs should ensure an adequate supply of toilets, baths, basins and showers, all of this in addition to their fire safety responsibilities. HMOs, the argument runs, should be viewed holistically, rather than simply as a fire issue. One urban authority states:

> The Local Authority should take lead responsibility for fire safety in HMOs. My reasons are that when HMOs are inspected, they are looked at for a whole number of issues i.e. adequate amenities such as bathrooms, W.C.s and adequate ventilation in the kitchen. Whilst fire safety is important, it is only one factor out of a number that need to be considered when judging if the property is fit for the number of occupants. The works required to improve means of escape in case of fire can also have an effect on other requirements, so it is important to ensure that fire precaution works are part of an overall package.

Environmental health officers argue: they have the existing database of HMO premises within their area; they have the knowledge of local landlords; an EHO can ensure structural fire precautions reflect the mode of occupation of the premises; they prevent duplication, lessening confusion and increasing efficiency; they act as a single point of contact for tenants, who may complain to EHOs about a multitude of issues; environmental health officers also indicate that if fire safety is so poor that a house must be 'closed', it is the housing authority which deals with the resultant homelessness. One environmental health officer in a large urban authority went so far as to indicate that 'we should enforce all legislation, i.e. fire safety of furniture, currently trading standards officers, gas safety, currently HSE'.

A strong argument can be made to retain the status quo of EHO enforcement. Many of those employed in the environmental health arena have the skills, knowledge and ability to effectively upgrade standards of safety within multiply occupied accommodation. It is important, however, to ensure that entrenched positions, protecting roles within which individuals are comfortable or believing that because an issue is currently dealt with in this way it cannot be equally well arranged through alternate means, does not provide the justification of keeping fire safety in HMOs as an EHO responsibility. At the time of writing this chapter, both the Department of the Environment, Transport and the Regions and the Home Office are writing consultation documents which will, inter alia, consider fire safety within HMOs. It is hoped that all concerned will be able to offer an objective view of fire safety enforcement as the new millennium approaches. Too many people die in HMO fires for enforcing authorities to waste their energies in inter-departmental disputes.

The subsequent questions raised by this section of the research focused on legislative amendments and their potential effect on HMO practice of landlords/managers and LHAs. The impact of a new duty to keep premises fit for the number of occupants, to be placed on owners and managers of HMOs, received a mixed response. LHAs were asked whether the new duty would enhance fire safety. The strong response from mixed/rural authorities was that it would have little, if any impact. The general view of these areas was that the welfare of tenants was not a high priority for landlords. Further, there were already sufficient controls in this area to allow an authority to act, and landlords were unlikely to be aware of the duties placed upon them. Larger, urban councils, on the whole, had a more supportive view of the new duty. One authority indicated:

> It is a single point of reference which can form the basis of improvements in service delivery by private landlords. It acts as a bench mark and it is a clear statement about responsibility.

Difficulties are, however, envisaged with the wording of the provision. The provision states:

> It is the duty of the person having control of a house in multiple occupation, and of the person managing it, to take such steps as are reasonably practicable to prevent the occurrence of a state of affairs calling for the service of a notice or a further notice under section 352 (notice requiring execution of works to render the house fit for number of occupants).

Issues raised here incorporated how the courts would interpret the phrase 'reasonably practicable'. The fear amongst some authorities was that this phrase could be used as a 'get out clause' to allow a landlord to argue that it was not 'reasonably practicable' to undertake particular works. The issue of costs would appear to be pertinent here, particularly if the value of the property was low and the works required extensive. One further issue identified was whether tenants would have the financial ability to take action against a defaulting owner. Additionally the fear of eviction may deter others from taking action. It does appear somewhat idealistic to expect landlords who have responsibilities to uphold safety and amenity standards to suddenly change their attitudes to these matters. The management regulations, albeit implicitly, already place HMO owners and managers under similar duties to those envisaged by the new duty. This appears to have made little difference to practices within the sector.

A further issue addressed within this stage of the research was the question of 'minded to' notices. These are a 'shot across the bows' type notice, see *Torridge D.C. v Jones* (1985) 18 HLR 107, requiring the authority, save where immediate remedial action is required, to issue a written notice, prior to a 'works notice', under sections 352 or 372 of the 1985 Act. These 'minded to' notices must stipulate works the authority believes should be undertaken, give an account for the grounds of this belief, and indicate a right of appeal and the right to make representations. Thus a further step in the enforcement process will usually be necessary: the service of a warning notice, followed by a right to make representations and appeal; followed by an enforcement notice, with a right to appeal. LHAs are generally opposed to this procedure, viewing it as another opportunity to delay the upgrading of fire safety and amenity standards. One of the more strident replies indicated this measure to be 'ridiculous, will not use unless challenged'. The potential benefit flowing from this process is recognized by a minority of respondents who envisage the possibility of greater contact with landlords during the representation process, and the possibility of involving the landlord in coming to a joint view. For some authorities this notice merely enshrines current practice.

> It will have little practical impact as in most instances this authority uses informal consultation procedures with owners before sending statutory enforcement notices.

Whilst there is a danger owners and managers of HMOs will simply foresee this measure as a means of at least delaying necessary work, the proposal undoubtedly has the potential within it to increase landlord participation within a system currently managed by LHAs.

Liaison Between Fire and Housing Authorities

The primary controversy within enforcing circles is the question of which profession, fire or environmental health, should have overall responsibility for enforcing HMO fire safety matters. The issue of consultation between authorities is, perhaps, the next most unsettled area of dispute. Under section 365(3) of the 1985 Act there is a duty on housing authorities to consult with the fire authority where they are under a duty to act or where the house is of such a type specified by the Secretary of State.

Research focused upon: how LHAs and fire authorities liaise; whether difficulties in consultation occur; joint fire and housing authority policies; and joint visits to HMOs. The majority of authorities within the study indicated they had regular meetings with the fire precautions officer in the attached fire service. The number of encounters appeared to be dependent upon the size of the authority and number of HMOs. An illustration from a large urban authority indicated that:

> Individual officers preparing schemes attend a weekly meeting with the Fire Prevention Officer under the guidance of a senior officer from Urban Renewal. Complex or unusual cases will often be the subject of specific on site meetings. They are very useful for establishing a practical response.

Smaller authorities, although again holding helpful discussions, tended to organize meetings on a more ad hoc basis. Of the authorities who found the meetings worked well comments included

> Meetings between fire and environmental health officers are very helpful in establishing a practical response.

> We have consulted and liaised with the fire authority for many years, their input is extremely useful.

A minority of LHAs, however, concluded that liaison was not all it could be; after commenting on the consultation process in the area one environmental health officer remarked, 'I find this a totally unsatisfactory method of working'.

In addition to consultation through regular or ad hoc encounters EHOs must confer with fire service personnel over notices where the LHA is required to act or may choose to consult where they have a discretion to act. This form of paper consultation, where an EHO forwards a proposed schedule of work to a fire precautions officer does not always operate effectively. One response received from an urban area indicated that consultation in relation to section 352 notices was a 'paper exercise', other EHOs indicated problems of inconsistent decision-making from fire precaution officers, or different fire precautions officers offering differing views. Disagreements were particularly apparent at the interface between fire and housing legislation. One case mentioned by an urban authority identified special disputes in relation to hotels, with existing fire certificates, now run as hostels for the homeless. Ultimately, it appears in this case the LHA decided to ignore fire service advice and undertake its own course of action. Of course the LHA is authorized to do this, consultation here is simply seeking the views of another organization, those views may be accepted or rejected. Broadly, consultation works most effectively where there is a mutual respect for the professional expertise of all involved. An awareness that if consultation is more than a paper exercise there must be an understanding that fellow professionals can differ in their views. Stability of personnel appears an important aspect in developing respect, relationships and a consistency of approach.

One further important and developing aspect of liaison between housing and fire authorities is the instigation of joint fire safety policies. One of the themes of the responses received to the questionnaires was a distinct move towards joint policies. Of the districts surveyed, four had already established such a policy with their respective fire service and four others were in the process of doing so. An example of such a document was provided by an urban authority that had developed a Code of Practice between the Director of Housing and Environmental Services and the Chief Fire Officer. This set out a joint approach by the two services, indicating standards of safety to be adopted by both services.

Local Housing Authority Practical Responses

LHAs were asked to consider here a number of areas such as: when the authority takes a leading role on fire safety; whether the authority has an operational registration scheme; the number of section 352 and section 365 1985 Act notices served on HMO owners; and whether, in their opinion, fire safety standards had improved or deteriorated in their area as a result of their actions, or the actions of others. Overwhelmingly, the view forwarded by environmental health officers indicated LHAs adopted the primary role in tackling fire safety within multiply occupied housing. Whilst this is unsurprising given their responsibilities under the 1985 Act there appears very few joint initiatives between fire and housing authorities in addressing safety matters in multiply occupied housing. Fire authorities appear to assume a lead position in non domestic situations, for example commercial or retail premises, leaving LHAs to deal with residential matters. Occasionally, smaller authorities will ask a fire precautions officer for assistance if they wish to close a property, or in an emergency.

The possibility of LHAs adopting a registration scheme for their area was referred to earlier. Five of the areas surveyed had undertaken such action, with another area having a registration scheme for hostels for the homeless, made possible by a local Act. Of the seven urban authorities four had a registration scheme, either of the notification or regulatory variety. Only one mixed/rural authority embraced registration. During the passage of the 1996 Act the then Housing Minister, David Curry stated (Hansard, Standing Committee G, February 20, 1996, col. 248):

> We are moving towards a scheme that will give permissive power to a local authority to introduce wide-ranging control measures if it chooses to opt into the scheme. It is common consent that an overwhelming majority of local authorities will do so.

Contrary to Mr Curry's view, of the authorities surveyed only one without an operational scheme indicated a desire to adopt registration. To an extent, events and particularly the result of the 1997 general election will mean that all LHAs will have to adopt a scheme of registration, but it is interesting to note that less than half, at the time of the questioning process, either had a scheme or indicated a wish to approve one.

Authorities were also asked to provide an indication of the number of section 352 and section 365 1985 Act notices issued within the last five years. What is particularly noticeable are the differing levels of use within authorities, not simply due to their size, but also through apparent LHA officer decisions to use proportionately more of one mechanism of enforcement rather than the other type. For example, one urban authority has used more section 365 notices, accepting undertakings from landlords, than the general works notice. However, other areas of comparable size appear to use the undertakings mechanism very infrequently. This would appear to be the result of preference and tradition in some areas, with a belief that one type of notice may have a greater practical effect.

One final issue raised in this section was the question whether fire safety standards in HMOs had improved or worsened over the last five years in the LHA area. The answer was a clear vote in favour of improvement. Eleven of the 14 authorities identified an improved position, and only two felt the situation had deteriorated. Reasons given concentrated on increased activity by LHAs to ensure premises are dealt with thoroughly. One authority highlighted that improvements in their area were:

> Because of local authority activity to ensure all premises are dealt with. Introduction of early warning systems. Replacements of unreliable secondary escapes. By April 1997 98% of all Category A premises (flatlets and bedsits) and 95% of all Category D properties (hostels, guest houses and boarding houses) operated by private and commercial landlords will be at or above the current fire safety standard. This compares with five years ago when 80% of such premises had no or had inadequate fire safety provision.

A further larger authority identified a more pro-active approach in enforcement strategies, particularly through consultation with landlords. Another aspect of this improvement has been the creation in LHAs of dedicated teams of EHOs with specific HMO responsibilities, even in smaller authority areas. Safety standard in multiply occupied housing does appear to have moved forward in the last few years according to these results. Whilst this part of the survey is inevitably subjective, relying as it does upon the impression of individual environmental health departments, these findings are perhaps some of the most welcome of all within this survey. Maybe the position identified by research in the 1980s that, for example, 81 per cent of HMOs lacked a satisfactory means of escape is at last being addressed (Thomas and Hedges, 1986). By no means, however, has the problem of fire safety in HMOs been solved.

LHA Views on the Registration and Licensing of HMOs

The previous government rejected the need for a mandatory national licensing or registration scheme for monitoring safety and amenity standards in HMOs, despite a clear view in favour from respondents to a consultation process. Of the LHAs questioned within this research, 12 indicated a wish for a mandatory scheme. This would appear at odds with the earlier indications that only six authorities had, or planned to have, an operational scheme of registration. The possible solution may lie in some of the reasons indicated for the introduction of a mandatory scheme; the arguments adopted in favour of such a process by an urban area included:

> Instil confidence in the sector. Be beneficial in terms of addressing the needs of tenants. Professionalise and increase investment in the sector. Alleviate homelessness and ill health brought about by poor housing conditions. Level Playing field. Single point of reference. National standard. Reduces regulation.

Possibly authorities would be more prepared to introduce a scheme if they could be guaranteed sufficient resources and all of their neighbouring authorities were embarking upon the same venture. One area opposed to licensing, however, argued that '[l]ocal housing authorities should be allowed to make their own strategic consideration of the level of significance of HMOs in their district'. The matter, they argue, should be left to individual authorities to determine the most effective course of action for their area. Additionally, one authority questioned the allocation of resources from central government and queried whether exclusions from any scheme, in terms of size of accommodation for example, would devalue a future licensing programme.

Following questions on the view of whether a mandatory scheme should be supported, LHAs were asked what type of scheme they envisaged would be the most effective in addressing safety and amenity matters in multiply occupied housing. One of the fundamental issues here is whether authorities should be required to licence property or people or property and people. The majority view was that licensing both the person in control of the property and the property itself was required for an effective system of management to operate. One response indicated that the essential features of such a scheme should include:

> National Code of Practice. Satisfactory resources to enable suitable implementation of such a scheme Fixed penalty system for non-compliance. Scheme should be relevant to persons and premises.

The minority view favoured a property based licensing system. Authorities further indicated the need for sufficiently severe penalties to ensure compliance with any scheme, with the requirement that it should be an offence not to register, and an offence to operate a HMO without a licence. The question of paying for a system of licensing was referred to, with a clear view emerging of the need for a system based on contributions from owners and managers to pay for the licensing operation. This would obviate the need for a large central government contribution to the running costs of such a programme.

One of the more controversial views forwarded by an EHO within an urban authority was the proposal that all private sector accommodation should be licensed, HMOs being simply one part of the sector.

> It should cover the whole of the private rented sector and not just HMOs. It must be linked to conditions and standards, with only properties of an acceptable standard receiving a licence. In addition landlords should be licensed.

This, in the opinion of the author, would be a radical step forward in upgrading the standards of accommodation and safety throughout the private rented sector. Given the findings of the Law Commission report into the state and condition of properties in the sector (Law Commission, 1995), this cannot be simply dismissed, and should be worthy of consideration by the new Labour government. However, given the deregulatory and decontrol process undertaken over the past two decades and the laissez faire attitudes adopted, New Labour are much more likely to introduce a mandatory licensing scheme for HMOs, rather than for the sector as a whole.

Ultimately, however, licensing is a means to an end rather than an end in itself. The rationale behind licensing HMOs must be to improve safety and amenity standards. If that is the rationale, the question needs to be asked whether licensing in the most appropriate manner in which to achieve that goal, are scarce resources best deployed in favour of a licensing system? If there is an affirmative answer to this question there would appear to be little room for wholesale exclusions from a licensing system, as is the case with the present arrangement which excludes any house of which the person responsible is a social landlord registered in accordance with Part I of the 1996 Act, and also excludes halls of residence and student hostels. However, it is important to be aware that some HMOs do represent a higher fire risk than others. This being the case, the issue arises of whether licensing should be limited to that type of HMO, to enable resources to be allotted accordingly. The EnTec report recommends:

> In the event that it is considered appropriate to regulate fire risks in all privately rented and social housing HMOs, it is suggested that consideration be given to developing a 'lower tier' registration scheme for lower risk HMOs, perhaps based on the accreditation schemes operated by a number of universities.

Licensing is no panacea, but it can provide, if operated efficiently, a mechanism to trace and enforce safety provisions in all higher risk HMOs.

Conclusion

This chapter is appropriately placed within the context of exclusion. Those who inhabit multiply occupied housing, many of whom are students or young single people, often have little choice of tenure type due to financial constraints. This position will probably be exacerbated for students with the introduction of tutorial fees and the abolition of the maintenance grant. Once living within a HMO, the standards of accommodation endured are often poor, both in the sense of physical condition of the premises and the provision of amenities. Upgrading of accommodation has traditionally been a matter for discussion between enforcing authorities and the landlords, tenants and licensees have been denied input into this process. Those who are accepted as homeless by local authorities will often be housed, at least initially, within a HMO and told to remain even if it is found to be unsafe *(R v RB Kensington and Chelsea ex parte Bel-el-Mabouk* (1995) 27 HLR 564). Those found homeless have little alternative.

On a policy level, central government appears to have ignored the views of local government for many years on HMOs. Whilst consultation has taken place on the introduction of a registration scheme, it is highly questionable whether the essence of this consultation was 'the communication of a genuine invitation extended with a recipient mind' (see Donaldson J in *Agricultural, Horticultural and Forestry Training Board v Aylesbury Mushroom Ltd* [1972]). The impression received was that decisions had already been made, the consultation was simply a facade. Thus, authorities have been excluded from offering valuable input to the development of safety policies.

With the election of a new government the task for those involved in the HMO field is to argue for a more inclusive approach. Responses received thus far are encouraging, with a DETR official indicating to the author the department will engage over the next three years on three formal consultation processes. Two of these consultations will involve consideration of a national mandatory licensing scheme, which the government is committed to, the third will concentrate upon the introduction of a Code of Practice. Additionally, some LHAs are beginning to move towards a system of involving occupiers in tenants' forums to consider upgrades and developing stronger links with landlords and landlord groups. The way ahead for HMOs, and for all private sector and social housing, must be to adopt a process which enables those involved, be it as a professional or a user, to be included in moving housing provision forward into a new age.

Bibliography

Arden, A. and Hunter, C. (1997), *Manual of Housing Law*, 6th edn, Sweet & Maxwell, London.

Department of the Environment (1993), *English House Condition Survey (1991)*, HMSO, London.

Department of the Environment (1994), *Houses in Multiple Occupation. Consultation Paper on the Case for Licensing*, Department of the Environment, London.

Department of the Environment (1995), *Improving Standards in Houses in Multiple Occupation*, Department of the Environment, London.

Department of the Environment, Transport and the Regions (1997), *Fire Risk in HMOs: A Summary Report*, Department of the Environment, Transport the Regions, London.

Department of Trade and Industry (1994), *Fire Safety Legislation and Enforcement Report of the Interdepartmental Review Team*, Department of Trade and Industry, London.

Everton (1997), 'Fire precautions – legal controls in houses in multiple occupation: safe havens ... or ... any port in a storm?', *Journal of Social Welfare and Family Law*, Vol. 19, No. 1, pp. 61–71.

Home Office (1994), *Fire Statistics United Kingdom 1994*, Home Office, London.

Law Commission (1995), *Landlord and Tenant Responsibility for the State and Condition of Property*, Law Commission 236, HMSO, London.

National Consumer Council (1991), *Deathtrap Housing*, National Consumer Council, London.

Randall, G., Brown, S. and Piper, J. (1993), *Houses in Multiple Occupation Policy and Practice in the 1990s*, Campaign for Bedsit Rights, London.

Smith, N. (1997), 'Determining a household for the purposes of Part XI of the Housing Act 1985', *The Conveyancer and Property Lawyer*, September – October, pp. 395–401.

Thomas, A. and Hedges, A. (1986), *The 1985 Physical and Social Survey of Houses in Multiple Occupation in England & Wales*, HMSO, London.

9 Researching the 'Impact' of Judicial Review on Routine Administrative Decision-making

SIMON HALLIDAY

Introduction[1]

The impact of judicial review on administrative decision-making is well established as a contemporary concern of socio-legal scholars of public law in Britain (Galligan, 1996; Richardson and Sunkin, 1996) and reflected by a growing literature. The current literature contains works with differing aims and concerns which, accordingly, approach the issue in differing ways. Nevertheless, it might be broken down into three rough categories. The first category contains works which propose links between judicial decisions and administrative reaction, thereby setting the agenda for close empirical examination (Harlow, 1976; Prosser 1983; Loughlin and Quinn, 1993; Richardson, 1993; Livingstone, 1995). The second category comprises work which reflects on the impact of judicial review by way of personal professional experience (Kerry, 1986; Alexander, 1989; Barker, 1996; James, 1996). The third category in this rough scheme comprises the findings of research projects which have sought to investigate empirically the impact of judicial review on administrative decision-making. This third kind of work has looked at the impact of judicial review in relation to a number of kinds of administrative decision-making in a number of different settings (Bridges et al., 1987; Sunkin and Le Sueur, 1991; Mullen, Pick and Prosser, 1996).[2] However, empirical research in this field is still relatively young and, accordingly, sparse. This essay aims to contribute to the conceptual preparatory work which is necessary to the empirical enquiry. It arises out of research I am undertaking concerning judicial review and homelessness decision-making in local government. By reflecting upon methodological issues in relation to this project and by presenting some initial findings of a first period of fieldwork, I will explore some difficulties surrounding the concept of 'impact' and argue for a methodological approach which stresses the social construction of administrative reality. By this I mean an approach which pays close attention to how the meanings of the phenomena that comprise the subject of administration are achieved within the administrative process.

I suggest that we must adequately grasp the nature of decision-making before we can progress to consider specific questions of impact. The way in which we think about 'impact' and about how to research the impact of judicial review must be driven by, and situated within, a proper conceptualization of discretionary decision-making. Such a conceptualization represents administrative decision-making as an evolving process of interpretive work and would locate experience of judicial review within the limitless number of potential influences on the interpretive processes which interact and culminate in administrative behaviour. I conclude that a rich theoretical and empirical understanding of decision-making presents us with a number of important obstacles to overcome before we can begin to speak of the 'impact' of judicial review.

The essay begins with an outline of the aims of the research project and a brief examination of some of the theoretical foundations of the research technique adopted. The essay goes on to explore the concept of 'impact' and presents some initial observations of a first period of fieldwork in order to illustrate the difficulties associated with assessing the 'impact' of judicial review on the administrative process. In this sense the essay comprises some reflections on the challenges implicit to this kind of research on the basis of preliminary fieldwork.

Researching Impact

It is important to be clear about exactly what one means when discussing the impact of judicial review (Richardson and Sunkin, 1996). We should be cautious about talking in simple terms about this topic. Rather, we should be explicit about the limits of our given focus. As Mullen et al. (1996) have noted, 'there are a number of dimensions to the impact of judicial review'.

Distinctions have been made between particular and general impact, and between implementation of actual judicial review decisions and action which anticipates potential judicial review (Bridges et al., 1987; Mullen et al., 1996). Issues may be drawn out concerning the intensity and duration of impact, the spread of impact and the significance between formal and informal reaction (Richardson and Sunkin, 1996). On the basis of their pilot study of central government decision-making, Sunkin and Le Sueur (1991) suggested that an increased awareness of the possibility of legal challenge would have different effects across different levels of administration. Bridges et al. (1987), whose research focused on local government reactions to the 'Fares Fair' case,[3] whilst recording that the uncertainty caused by the case brought about an increased bureaucratization in a majority of the local authorities examined, nevertheless noted a variance of reaction within the sample of local authorities. Mullen et al. (1996) carried out an impact study of two Scottish local authorities in relation to homelessness decision-making. Although discovering that judicial review actions achieved tangible gains for individual applicants, they also considered the more general effects of judicial review, noting differences between the two authorities in this regard. The quality of decision-making seemed to improve around the same time as an increase in the amount of judicial review litigation in one authority. In the other authority, however, attempts to increase awareness of legal issues seemed to become ineffective at a local neighbourhood office level.

To speak, then, of the 'impact' of judicial review requires elaboration about the sense in which the term is used. However, it is also unhelpful to talk in simple terms about 'judicial review'. Judicial review actions can be broken down into different types of case. The grounds under which judicial review may be invoked can be subsumed under the 'Diplock catalogue'[4] – illegality, irrationality and procedural impropriety. Judicial review has also been categorized as having different types of effects on administrative behaviour (Feldman, 1988; James, 1996). Feldman's typology of decision effects is threefold: decisions may direct, limit, or structure administrative behaviour. James' typology is fourfold: decisions may have a cancelling effect, a corrective effect, a restrictive effect or an inhibitive effect.

In light of the need for clarity of focus, therefore, it is important to be explicit about the aim of the research project discussed here. This research focuses upon the routine decisions of local government housing departments which determine the housing rights of homeless applicants. The fundamental concern of the research is to gain insights into how judicial review litigation may influence the way in which the social reality of homelessness decision-making is constructed by decision-makers within local government organizations. The project's aim is to move towards an understanding of how judicial review influences the way in which administrators ascribe meanings to the 'facts of the case' and the 'rules' and 'procedures' which comprise the decision-making processes and culminate in decision-outcomes. My concern is, therefore, limited to what might be termed the 'general effects' of judicial review on routine administrative decision-making. I have not set out to examine the impact of particular judgments on particular homeless applicants' circumstances, although this clearly may become of interest in the course of further fieldwork. Rather, as I shall explain further below, I am primarily concerned with the effect of prolonged exposure to litigation on the day-to-day administrative reality as constructed by administrators.

To this end I have adopted an ethnographic research methodology. The fieldwork consists of periods of participant-observation with three local authority housing departments, each of which has had considerable experience of judicial review litigation. By 'litigation' I mean judicial review actions which have proceeded to full judgment. This definition does not, however, reflect a view that experience of litigation which ends prior to full judgment (for example, by way of settlement, or at the stage of application for leave, or application for legal aid) may not have its own effects or influence. To gain a proper understanding of the impact of judicial review, such questions need to be addressed (Richardson and Sunkin, 1996). We know that in England and Wales a large proportion of applications for judicial review do not proceed to judgment despite leave to apply having been granted (Bridges et al., 1996). In Scotland also, a significant proportion of petitions do not proceed to full judgment and a greater proportion of actions are halted at the stage of application for legal aid (Mullen et al., 1996). However, the choice to conduct research with local government departments which have had significant experience of litigation in the sense in which I have defined it, was based on the desire to work with administrators whose decisions had been subject to full review and comment by judges. Such experience, I would suggest, *symbolizes* the fullest immersion of the administrative decision-making process into the legal world. The choice is one which clearly and inevitably limits the focus of the enquiry, but which may, nevertheless, afford opportunities to reflect on some of the issues mentioned above.

Of course, there is another sense in which this choice of research subjects imposes limits on the enquiry. The local authorities with which I have spent (and will spend[5]) periods of participant-observation, unlike many others, are particularly experienced in defending judicial review actions, both in terms of the amount of litigation they have been involved in, and the number of years over which they have been involved. However, it is also important, in contrast, to consider the impact on routine decision-making of sporadic judicial reviews (see Loveland, 1995, ch. 10 in this regard).

Nevertheless, despite the particularities of this project's focus, ethnographic data of such local government departments has an important contribution to make to the broader academic endeavour of understanding the impact of judicial review. Implicit to my approach is a starting point which holds that meanings are imposed upon the social world by individuals (Schutz, 1967). Social reality is constructed by each of us through interpretive processes. These processes of interpretation take place within what might be termed 'interpretive communities' (Fish, 1989). Shared meanings and understandings emerge and evolve within interpretive communities. These communities are infinite and various and are neither closed nor mutually exclusive. As Fish remarks of himself, 'I am, among other things, white, male, a teacher, a literary critic, a student of interpretation, a member of a law faculty, a husband (twice), a citizen ...' (Fish, 1989, p. 30).

The starting point, therefore, is at the level of the individual, in the sense that we encounter the world pre-interpretively as individuals (Schutz, 1967). However, a picture of interpretive communities illustrates how the meanings of the social world are ascribed. Although our absolute starting point may be individualistic, we learn to understand our worlds in community. We *engage* with the social world not as individuals, but rather as members of communities. In relation to organizational decision-making, or more particularly as we shall see below, in relation to decision-making within a single team of administrators, individuals become initiated into the interpretive schema of the team. As new officers (and, indeed, as participant-observers) 'learn the job', so they come to learn what meanings are attached to the phenomena that make up the subject and fabric of the administrative process. As regards organizational matters, therefore, the interpretive mandate comes from the organization itself. The organization is the interpretive filter by which workers come to understand the business of the organization (Cicourel, 1968; Waegel, 1981; Emerson and Paley, 1992). Attention to the shared meanings and organizational interpretive schema then becomes central to our understanding of decision-making.

It is important to realize, however, that within organizations there may be departments and subgroups. Such subgroups may well act autonomously and in conflict with other subgroups. Similarly, the notion of organizational social constructs does not seek to deny the ability of individual workers within an organization to choose whether to follow rules, guidelines or accepted practice (see, for example, Sainsbury, 1992). The use of procedural guidance may well inform the construction of the 'facts' of a case (see below, and Halliday, 1997). However, in seeking to understand organizational decision-making we should regard the organization itself as the interpretive unit. The importance of an organizational perspective and the organizational limits upon the use of discretion should not be underestimated (Emerson, 1983; Feldman, 1992).

When the above approach is applied to the study of homelessness administration and decision-making it means that matters such as an applicant's housing history, or a 'typical' case, or whether it was reasonable for an applicant to have carried on living in her old home, are socially constructed within individual local authority housing departments. Such matters are ascribed meanings by the administrative organization. Similarly, an organization's self-awareness of how its decisions are made is also a construct. The appreciation which an organization has of its own activities is not itself straightforward or exempt from the process of construction. How an organization understands itself, the accounts it gives (both formal and informal) of how it has carried out its functions, will be informed by a variety of influences. The aim of the research I am undertaking is to move towards an understanding of what influence the exposure to judicial review litigation may have on these processes of construction, on how the homeless persons' unit understands its own work and constructs its 'decisions'. This requires more than just looking at how homeless persons' units articulate their formal decisions, although this is clearly a part of it. It demands also a close examination of how they produce 'facts of the case' and 'rules' which culminate in 'decisions' (Baldwin and Hawkins, 1984). Such an approach requires an examination of what concepts the organizations employ, how they categorize their work, how they typify their applicants, and so on.

This locates judicial review alongside other influences upon the interpretive processes that comprise administrative behaviour. Experience of judicial review becomes one of a number of potential influences on the social construction of administrative reality. This sets up the need to understand the complexities of decision-making as a prerequisite to understanding the impact of judicial review upon it. We must adequately grasp the nature of decision-making before we can progress to consider specific questions of impact. This in turn leads us down the path of ethnographic research whereby the complexities of the social construction of decision-making can begin to be teased out. As Emerson et al. (1995, p. 2), have noted:

> the field researcher must be able to take up positions in the midst of key sites and scenes of other's lives in order to observe and understand them. But getting close has another, far more significant component: the ethnographer seeks a deeper *immersion* in others' worlds in order to grasp what they experience as meaningful and important. With immersion, the field researcher sees from the

> inside how people lead their lives, how they carry out their daily rounds of activities, what they find meaningful, and how they do so. In this way immersion gives the fieldworker access to the fluidity of others' lives and enhances his sensitivity to interaction and process.

Such a path initially takes us to the particular rather than the general. However, if we set ourselves the task of enquiring whether judicial review 'shapes or influences the administrative process' (Mullen et al., 1996), then close and rich descriptions of the construction of administrators' worlds is the most appropriate place from which to begin. Such descriptions are most reliably gained by immersion in the world of the administrators.

The research methods adopted in the empirical research carried out so far comprised interview-based studies (Bridges et al., 1987; Sunkin and Le Sueur, 1991) and interviews and documentary analysis (Mullen et al., 1996).[6] Clearly, interview data is of great importance and indeed is usually part of the ethnographic process (Ellen, 1984). However, the significance of participant-observation to the goal of understanding routine decision-making lies in its greater ability to facilitate an intimate and particular appreciation of the complex of processes whereby 'knowledge' is produced for the purposes of decision-making. It aims 'to develop the ability to think, feel, and articulate ... understandings of the studied culture in terms of the categories utilized by the observed to order and provide significance to their experience' (Van Maanen, 1981, p. 192). It presupposes the need to participate in and observe the activities of the research subjects in order to appreciate the meanings attached by them to the various aspects of their world and the processes by which this knowledge is achieved.

In short, our route to understanding the impact of judicial review is through understanding the social construction of administrative reality, and our best chance of understanding the social construction of administrative reality is by way of participant-observation.

Conceptualizing Impact

When conducting research about the impact of judicial review on administrative decision-making, in addition to being clear about the senses in which one uses the terms 'impact' and 'judicial review', it is also important to unpack the assumptions implicit to the way that one speaks about 'impact'. A proper conceptualization of 'impact' must be striven for.

As I suggested earlier, the way in which we think about 'impact' and about how to research the impact of judicial review must be driven by a proper conceptualization of discretionary decision-making. Decision-making should be conceptualized as a continually developing process of social construction, as 'a subtle and shifting affair which is a matter of seemingly endless human interpretative work' (Baldwin and Hawkins, 1984, p. 581). We must be careful not to think of historical events such as judicial review as being somehow 'fixed' in time, and therefore as having an eternal, unchanging meaning and relationship to current practice. The decision-making process inevitably involves interpretive work. The 'impact' of judicial review should, therefore, be recognized as being dynamic, organic and changing. As administrators continually engage in the process of interpretation and reinterpretation, so the 'impact' of judicial review mutates. In an important sense, then, the 'impact' of judicial review exists in the current perspectives of decision-makers. The risk in talking about 'impact' is to conceive of the process of decision-making as comprising a series of discrete and overly straightforward cause-effect relationships between 'informing factors' and decision outcomes. Under this model of decision-making, judicial review (cause) may be deemed to have a fixed and determinant effect on decision-outcomes. Under this notion the relationship between judicial review and decision-outcomes is one of linear cause and effect. However, if we conceptualize the 'context' of decision-making as being internal rather than external to the decision-making process (Emerson and Paley, 1992), as being fluid and having multiple possible constitutions, it becomes potentially misleading to talk about the *impact* of various factors upon decision-making. A picture of 'factors' external to the 'decision' sustaining a discrete cause-effect relationship to the 'decision' becomes problematic. Rather, we should picture the decision-making process as a complex of interpretive processes that may draw on a number of informing influences. The question of what impact judicial review has may, then, be better conceived as one of how the influence of experience of judicial review interacts with other informing influences.

There is, however, a further sense in which caution should be exercised when speaking of the impact of judicial review. If we accept the view that judicial review is but one of many influences upon the complex of interpretive processes, then we are left with the difficulty of how to isolate and assess one particular influence from amongst the many, even within the particular setting of one research site. This is a difficulty which is explored further in the next section.

Fieldwork

The above sections looked at some of the difficulties attached to the notion of the impact of judicial review. It was suggested that the problem might be helpfully reformulated in terms of asking how the informing influence of judicial review interacts with other informing influences on the interpretive work that comprises administrative decision-making. This representation of the problem raises the difficulty of how to disentangle the influence of judicial review on routine decision-making from the complex of influences upon it. By presenting some brief initial findings of a first period of fieldwork, the following section aims to illustrate how informing influences may combine in their effects on the administrative process.

First, however, some comments should be made concerning the legislative context within which the decision-making took place. Some further introductory remarks about the local authority with which the first period of fieldwork was conducted will also be made. This fieldwork took place in the last quarter of 1996, with a shorter follow up visit in the spring of 1997.

Legislative Context

As mentioned above, the focus of this research project is upon decision-making within local government concerning the housing rights of homeless applicants. At the time of this first period of fieldwork, so far as the legal jurisdiction of England and Wales was concerned, the legislation governing the rights of homeless applicants was contained in Part III of the Housing Act 1985 ('the 1985 Act'). Since the completion of this fieldwork, the Housing Act 1996 ('the 1996 Act') has come into effect. Part VII of the 1996 Act has replaced Part III of the 1985 Act as the legislation governing the rights of homeless applicants.[7] One of the changes effected by the 1996 Act is that homeless applicants have been given a right to request a review of the local authority's decision.[8] Further, homeless applicants now have a right to appeal to the county court concerning a decision or review decision on any point of law.[9] This right of appeal to the county court effectively replaces the role of judicial review as a legal remedy in relation to many of the aspects of the homelessness decision-making process.

So far as the jurisdiction of Scotland is concerned, the legislation governing the housing rights of homeless applicants is contained in Part II of the Housing (S) Act 1987. This legislation has been unaffected by the Housing Act 1996 and is substantially identical to the terms of Part III of the 1985 Act. Both pieces of legislation are re-enactments of the Housing (Homeless Persons) Act 1977 which applied to the whole of Great Britain. The reforms contained in the 1996 Act are restricted to England and Wales. Accordingly, judicial review, at the time of writing, is still the appropriate legal remedy for aggrieved homeless applicants in Scotland.

As noted above, fieldwork for this research project comprises periods of participant-observation with three local authorities. All three local authorities are located within the jurisdiction of England and Wales. During fieldwork with the second and third local authorities, therefore, these authorities will be implementing the terms of the 1996 Act. This raises two questions which should be addressed briefly. First, can fieldwork with local authorities which are no longer subject to the threat of judicial review in relation to most substantive issues within the decision-making process tell us anything about the impact of judicial review? Second, can fieldwork with local authorities whose experience of judicial review relates to a separate piece of legislation tell us anything about their implementation of new legislation?

In relation to the first question, it is important to note that the role of the county court in hearing appeals on points of law mirrors substantially the role of the High Court in relation to judicial review. In short, the county court will be asking itself substantially similar questions to those which the High Court asked previously. More importantly, however, it remains to be seen whether such a legal change is of significance to the processes of social construction within the administrative process. Data which confirms or denies the significance of the legal change will be of great interest.

This leads on to the second question raised above. It should similarly be noted that the legislation concerning the meaning of homelessness, priority need, and intentional homelessness remains substantially the same. This part of homelessness law comprises the 'obstacle race' (Robson and Watchman, 1981) which must be overcome in order for the homeless applicant to win the right to housing. These obstacles represent the threshold to the right to housing, and decision-making about these obstacles, as will be explained below, was the focus of my first period of fieldwork. It will also be the focus of subsequent fieldwork. However, more importantly, the purpose of conducting ethnographic research is to gain an appreciation of the administrative process from the administrators' perspective. Questions about the influence of judicial review under the 1985 Act remain to be answered, and answers will be of significance to the broader goal of understanding the impact of judicial review.

Having put these matters which relate to future fieldwork to one side, we can now turn to the completed fieldwork.

Timbergreens Council

The local authority with which fieldwork was conducted, and which I have called Timbergreens, is situated within a large city. It is one of the poorest areas in Great Britain and levels of applications to the Homeless Services Section for help with housing have been high.

The Homeless Services Section

The Homeless Services Section forms part of Timbergreens' Central Housing Services. The Homeless Services Section comprises four subsections: Assessments, Rehousing, Finance and Temporary Accommodation. The fieldwork was spent exclusively with the Assessments Team, the job of which is to determine whether homeless applicants have a right to permanent accommodation.[10] This required it to decide whether applicants are homeless, in priority need and whether they have become homeless intentionally (Robson and Poustie, 1996).[11] If applicants were deemed to be not homeless, or not in priority need, or to have become homeless intentionally, then they were refused permanent housing. The Temporary Accommodation Team is responsible for securing and managing temporary accommodation for homeless applicants while a decision on their application is pending. The Rehousing Team are responsible for securing long-term housing for homeless applicants who are deemed to be entitled to it. The Finance Team are responsible for the payment of Housing Benefit to those applicants in temporary accommodation, for the collection of rent, and for other miscellaneous financial duties. The Assessments Team, therefore, comprised the front-line workers who initially saw homeless applicants and determined whether any of the other teams became involved in the applications.

The Assessments Team

At the time of fieldwork, the Assessments Team had one manager, three team leaders, 13 homeless officers, and two administrative staff. In one sense the functions of these different levels of hierarchy within the Assessments Team are quite clear, although in practice there is a blurring of distinctions. The administrative staff support the homeless officers and carry out routine administrative tasks – data entry into computer systems, and so on. The homeless officers are the front-line workers who interview homeless applicants and conduct enquiries into their circumstances. The homeless officers are divided into three teams, each with their own team leader. The team leaders are responsible for issuing decisions on the cases passed to them by their team members. The manager oversees all the case work in this section, although not being directly involved in it, and manages the personnel within it.

The Assessments Team is marked by a particular longevity of service from its members. At the time of fieldwork, the least amount of continuous years worked by an officer in the team was four. The manager has worked in the team since 1985. One of the team leaders joined the team prior to the enactment of the Housing (Homeless Persons) Act in 1977.

Legal competence – knowledge of legislation and case law, the ability to develop legal arguments – is regarded as a professional attribute within the Assessments Team. Officers are encouraged to develop their legal knowledge. Training in homelessness law and related areas of law, both in-house and from external personnel, is a regular and not infrequent aspect of organizational life. Two of the homeless officers, one senior and one junior, at the time of fieldwork were studying for a degree in law on a part time basis. Information about legal developments, in terms of legislation or litigation, is generally issued to all officers. During the period of fieldwork considerable information was disseminated concerning the terms of the Asylum and Immigration Act 1996 which had recently come into force. Similarly, a mass of information was distributed concerning the Housing Act 1996 which was due to come into force shortly after the expiry of the fieldwork. This dissemination of information about legislative developments generally comprised the handing out of Voluntary Agencies' guidance on new law. Information concerning case law developments was disseminated by the distribution of photocopies of a broadsheet's law report.

On a more personal basis, where an officer is considered by his/her colleagues to have good legal knowledge, this is the source of professional respect. This is particularly so in relation to the manager, who is widely regarded by his staff as being 'clued up' on housing law. Conversely, where an officer is regarded to have an absence of legal skills this is the source of some scepticism concerning the officer's overall competence.

Relations between the Assessments Team and Timbergreens' Legal Department

The relationship between Timbergreens' legal department and the Assessments Team is very strong. Since the mid-1980s the Homeless Services Section has had an appointed legal adviser. The present legal adviser has been carrying out this role since 1990. However the relationship between the Assessments Team and the legal adviser was strengthened in late 1991 when she became a formal member of the Homeless Services Section's management team. In the summer of 1995, as a result of restructuring in the legal department, her position was altered. She ceased to be on the management team of the Homeless Services Section and reverted to simply being the appointed legal adviser. At this stage she also ceased to be responsible for legally administrating judicial review actions, and instead acted solely in an advisory/consultancy role to the Homeless Services Section relating to legal aspects of its functions. Judicial review actions are now legally administrated by various other legal officers within a designated team in the legal department.

The legal adviser has both scheduled and ad hoc contact with the Assessments Team. The relationship between individual homeless officers and the legal adviser are very friendly and familiar to the extent that they will occasionally approach her directly for advice on legal questions. Although this is a practice which is not formally recognized or condoned, the homeless officers are sufficiently familiar with the legal adviser for this to be an acceptable, albeit infrequent, practice. Team leaders contact the legal adviser more frequently on an ad hoc basis, although their main point of contact with the legal adviser is on a scheduled basis (see below). In the main, however, the manager has the most frequent informal contact with the legal adviser with whom he has a close working relationship. The manager regularly consults the legal adviser on legal questions relating to the Assessment Team's decision-making on an ad hoc basis.

The legal adviser also has scheduled meetings with the team leaders concerning certain cases within their overall workload. These are called the 'intentionals meetings' and happen on average every two weeks. A decision of intentional homelessness is never made by a team leader without consultation with the legal adviser. The legal adviser acts as a legal safety check in relation to decisions where a homeless applicant is provisionally deemed to be intentionally homeless. The nature of this check is to determine whether a decision to refuse assistance is legally defensible – whether it can be made without the risk of successful legal challenge.

It is only in relation to decisions about intentional homelessness that the legal adviser has meetings with the team leaders. She has no formal or regular input into decisions about whether or not an applicant is homeless or in priority need, or has a local connection with Timbergreens. She is contacted on an ad hoc basis concerning such matters if the team leaders or manager thinks a case merits this, but there is no requirement for her to be involved in these decisions and it is the general practice of the team leaders not to contact her.

'Settlement Cases'

In the remainder of this section I will examine aspects of the decision-making process concerning 'settlement cases'. This is a specific type of case within the Assessments Team's typology. By focusing on particular aspects of the process I will explore how different informing influences on decision-making may combine and interact.

A typology of cases For reasons of administrative efficiency the Assessments Team has developed a written case typology. All homeless applications which are registered for casework ('cases') are allotted a 'case type' by one of the team leaders. This typology was devised by the manager some years ago in order to streamline the processing of cases from registration as a new case to the issuing of a formal decision. By categorizing cases it was possible to allocate more 'difficult' cases to the more experienced officers who would be able to process these cases more quickly and efficiently.

There are 12 case types in total. However, we need only look at two types for the purposes of this essay. They are as follows:

'A' cases: possibly intentionally homeless – settlement grounds This ascription is made where the team leader believes that a decision of intentional homelessness is possible for 'settlement reasons'. 'Settlement cases' involve the situation where the homeless applicant has lived abroad and has given up this accommodation prior to coming to Great Britain and applying to Timbergreens for housing.

'B' cases: possibly intentionally homeless – non-settlement grounds This case type is allotted to an application when the team leader thinks that a decision of intentional homelessness is possible for reasons other than 'settlement' ones.

Some of these terms require further explanation. The Assessments Team has its own vocabulary and language which officers learn. Its language is characterized by routine abbreviations and shorthand phrases, as well as by idiosyncratic distortions of the normal rules of grammar – nouns become verbs (files are 'deaded'; one may 'section 64' a case), adjectives become nouns (cases are referred to as being 'intentionals'), and so on. Both 'A' and

'B' cases are classified as being 'possibly intentionally homeless cases'. These are generally referred to in the vernacular as 'possible intentionals' or, more often, as 'PIH' cases. The phrase 'possibly intentionally homeless' has originated from within the Assessments Team. It is not part of homelessness legislation or case law. When a case is deemed to be a 'PIH' case, it means that the homeless officer is formally put on notice that the team leader, from a first reading of the application, considers that a decision of intentional homelessness is an active possibility.

The term 'settlement case' is also part of the esoteric language of the Assessments Team. The manager explained the distinction between 'A' (settlement) and 'B' (non-settlement) cases:

> It's complexity ... [I]n this authority people who come from abroad predominantly come from [Southern Asia],[12] often for the same reasons – there's a better lifestyle available over here than there was over there – and if you look at a 'B' case there's a million and one reasons why a case could fall into a 'B' category. It could be rent arrears, mortgage arrears, tied tenancies which are a nightmare, people who just abandon properties.

The root of the term 'settlement' lies in the first judicial review case in which Timbergreens was involved. The manager explained

> It all resulted from the [X] case. We had a number of people in a similar situation, whom the Council argued were settled in [Southern Asia]... Now the Council was arguing that ... for the four years immediately prior to [Mr X] approaching as homeless, they were settled as a household in the accommodation in [Southern Asia]. And that's where it comes from.

Processing Settlement Cases

Settlement cases comprise a very significant proportion of the judicial review history of the Assessments Team. Although both settlement and non-settlement cases are deemed to be PIH cases, different administrative procedures follow on from the ascription of case type. Once a case has been designated as a PIH case it is allocated to a homeless officer. This homeless officer will then call the applicant in for the 'first PIH interview' where detailed questioning about the applicant's present circumstances and housing history will take place. In 1991 the manager introduced a procedures manual which contains specific guidance to homeless officers about how to carry out this interview in relation to settlement cases.

This procedures was designed as a guide. Guidance, however, was only introduced in relation to settlement cases. There is no similar guidance in relation to non-settlement cases. This is because settlement cases, unlike non-settlement cases, are perceived within the Assessments Teams to be homogeneous (Halliday, 1997). The manager explained:

> If you can write a procedures guide then you should do so, so that people know what they're supposed to be doing and why they're supposed to be doing it. It was done on settlement intentionals because they do follow a fairly similar format in the vast majority of cases. There are too many 'ifs' and 'buts' on things like rent arrears.

The guidance instructs the homeless officer to explain to the applicant what intentional homelessness means, and why it may be relevant to the applicant's case. The homeless officer must also emphasize that the applicant's comments will form a basis for the assessment of the application. The guidance then goes on to list specific questions that must be asked, of which there are almost 30. This list was drafted by the manager and has been supplemented on a few occasions. The content of the list has been partly, although not exclusively, informed by lessons learned from judicial review actions in which Timbergreens has been involved.

Homeless officers take this list of questions to PIH interviews and adhere to them very strictly, even to the point where they obtain information which does not appear to be pertinent to the case in hand. Interviews will generally take from 60–90 minutes to conduct and produce very detailed reports. The manager explained that Timbergreens learned early on from its experience of judicial review that it needed to be able to *demonstrate* that it had considered the relevant factors in an applicant's case. Accordingly, as much information is obtained as possible so as not to be caught out in a subsequent legal challenge by the claim that it has not considered all the relevant factors. He summarized this by saying, 'a [decision letter] can never be too long. It can be too short, but never too long.' The PIH interview operates as a kind of information binge to enable Timbergreens to be able to claim that it has considered all the relevant factors in an applicant's case.

However, another reason lies behind information bingeing. A general culture of suspicion exists in the Assessments Team in relation to the openness and truthfulness of homeless applicants. The widespread view is held that applicants 'change their stories' in order to circumvent the legal barriers which may prevent them from being eventually offered housing. Many of the staff, from homeless officers, to the manager, to the legal adviser, expressed a general suspicion that homeless applicants learn how to 'play the game' when making a homeless application – that they become aware of how to fill in applications and answer interview questions in order to secure an offer of housing. For example, in case T21 the applicant offered a different account of events in the PIH interview than she had offered in her first interview on approach to the Assessments Team. The interviewing homeless officer remarked after the PIH interview that the applicant had 'changed her story and [was] trotting out the right phrases to get a house'. The homeless officer suspected that the applicant's cousin, who had accompanied the applicant to the interview, '[was] very bright and [had] told the applicant what to say'. Another homeless officer remarked that it was amazing how, as 'stock questions' in settlement cases had changed over the years, so had the 'stock answers' given by applicants, adding, 'a lot of priming goes on in the [Southern Asian] community'.

The legal adviser shared the view that 'stories change' during the course of applications, but offered an alternative explanation of why this happened. She explained that the general policy of the Assessments Team was to defend a judicial review application if the Assessments Team thinks that they are right about a case. I asked what she meant by being 'right'. She explained:

> [Timbergreens] is good at homelessness work. We write much better letters than other authorities, some of the best I've seen ... We make decisions based on what is known at the time. Applicants often change their story after they've been to a solicitor. [Timbergreens] takes a stand on this. The first interview is probably the most honest account you'll get.

Regardless of whether the perceived source of 'story changing' is advice from members of an ethnic community, or family and friends, or solicitors, a general suspicion on the part of officers nevertheless exists about the truth of applicants' claims and about why accounts of their circumstances alter.[13] One tactical way the Assessments Team counters this is to get as much information as early as possible, regardless of whether it seems pertinent at the time. In doing this it is storing up defences against potential challenges based on a change of information about the applicants' circumstances.

Another aspect of PIH cases in general relates to the decision of how to categorize the situation where more than one adult approaches Timbergreens for help as homeless people – whether to class them as joint applicants, or to class one of them as the sole applicant and the other as a dependant of the applicant. Although homeless officers indicated that ultimately this could be the decision of the applicant(s) rather than Timbergreens, in practice the decision is made by the homeless officer and is generally not challenged by the applicant(s). Effectively, unless the individuals seeking assistance actively object to the decision about who is to be treated as the applicant, the decision is one for Timbergreens to make. For example, one homeless officer explained that she normally says to the applicants when conducting initial interviews, 'OK, we'll make this a joint application'. She would only alter this position if the 'applicants' objected. Decisions are also made to change applications which have been registered with single applicants into joint applications; that is, to make the partner of the sole applicant into a joint applicant. For example, in case T56 the homeless officer's opening words to the male applicant of a married couple in the first PIH interview were, 'I'm going to put Mrs [Applicant] up as a joint applicant coz you're married and it's reasonable to make you joint applicants'. The applicants made no response to this, and so the decision was made. It seems unlikely that applicants understand the implications of such a decision and similarly unlikely that they would choose to make any objection to it.

The reason for this policy was explained by another homeless officer. He explained that Timbergreens had been 'caught out' some years previously when the partner of a single applicant who had been deemed to be intentionally homeless applied in her own right claiming that she had not acquiesced in her husband's actions on which the decision of intentionality was based. This partner was able to claim that she had no part in the actions which led to her homelessness and could not then be regarded as being intentionally homeless. Accordingly, the officer explained, the Assessments Team now 'like to do them together'. This is done so that, should a wife make a subsequent application claiming that she had no part in the activities on which the first decision of refusal is based, Timbergreens will be able to base a defensible refusal of this second application on the wife's status as joint applicant in the original application. By making both partners to a relationship joint applicants, Timbergreens feels that it will be able to refute the credibility of any subsequent claims of one partner that she herself cannot be tied to the intentionality of her homelessness.

The converse practice also exists where the homeless officer will actively decide *not* to make two individuals joint applicants. The homeless officer will not classify two individuals as joint applicants where she feels that having a single applicant will conduce to a decision of refusal, or that having a joint application will preclude Timbergreens from being able to make a legally defensible decision of intentional homelessness. So, in case T60, a 45-year-old woman and her 25-year-old son approached Timbergreens for assistance as homeless people. The mother had been the sole tenant of privately rented accommodation from which they had both been evicted. The homeless officer told the mother and son that the mother would have to be the sole homeless applicant and conducted the interview accordingly. The mother and son made no objection. After the interview the homeless officer explained that she made the mother the sole homeless applicant because the tenancy from which they were evicted was in her sole name. She did not think that Timbergreens would be able to 'make them both intentional'. By this she meant that she did not believe that a decision of intentional homelessness which related to them both as joint applicants would withstand the pressure of legal scrutiny. The homeless officer did not believe that Timbergreens would be able to legally hold the son (in conjunction with the mother) responsible for the loss of the mother's tenancy. Accordingly, she classed the application as a sole application in the name of the mother so that a refusal of housing was legally possible.

Social Construction and Administrative Process

From these initial findings concerning the processing of PIH cases by Timbergreens we can see that a number of influences are contributing to the social construction of decisions. We know that the content of the procedural guidance to homeless officers has been fuelled in part by the lessons which the Assessments Team has learned from its experience of judicial review. This guidance is adhered to strictly and the PIH interviews are highly routinized. However, each member of the Assessments Team, from the homeless officers to the manager, feels overworked. The feeling of not having enough time to do one's work is part of the cultural identity of the Assessments Team.[14] When feeling under pressure of time the goal of getting through the routine can obscure the aims of the routine itself. Homeless officers generally do not feel they have the luxury of the time to use the questions merely as a guide to understanding the full circumstances of the applicant. Instead, the answering of these questions becomes an end in itself. The questions take on the form of obstacles which must be successfully negotiated before being able to move the case on to its next stage. The content of the questions, therefore, determines the content of the interview to the exclusion of information which may lie outside the limits which they impose (Halliday, 1997).

Prescriptive guidance, however, as I noted earlier, does not exist for non-settlement cases. This is due to the perception of settlement cases as homogeneous and non-settlement cases as heterogeneous. This kind of homogenization pervades much social decision-making (Waegel, 1981; Emerson, 1983). It is critical to our understanding of administrative decision-making and, in relation to fully understanding the administrative process within Timbergreens, begs the question of *why* settlement cases in particular are constructed in this fashion. However, for the purposes of this essay, it is important to note that this is another influence upon the social construction process within the administration process.

We have also seen that what I have termed a 'culture of suspicion' further informs the administrative process. This means that homeless applicants are frequently regarded as 'trying it on' when officers perceive a break in the consistency of the applicants' 'stories'. This in turn informs the determination of the facts of the application which feed into to the formal decision.

Finally, we saw that the identity of the applicant(s) is not unproblematic. Effectively this is decided by homeless officers on the basis of how best to store up defences in relation to potential legal challenges against refusals of housing. This is part of an ethos within the Assessments Team whereby officers gain an initial sense of the 'intentionality' of applicants and seek to be able to confirm this through their casework. In this sense it is linked to the culture of suspicion discussed above. An example of this is seen in case T21 already discussed. Here the homeless applicant offered an alternative version of events in a PIH interview to the version she had offered in her initial interview. After the PIH interview the interviewing officer suggested that the homeless applicant was 'trotting out the right phrases to get a house'. In response, a fellow officer asked, 'Do you think you'll get her?'. By this, the second officer was asking whether the interviewing officer would be able to secure a decision that the homeless applicant had become homeless intentionally. This ethos of 'getting intentionals' is in keeping with the character of decision-making suggested elsewhere as being 'a process of gradual affirmation or denial of a provisional solution to a problem by informally employing typical or typical whole case stories' (Tata, 1997). This is another aspect of the decision-making process which informs the constructions of 'cases' and decisions. Of course, the sense which the officers have of *how* to secure a decision which fits with their initial perceptions has been informed in part by their experience of judicial review.

In this examination of the processing of one particular type of case, we can detect the influence of judicial review. However, this is not the same thing, I would suggest, as being able to separate out and assess the 'impact' of judicial review. The complex of influences is such that they intertwine and combine in their effect. A separate treatment of judicial review may then be difficult to achieve. Rather, a continued attention to the particularities of the decision-making setting and the combination of influences at any given time is required. This, of course, is not to say that we cannot move forward in our attempts to understand the relationship between judicial and administrative decision-making, but only that we must exercise caution in doing so.

Conclusion

The impact of judicial review is a matter of contemporary concern for public law scholars. Empirical investigation of judicial review's impact, although still a fairly new endeavour, is increasingly recognized as being of crucial significance to a proper understanding of the subject. In this essay I have argued for an approach to the research process which begins with an empirical investigation of decision-making and moves on to consider the influence of judicial review on the processes of social construction which comprise the administrative process. I have suggested that we must reject a picture of 'impact' whereby external factors make contact with the decision-making process and produce determinant 'effects' which are fixed and observable. Instead we should embrace a conceptualization of 'impact' which is organic rather than mechanistic, where 'impact' gains its meaning from the current interpretive schemes of decision-makers rather than from any frozen historical moment.

By presenting some findings from a first period of fieldwork I have tried to demonstrate how the complex of influences on the interpretive processes can combine in the construction of facts and rules which culminate in decisions. Within that complex we can detect traces of Timbergreens' experience of judicial review. However, the nature of this complex of influences renders it difficult to isolate and assess the 'impact' of judicial review alone. This poses a challenge for further research in this area and presents us with some difficulties in speaking about the impact of judicial review on the administrative process.

Notes

1 I would like to acknowledge the help of David Cowan, Neil Hutton, Peter Robson and Cyrus Tata who offered helpful comments on earlier drafts of this essay.

2 Loveland's research (1995), although broader in its aims, also contains important empirical data on this question (see ch. 10).
3 *Bromley LB.C. v Greater London Council* [1983] 1 AC 768.
4 This scheme of categorization is taken from the influential judgment of Lord Diplock in *Council for Civil Service Unions v Minister for the Civil Service* [1985] AC 374.
5 At the time of writing one period of fieldwork has been completed and the remaining fieldwork is about to be commenced.
6 Of the empirical research, only that of Bridges et al. (1987) comprised a full research project. Sunkin and Le Sueur's work (1991) was a pilot project aimed at highlighting areas for further research. Mullen et al.'s work (1996) was a 'limited' impact study carried out as part of a broader project aimed at examining the volume and nature of use of judicial review in Scotland, along the lines of other projects in other jurisdictions (Hadfield and Weaver, 1995; Bridges et al., 1996).
7 For a discussion of the terms of the 1996 Act, see Arden and Hunter (1997a).
8 Housing Act 1996, section 202.
9 Housing Act 1996, section 204.
10 At the time of fieldwork it was the practice of Timbergreens to offer permanent accommodation to applicants who are deemed to be unintentionally homeless and in priority need.
11 If a homeless applicant was deemed to have the right to permanent housing, the Assessments Team also had the job of determining whether she had a local connection with Timbergreens. This issue was examined in order to determine whether the duty to house rested with Timbergreens.
12 I have described the particular country to which the manager is referring here as 'Southern Asia'. This term will be used throughout the essay.
13 I am not implying here that the homeless officers' constructions of applicants' circumstances can be contrasted with any 'truth' of what happened. Rather, I am merely attempting to illustrate one of the aspects of the way in which applicants' 'stories' are constructed by homeless officers.
14 This is not to say, of course, that the team was not overworked. However it is the sense which the team members have their own constraints of time which is of significance.

Bibliography

Alexander of Weedon, Lord (1989), 'Judicial Review and City Regulators', *Modern Law Review*, Vol. 52, pp. 640–48.

Arden, A. and Hunter, C. (1997a), *Homelessness and Allocations*, Legal Action Group.

Arden, A. and Hunter, C. (1997b), *Manual of Housing Law*, Sweet & Maxwell, London.

Baldwin, R. and Hawkins, K. (1984), 'Discretionary Justice: Davis Reconsidered', *Public Law*, pp. 570–99.

Barker, A. (1996), 'The Impact of Judicial Review: Perspectives from Whitehall and the Courts', *Public Law*, pp. 612–21.

Bridges, L. et al. (1987), *Legality and Local Politics*, Gower, Aldershot.

Bridges, L., Meszaros, G. and Sunkin, M. (1996), *Judicial Review in Perspective*, Cavendish, London.

Cicourel, A. (1968), *The Social Organization of Juvenile Justice*, John Wiley & Sons, London.

Ellen, R.F. (1984), *Ethnographic Research*, Academic Press, London.

Emerson, R. (1983), 'Holistic Effects in Social Control Decision-Making', *Law & Society Review*, Vol. 17, pp. 425–55.

Emerson, R., Fretz, R. and Shaw, L. (1995), *Writing Ethnographic Fieldnotes*, University of Chicago Press, Chicago, Illinois.

Emerson, R. and Paley, B. (1992), 'Organizational Horizons and Complaint-Filing' in K. Hawkins (ed.), *The Uses of Discretion*, Oxford University Press, Oxford.

Feldman, D. (1988), 'Judicial Review: a Way of Controlling Government?', *Public Administration*, Vol. 66, pp. 21–34.

Feldman, M. (1992), 'Social Limits to Discretion: An Organizational Perspective' in K. Hawkins (ed.), *The Uses of Discretion*, Oxford University Press, Oxford.

Fish, S. (1989), *Doing What Comes Naturally*, Oxford University Press, Oxford.

Galligan, D. (1995), 'Introduction' in D. Galligan (ed.), *Socio-Legal Studies in Context*, Blackwell, Oxford.

Galligan, D. (1996), 'Introduction' in D. Galligan (ed.), *A Reader on Administrative Law*, Oxford University Press, Oxford.

Hadfield, B. and Weaver, E. (1995), 'Judicial Review in Perspective: An Investigation of Trends in the Use and Operation of the Judicial Review Procedure in Northern Ireland', *Northern Ireland Legal Quarterly*, Vol. 46, No. 2, pp. 113–45.

Halliday, S. (1997), 'Decision-making in Public Administration: Routine Decisions and the "Fettering of Discretion"', conference paper, Law and Society Association Annual Meeting, St Louis, Missouri.

Harlow, C. (1976), 'Administrative Reaction to Judicial Review', *Public Law*, pp. 116–33.

Hawkins, K. (1992), 'Using Legal Discretion' in K. Hawkins (ed.), *The Uses of Discretion*, Oxford University Press, Oxford.

James, S. (1996), 'The Political and Administrative Consequences of Judicial Review', *Public Administration*, Vol. 74, pp. 613–37.

Kerry, Sir M. (1986), 'Administrative Law and Judicial Review – the Practical Effects of Developments over the past 25 years on Administration in Central Government', *Public Administration*, Vol. 64, pp. 163–72.

Livingstone, S. (1995), 'The Impact of Judicial Review on Prisons' in B. Hadfield (ed.), *Judicial Review: A Thematic Approach*, Gill and MacMillan, Dublin.

Loughlin, M. and Quin, M. (1993), 'Prisons, Rules and Courts: A Study in Administrative Law', *Modern Law Review*, Vol. 56, pp. 497– 527.

Loveland, I. (1995), *Housing Homeless Persons*, Oxford.

Mullen, T., Pick, K. and Prosser, T. (1996), *Judicial Review in Scotland*, John Wiley & Sons, Edinburgh.

Prosser, T. (1983), *Test Cases for the Poor*, Child Poverty Action Group, London.

Richardson, G. (1993), *Law, Process and Custody: Prisoners and Patients*, Butterworths, London.

Richardson, G. and Sunkin, M. (1996), 'Judicial Review: Questions of Impact', *Public Law*, pp. 79–103.

Robson, P. and Poustie, M. (1996), *Homeless People and the Law*, Butterworths.

Robson, P. and Watchman, P.Q. (1981), 'The Homeless Persons Obstacle Race', *Journal of Social Welfare Law*, pp. 1–15 and 65–82.

Sainsbury, R. (1992), 'Administrative Justice: Discretion and Procedure in Social Security Decision-Making' in K. Hawkins (ed.), *The Uses of Discretion*, Oxford University Press, Oxford.

Schutz, A. (1967), *The Phenomenology of the Social World*, Northwestern University Press.
Sunkin, M. and Le Sueur, A.P. (1991), 'Can Government Control Judicial Review?', *Current Legal Problems*, Vol. 44, pp. 161–83.
Tata, C. (1997), 'Conceptions and Representations of the Sentencing Decision Process', *Journal of Law and Society*, Vol. 24, pp. 395–420.
Van Maanen, J. (1981) 'Notes on the Production of Ethnographic Data in an American Police Agency' in R. Luckham (ed.), *Law and Social Enquiry: Case Studies of Research*, Scandinavian Institute of African Studies.
Waegel, W.B. (1981), 'Case Routinization in Investigative Police Work', *Social Problems*, Vol. 28, pp. 263–75.

10 Too Poor To Stay Here: 'Illegal Immigrants' and Housing Officers

MATTHEW WADDINGTON

Introduction

This paper offers an analysis of the increasing use of immigration status to restrict access to council housing. The paper focuses on the treatment of 'illegal immigrants', a category which has been less studied than the more controversial category of (bogus) asylum-seekers (for which see Tuitt, 1996).

Increasingly Draconian restrictions have been introduced against access to social housing by immigrants other than asylum-seekers. Housing officers are obliged to ascertain the immigration status of housing applicants and refuse access to housing on certain immigration grounds. However, there is no statutory duty on housing officers to report people to the immigration service, which might render the applicant open to immigration detention and removal abroad. The paper argues that housing officers are, in practice, compelled to report applicants by the complexity of the immigration tests, the arrangements for how applicants are checked, and the fact that two of the immigration questions are unanswerable without contact with the Home Office. This reporting of applicants to the Home Office has serious consequences for civil liberties and data control, but also for race equality and the promotion of good race relations.

The attack on the housing rights of immigrants other than asylum-seekers was made with remarkably little introduction. What little explanation the previous government offered was about the burden to the taxpayer of illegal immigrants obtaining social housing. However, there is practically no evidence of any such housing problem, nor is there any clear definition of the penumbra of the term 'illegal immigrant'. This paper argues that the real purpose of the attack was to force housing officers to participate ever further in the process of immigration control. This purpose is examined in the light of criminological concepts of 'elimination', 'moral panics', and 'responsibilization'. The concept of responsibilization is reworked to adapt it to a moral panic, so as to account for the relatively quiet way that the restrictions on other immigrants were introduced, compared to those on asylum-seekers. The paper uses concepts from other work on inter-agency collaboration to analyse how housing officers are led into participating in immigration control. The paper argues that the purpose behind this viciously exclusionary programme is partly to distract attention from the housing shortage. However, the purpose is also to responsibilize housing authorities in an ongoing racist 'moral panic' and to increase the policing of a multi-cultural society.

The Problem

The impression is given, by the drastic and complicated steps taken to deny immigrants access to social housing, that a serious problem is being tackled. It is argued here that the alleged problem does not exist, that the impression of seriousness is illusory, and that the point of the reaction was to give this illusory impression.

Housing officers and housing lawyers generally regarded immigration as irrelevant until 1993 when it was brought to their attention by the Asylum and Immigration Appeals Act 1993 and *Tower Hamlets L.B.C. v Secretary of State for the Environment* (1993) 25 HLR 524. Menski noted the absence of work on the overlap between housing and immigration, pointing out that housing law text books hardly mention immigration (1996). The same can be said for housing policy text books (except for example Power, 1993). Housing officers did not see immigration status as their problem because they did not need to resort to eviction to recover the properties if the immigration authorities deported council tenants. Immigration status therefore only gave difficulties to housing officers when the immigration authorities delayed decisions on immigration status. Delays on asylum applications have led to a backlog which at the time of writing was over 50,000 cases (Home Office, 1997).

However, no suggestion was made of delays in the processing of illegal immigrants, as opposed to asylum-seekers. In fact, the consultation papers and the White Paper leading up to the Housing Act 1996 contain no attempt to justify why the Act should exclude illegal immigrants from housing (DoE, 1994a, paras 14.1–14.2; 1995, no mention; 1996, para. 12). The only justification came in a Home Office press release which announced £100 million of savings through an 'efficiency scrutiny' which would 'ensure that illegal immigrants and temporary visitors do not receive social security benefits and social housing for which they have no entitlement' and 'establish a procedure for staff across both Central and Local Government to notify immigration officials about suspected illegal immigrants' (Home Office, 1996a). It ended with the statement that:

> We, as a society, cannot bear the burden of illegal immigrants who seek to obtain publicly funded services that they have no right to receive. Resources must be spent upon those who have a right to live here and who contribute to our society. Anyone legally entitled to be here has nothing to worry about.

However, no empirical evidence was offered to justify the belief that 'illegal immigrants' or people with temporary leave were causing any housing problem, or even that there were any significant numbers of illegal immigrants in the country. In fact the extensive, often government funded, empirical research on the housing allocations and homelessness processes has not looked at the issue in any depth. Evans and Duncan's research did not consider illegal immigrants, but did find 93 per cent of English and Welsh councils had not accepted as homeless anyone with a temporary visitor visa, and that the average number accepted in 1985/6 was less than half a case each. They pointed out that even in London, where the average number of such households accepted was ten, the figures were distorted by two councils with exceptionally high figures of 'over 30' and 'between 16 and 20' (Evans and Duncan, 1988, p. 26). The research on which the Department of Environment claimed to base their 1994 Consultation Paper (DoE, 1994a) did not gather direct evidence of immigration status but simply extrapolated that it was likely that 'a large number of those who described themselves as black African were recent refugees' (Prescott-Clarke et al., 1994, pp. 70 and 87).

'Illegal Immigrants'

This lack of statistical evidence might have arisen because there is no clear basis to define what is meant by an 'illegal immigrant'. The concept is in fact a very convenient use of language to stigmatize visible minority communities. The loose term 'illegal immigrant' is easily confused with the properly defined immigration term 'illegal entrant', which carries the most serious of all immigration consequences, administrative removal with no right of appeal. The courts invented the category of 'illegal entry by deception', prompted by Home Office practice (Macdonald and Blake, 1995, pp. vii and 14–16; Griffith,

1991). The courts also went on to invent, through *obiter dicta*, exclusion from homelessness rights on grounds of illegal entry by deception explicitly without foundation in any of the legislation: *Tower Hamlets L.B.C. v Secretary of State for the Environment* (1993) 25 HLR 524.

The concept of the 'illegal immigrant', however, is not used anywhere in the immigration or housing legislation. The main problem in the term 'illegal immigrant' is the all-encompassing way it confuses various categories such as illegal entrants, overstayers, people facing deportation, or people with valid leave to be here who either breach conditions on their stay or lose the basis of their stay. It operates to make people in all these categories appear to be a serious problem and equally undeserving of housing or other services. In housing some examples show the range of the concept: an illegal entrant by deception (about the availability of accommodation in this country) which subsequently leads to homelessness; a woman legally in this country as a spouse on one year's leave who flees domestic violence; or someone in this country with valid leave who merely asks to go on a council waiting list. Each is viewed differently by immigration law, but the label is similar to branding everyone who has ever speeded as an 'illegal driver'.

If illegal immigration is not a problem that may indicate a perception of immigration itself as the problem. But if an approach of economic self-interest was taken then immigration would be seen as supporting the economy (Spencer, 1994), and a solution to problems over pensions (Vincent, 1996). In a European context 'economic migration', far from being a problem, is what is promoted by the right of free movement, a major right granted to citizens of European countries. If immigration is not a problem that may indicate a perception of the racial identity of immigrant communities itself as the problem. Debates on race and race relations have long been bound up with those on immigration (Paliwala, 1995).

The Harshness of the Reaction

The restrictions which have been introduced against access to housing by immigrants other than asylum-seekers have two key features. First, they have become increasingly complex and contradictory to the point where it is not only beyond the scope of this paper to set them out in detail but equally beyond the capacity of housing officers to integrate them into housing procedures. Second, they have become increasingly Draconian, excluding certain categories of person from abroad from the housing register and the homelessness service irrespective of any housing need.

The only statutory prohibitions imposed so far on access to social housing are for categories of 'person from abroad'. The Asylum and Immigration Act 1996 and the Housing Act 1996 introduced the first statutory restrictions on the housing rights of immigrants other than asylum-seekers (they also contain reworked versions of the restrictions on asylum-seekers in the Asylum and Immigration Appeals Act 1993). Narrower restrictions, relating only to immigration offenders and homelessness, had been introduced by the *Tower Hamlets* case. The statutory restrictions are much broader, covering people who have not committed any immigration offence and applying to the housing register as well as homelessness provision.

Related changes in immigration law in 1996 criminalized use of any council housing by certain immigrants lawfully present in Britain on temporary leave. This was achieved by including all council housing (instead of just homelessness provision as formerly) in the definition of 'public funds', introducing those public funds rules into all categories of temporary leave, and allowing prohibitions (breach of which is a criminal offence) against use of public funds to be imposed on the grant of temporary leave (Statement of Changes in Immigration Rules HC31 of 31 October 1996, and para. 1(1) of Sch. 2 Asylum and Immigration Act 1996).

The combined effect of these immigration law changes with the housing law changes is that an immigrant who is lawfully present in Britain, but then develops a need for social housing, can be refused housing and left homeless whatever the need, but also can be criminalized and forced to leave the country. Deportation can lead to disappearance at the hands of the person's home government or even to death at the hands of British officials carrying out the deportation as in the case of the death of Joy Gardner in 1993 (Bhabha and Shutter, 1994, pp. 158–60).

Elimination

This extreme reaction points towards ideas in criminology of the 'eliminative ideal' in which the state tries to solve problems by 'getting rid of troublesome and disagreeable people with methods which are lawful and widely supported' such as the current 'three strikes and you're out' policies (Rutherford, 1996). Rutherford points out, however, that these policies date back to transportation, which was disproportionately used against people of Irish extraction. Transportation is very similar to deportation in removing people abroad rather than into prisons, and in having a racial bias (justified in deportation on the grounds of nationality).

Garland adds a dimension to elimination by describing how, in tandem with following more rational policies on crime control, a weak state is drawn in to 'denial' in which shows of punitive force are used, with 'knowing and cynical manipulation', to give public displays of the state's power as a distraction from deeper social problems and to give the appearance that 'something is being done'. He suggests that 'the essential attractiveness of the punitive response is that it can be represented as an authoritative intervention to deal with a serious, anxiety-ridden problem' (Garland, 1996). It is a contention of this paper that this works in both directions, in that the severity of the punitive approach to immigrants is being used to foster an anxiety that there must be a correspondingly serious problem when none in fact exists. Carlen uses similar criminological concepts in a homelessness context to describe how the treatment of homeless young people deters them from applying as homeless and denies their experience as part of a disciplinary project of 'the management of social change and the denial of innovation' (Carlen, 1994). In a similar way the policing of housing applications is part of the management of social change and innovation which is caused by immigration and multi-culturalism.

Moral Panic

The following elements have therefore been shown to be present in the creation of the restrictions on immigrants' access to social housing: a nonexistent or exaggerated problem; the labelling as 'folk devils'; and drastic action in response. These would fit within the concept of a 'moral panic' as set out by Cohen (1972) and developed since (see, for example, Goode and Ben-Yahuda, 1994). Research in related areas has detected moral panics in attitudes to national identity (Husbands, 1994), the nexus between race relations and immigration (Paliwala, 1995), and the linkage of race with immigration and benefit fraud (Cook, 1997). However, the model does not appear to fit precisely to the restrictions on access to social housing by immigrants other than asylum-seekers.

A key element in a moral panic is the way the media are sensitized to, and then define and exaggerate the alleged problem. The media coverage of immigration has been examined by Layton-Henry (1984) for 1978, Billig and Golding (1992) for 1992, and Cowan (1997) for 1996. It appears that the media coverage has been largely about asylum rather than about other forms of immigration, as though the evils of illegal immigration can be taken as read. There is also little sign of the 'moral entrepreneur' who is a crusading reformer who drives a moral panic. Instead, the timing and sources of the press coverage would seem to indicate that the press were largely taking a lead from government or political sources (see Hall et al., 1978, who discuss a process of news management by 'primary definers'). The media outbursts considered in each of the three studies mentioned above were all in periods leading up to a general election. The Asylum and Immigration Appeals Act 1993, the Asylum and Immigration Act 1996 and the Housing Act 1996 are the only three pieces of legislation making immigration status relevant to housing. They originated in the campaigns for the last two general elections, when the Conservative governments believed they would lose. The media coverage and the legislation both therefore appear to owe more to political gesture than to coherent planning for practical solutions to real housing problems.

However, using the concept in relation to immigration and housing emphasizes the way that attacks on illegal immigrants hardly need justifying, and that a government (without any other moral entrepreneur) can quietly introduce such severe changes on the back of attacks on asylum-seekers. This ease of action suggests a strong and persistent underlying source such as racism operating as a pool to be tapped as and when needed. Racism and opposition to immigration have deep historical roots in Britain (Dummett and Nicol, 1990, and Husbands, 1994). This might stretch the idea of a moral panic too far, although Goode and Ben-Yahuda describe witch-hunting as a moral panic even though it lasted for two centuries (Goode and Ben-Yahuda, 1994). This theme is returned to below when moral panics are considered in the light of the concept of 'responsibilization'. First, however, there is the question of how the reaction to the moral panic manifests itself in the relationship of housing authorities with the immigration service.

Inter-agency Partnerships

This paper argues that the real purpose of importing immigration questions into the rehousing process is not to tackle the alleged housing problem. This could be achieved just by denying access to social housing. Instead the paper contends that the imposition of immigration questioning is designed to force housing officers to participate ever further in the process of immigration control, and in particular to report details of people in whom the Home Office might be interested. This participation was achieved in a way which allowed the then government to maintain its fictional claims that 'it is not intended that local authority officials should act as quasi-immigration officers' (Home Office, 1996b), that 'anyone legally here has nothing to fear' (Home Office, 1996a), and that housing officers were only being made to ration social housing more efficiently. The legislation therefore does not explicitly order housing officers to report people to the immigration service. Instead, housing officers are in practice compelled to report applicants by the complexity of the immigration tests. This process is next examined through concepts derived from other work on crime control and multi-agency partnerships.

Housing authorities participate in many instances of multi-agency partnerships, with varying degrees of success (see Cowan, 1997). Some involve the police, such as those on crime prevention, racial harassment or domestic violence, some tend only to involve welfare agencies, such as those on the Children Act and community care. Sampson et al. warn against taking an over simple view of these relationships as either wholly conspiratorial or wholly benevolent (1988). Nevertheless, the relationship between housing and immigration is significantly different from most of the other partnerships in that the housing authority is forced to use immigration categories as the basis for housing activity. In the other relationships the housing authority normally keeps its definitions, for example of vulnerability or nuisance, and is required to cooperate only as far as is reasonable with other agencies, who for their part retain their definitions. Housing authorities have therefore been forced into a greater degree of 'inter-organizational homogeneity' in their relationship with the immigration service than they have with their more usual partners, and this should lead to more stable and cohesive collaboration (Hudson, 1987). However, this homogeneity has been one-sidedly forced onto housing authorities. This element of one-sidedness justifies considering how the relationship between housing and immigration may fit the 'conspiratorial' model of partnership.

Responsibilization and Governance-at-a-distance

The concept of 'responsibilization' describes an attempt by the state to achieve 'governance-at-a-distance' (Garland, 1996, p. 454). Responsibilization therefore offers a very useful model for how the immigration service operates by proxy through housing authorities. In crime control, private agencies and the community have been recruited into policing so that they might avoid becoming victims of opportunist criminals. There is a parallel between those developments and the way that housing authorities are being expected to protect themselves against housing applications by undeserving immigrants. As with 'neighbourhood watch' and 'designing out crime', the implications of the immigration changes go beyond protecting social housing and making housing officers into another line of unpaid immigration police.

One fundamental aim of the immigration service is to ensure that certain people who should not be present in Britain are forced to leave. This can be achieved directly, by deportation of people subject to immigration control who come to the attention of the immigration service. Britain, as an island, has traditionally relied on deploying immigration officers at ports of entry. Internal control is therefore heavily reliant on people being reported to the immigration authorities. The welfare state, and particularly the Department of Social Security, has long had a role in this reporting (see for example Storey, 1986).

Alternatively, people can be made to leave indirectly, by refusing welfare state services so that a person will leave the UK rather than stay in destitution. This method will work even if the immigration service is never contacted. The indirect method is the model for the housing restrictions considered in this paper and the related restrictions on welfare benefits, though the method has proved flawed because of maintenance and accommodation from Social Services under the National Assistance Act 1948.

The same effect can also, however, be achieved covertly against British citizens, again either directly or by proxy through the welfare state. The direct technique is to make the British citizen's family life hard enough that they are inclined to leave, through refusing entry for spouses or visitors from the country of origin of the person's community. The welfare state can be used to achieve a similar effect by proxy against British citizens without directly refusing benefits. A British citizen who is entitled to welfare state services may use those services, but then cannot sponsor their family or visitors to come to the UK. The British citizen then has to choose between claiming the benefits or going overseas for the reunion with family or friends. Even if these factors do not achieve a hidden induced repatriation, they act as a means of control over communities in this country which maintain links abroad.

There are therefore several ways in which the immigration service can achieve 'governance-at-a-distance' if it can persuade housing authorities to accept responsibilization. In the most open attempt at this the Home Office issued a circular in October 1996 to councils to 'invite' and 'encourage' them to report suspected immigration offenders encountered 'in the normal course of their duties', while emphasizing that 'it is not intended that local authority officials should act as quasi-immigration officers' (Home Office, 1996b). The circular draws a distinction between reporting people to the immigration authorities and asking those authorities to assist in assessing eligibility for housing. A housing authority is not compelled by the circular or any legislation to do either of these. Nevertheless, if it wishes to, a housing authority can by doing so take its place with the rest of the welfare state in serving immigration purposes. Even so, housing is less under central government control than other parts of the welfare state, so the question remains why housing authorities would want to take on this role.

Part of the answer is that there was an underlying incentive to cooperate even before the changes. On the face of it, the unit of exchange in the relationship between the housing authority and the Home Office is information. The housing authority can trade information on the existence, whereabouts and activities of a potential immigration offender. The Home Office can trade information about immigration status on which housing eligibility is dependent. There is therefore high 'resource reciprocity' and 'unit standardization', which would facilitate collaboration in the model put forward by Hudson (1987, p. 180–81).

However, no cooperation or exchange of this information actually needs to take place for the goals of both sides to be furthered. A person may instead be persuaded not to apply for housing rather than risk their information being passed on. In that case, the immigration service benefits in that life is made harder for an immigrant who may as a result leave the country, while the housing authority benefit from the reduction in demand for their limited stock. However, the pressure on housing authorities' stock could be counterbalanced by their political views or by worries about the legality of cooperation. Before 1993 the Commission for Racial Equality (CRE) had offered guidance twice on immigration and housing issues, in each case strongly discouraging cooperation (CRE, 1989 and 1991). Some other factor was therefore needed to produce closer collaboration.

Organizational Interdependence

The point of the responsibilization process is that the Home Office wish to be able to depend on housing authorities to report potential immigration offenders to them. If housing and immigration were to collaborate fully there needed to be 'organizational interdependence' between them, rather than just some incentives which may be outweighed by other factors (Hudson, 1987). Interdependence may be 'induced' by legislation, but 'such an approach may be tenuous and subject to rupture', as is seen in the relationships of housing and social services authorities (p. 180).

The Housing Act 1996 does not impose any duty on housing authorities either to report or check people with the Home Office. The legislation appears to leave the Home Office in the weaker position, given that there is a unilateral duty on the Home Office to respond to housing authorities' requests for information, whereas there is no corresponding duty on housing authorities to ask for information or to provide it (s. 187 Housing Act 1996). There is no time limit in the Act on the Home Office's response, but the Code promises responses 'without undue delay and within 10 working days at the latest' (DoE and DoH, 1996, Annex E4). The dependency must therefore be made mutual, so the housing authorities have to be made to need the Home Office.

There are three ways in which this is done practically. These are the Code's advice that there is still a case-law duty to report immigration offenders, the fact that two of the immigration questions are logically unanswerable without contact with the Home Office, and more generally the complexity of the immigration questions which housing authorities are required to ask.

The Code and Reporting

The Code confuses the issue by dealing specifically with illegal entrants and overstayers, even though they are not referred to in any of the housing legislation (DoE and DoH, 1996, paras 12.13–12.16). The Code relies on *obiter dicta* in the *Tower Hamlets* case to state that 'a housing authority are under a duty to inform IND where they are satisfied that a person is in the country illegally' (para 12.15). What the Code ignores is that the case should be regarded as being at least redundant after the Housing Act 1996. That Act now casts its net much wider, requiring councils to refuse people not on the basis of any offence but purely on the fact that they are subject to immigration control and do not fit any of the exceptions. An applicant can therefore be refused before the question of the currency or validity of their temporary leave ever arises. However, the fact that the Code still refers to illegal entrants and overstayers will confuse even councils which understand the Act and will make them more inclined to seek reassurance from the Home Office.

Unanswerable Questions

If a council is to implement the Housing Act 1996 fully then there will be two questions on which it is forced to check with the Home Office (or with the DSS who will normally liaise with the Home Office anyway). These are whether a European has been 'required by the Secretary of State to leave the United Kingdom' and whether an 'undertaking' has been given under the immigration rules (respectively Class G in Reg. 6 and Class C(i) in Reg. 4 of the Allocation Regulations, and Reg 4(b) and Class F(i) in Reg. 3(1) of the Homelessness Regulations). The applicant cannot otherwise provide any evidence, proving a negative, that either of these documents does not exist. Thus, the housing authority must consult with the Home Office in these cases.

Complexity and Confusion

As well as being harsh, the restrictions on immigrants' housing rights are extraordinarily complex. Essentially, people who are subject to immigration control are excluded from council housing unless they fall within certain exceptions, while people not subject to control will not be excluded subject to a further set of exceptions. There is, however, inevitable scope for confusion in importing immigration concepts into the work of housing officers, given the unfamiliarity and complexity of the immigration system. The scope for confusion is exacerbated by the way that the changes are bedevilled by inconsistencies and failures to think through the practicalities. To detail these is beyond the scope of this paper, but the following examples offer an idea of the problems they pose.

Instead of one set of housing restrictions there are, at the time of writing, three separate but similar sets of exclusions contained in s. 161(2)–(3) Housing Act 1996 for the housing register, s. 185–186 Housing Act 1996 for homelessness, and the amended s. 9(1) Asylum and Immigration Act 1996 for other cases. Between them these provisions have so far accumulated six Statutory Instruments (1996, Nos 1982, 2753, 2754; 1997, Nos 628, 631, and 2046).

There is no definition for the notorious habitual residence test, and the Code can do no better than simply refer to the Housing Benefit Guidance Manual (DoE and DoH, 1996, paras 4.18 and 12.21).

Where a homeless applicant is eligible but other people involved are ineligible, the ineligible people are ignored in assessing the eligible person's homelessness and priority need. So by implication they are taken into account in assessing intentionality, local connection and suitability of offers (s. 185(4) Housing Act 1996). This confuses the handling of cases such as where an ineligible person, who lives with a settled applicant, suffers a problem which makes it no longer reasonable to continue to occupy a property, or causes domestic violence, harassment, overcrowding, or intentional homelessness.

Uncertainties are introduced from European law on the purposes for which free movement can be exercised, the validity of claims to citizenship of other European countries, the effect of becoming a charge on public funds, the ability to require European nationals to leave, and the validity of the habitual residence test.

The DoE Code assumes all entitlements will have already been recognized by the Home Office and therefore evidenced by clear paperwork (DoE and DoH, 1996, paras 4.10, 12.4 and Annex E3). But, for example, claims to the right of abode or European nationality may not be apparent to the applicant and will then be overlooked.

This complexity serves to induce the dependence necessary for successful collaboration. Their relative lack of knowledge of immigration law renders housing officers dependent on the Home Office to complete their investigations. This imbalance is used to draw housing authorities into participating in the immigration system, while at the same time maintaining that 'it is not intended that local authority officials should act as quasi-immigration officers' (Home Office, 1996b). However, it is submitted that the distinction between reporting people and checking their eligibility is more apparent than real, because of the arrangements for how eligibility is checked.

While some councils will feel able to assess eligibility for themselves, most would be likely to find the issues so complex that they will need and want assistance. There is assistance available, and the new Code sets out in detail how to obtain it, in the form of an offer by the Home Office of a service checking eligibility for housing (DoE and DoH, 1996, Annex E4). The branch offering the assistance is the innocently named 'Immigration Status Enquiries Unit'. However, this is exactly the same Unit to which the Home Office circular invites councils to report immigration offenders (Home Office, 1996b). This implies that this Unit must be ready to take action to remove people. The policing function is therefore effectively being disguised as a voluntary means of ensuring accuracy in processing housing applications.

This form of collaboration avoids the risk of controversy and possible opposition if reporting were made compulsory. It has the further advantage of making councils, instead of the government, appear culpable if they choose to report people rather than being forced to. Instead the Home Office can claim simply to be offering a service to councils, and can brand as inefficient those which do not use it.

Responsibilization and Moral Panic

The application of the concept of responsibilization to the field of immigration control raises difficult but useful questions as to the nature of any failure of the state. If the failure of the state is seen as a failure to solve the housing crisis, then immigration (other than asylum) is largely irrelevant due to the lack of evidence of any figures for immigrants using social housing. If immigration control is considered instead of housing then there appear to be several differences from the crisis of rising crime rates considered by Garland (1996). In immigration there is no equivalent failure of the state, no rising crime as a fact perceived by its victims as a problem which they might have an interest in tackling themselves, no defining down of a problem of shallow-end deviance, no reformative penal-welfare system or solidarity project to abandon, and the agencies being co-opted in these changes are public agencies (housing departments) not private agencies or the community.

It is argued however that responsibilization is still useful in an immigration context if it can be reconceived to apply where there is a moral panic instead of a real rising crime rate. Responsibilization then becomes a method of institutionalizing the moral panic. This would help explain for example why there has been so little sign of 'moral panic' over immigrants other than asylum-seekers using housing. It was seen as worth the risk of the state pretending to fail, in order to secure the benefits of responsibilization to a programme of fuelling racist fears about economic migrants and cultural swamping, and to use this for ends which are not just about housing policy but about winning elections and fostering racism as a useful tool.

Victimization

Responsibilization is problematic in crimes such as immigration offences, which are seen as victimless. The supposed 'crime' of the immigrant who applies for council housing is to 'steal' tenancies from the council and from the other people on the waiting list. However, first, obtaining council housing is not an actual crime and, second, the effects on its 'victims' are too diffuse to produce the reaction necessary for effective responsibilization. Nevertheless, the process of responsibilization can be seen as being of enough benefit in itself to be worth inventing a problem and a failure. Such invention would require a twin approach of criminalization and victimization. Criminalization took the form described above in the changes to immigration law. Victimization was then essential if responsibilization was to be effective. Garland points out that real victims can be responsibilized by simple exhortation, by pointing out the full nature of their losses, or occasionally by 'more forceful methods' such as 'threatening to shift the costs of retail theft prosecutions on to the retailers themselves' (Garland, 1996, p. 453). It is only one step further to shift costs onto an organization in order to create a responsibilized victim in what was previously a victimless crime.

The model to hand was the success of the Immigration (Carriers' Liability) Act 1987. Through that Act the immigration service exercises 'governance-at-a-distance' by fining airlines, so persuading them to refuse to fly people with suspect visa paperwork. Airline companies were not victims of crimes, but the fines reponsibilized them. The result for asylum-seekers was that 'in essence, the migrant refugee is not seen as a person who may urgently require humanitarian assistance, but rather as a "risk" measurable in monetary terms' (Tuitt, 1996, p. 77). Risk management is at the heart of the responsibilization strategy.

The means used in the housing context is to restrict Housing Benefit, so as to create a rent arrears problem for a council which houses ineligible immigrants. In the middle of 1996 there was a gap of several months between the imposition of new severe Housing Benefit restrictions on certain categories of immigrants and the removal of the homelessness duties in respect of those immigrants. There was therefore for a time a severe problem for councils. They had to house people who could not use benefits to pay the rent, leading councils such as Westminster and Hammersmith and Fulham to threaten judicial review against the government over the implementation of the changes (Ellery, 1996). The negative effect for government policy was offset, however, by the way it was able to stoke up, and then meet, a demand from councils for the introduction of the Housing Act 1996 to level down homelessness and allocations eligibility to match Housing Benefit eligibility. A further bonus for government policy was that councils had then learnt a very important lesson that immigrants could cause severe problems for rent arrears management.

Even after the Housing Act 1996 reduced eligibility for social housing, there remains a difference between housing and housing benefit. If someone's immigration status changes to make them ineligible, then their housing benefit can be stopped immediately. However, secure tenants cannot be evicted on grounds of changes in immigration status, so they will start to build up rent arrears when housing benefit is stopped (*Akinbolu v Hackney L.B.C.* (1997) 29 HLR 259). Councils will therefore still face the risk of financial loss if they house the wrong kinds of immigrants. Councils are thus recast as potential victims who can be made to understand that they do have an interest in protecting themselves against the criminal immigrant, and can therefore be susceptible to the process of responsibilization.

Effects

Civil Liberties and Data Control

This reporting of applicants to the Home Office has serious consequences for civil liberties. The Home Office's discretionary powers are so strong that innocent people may have something to fear if they are reported. This is because applying for housing could lead to an assumption that the person knew before entry that their accommodation in Britain would be inadequate and therefore that they entered illegally by deception (the scenario in the *Tower Hamlets* case). There is no appeal from this country against removal after the Home Office decide someone is an illegal entrant. The person can be arrested and put on a plane with minimal procedural requirements. They have to show they did not know before they entered that the accommodation would fall through. The difficulty is that this involves proving a negative about a state of mind which is notoriously difficult. There is a risk that it can be easier for a guilty person to produce a prepared alibi than for an innocent person to understand how to defend themselves.

Apart from deportation and indefinite detention without trial (see Ashford, 1993), the immigration system also uses more subtle forms of control. If housing authorities are successfully co-opted further into immigration work, then these techniques of control will reach further and increase the threat to civil liberties. The powers available to the immigration service to allow surveillance of immigrants in the community include being able to impose conditions that an immigrant should report to a police station at regular intervals, should not work, or should only work for a particular employer (creating 'domestic slavery', on which see Bhabha and Shutter, 1994, p. 181–84), should live at certain address, or should continue living with their spouse (trapping women in domestic violence, on which see Bhabha and Shutter, 1994, p. 119–24). There is a long history of abuse of civil liberties through internal immigration controls such as these (see Gordon, 1981; CRE, 1985, ch. 8). The welfare state has played a significant role in that abuse (Storey, 1986). From this perspective, housing is being drawn in amongst the other welfare state services. The fact that it was relatively overlooked until 1993 would square with the belief that public housing has never fully been integrated into the welfare state (Cole and Furbey, 1994).

One of the main purposes of the 1993 Home Office review was to produce 'quicker and more efficient arrangements for staff of benefit providers to pass information on immigration offenders to the immigration authorities' (Home Office, 1996a). The previous edition of the Code did say immigration status should be treated as confidential, but allowed for it to be passed on to the Home Office (DoE, 1994b, para. 4.33). This statement was left out of the new Code but is assumed in Annex E4 para. 2 (DoE and DoH, 1996). Reporting people to the immigration service, as opposed to checking their status before rehousing them, may be *ultra vires*, a breach of confidence, racially discriminatory, or a breach of the Data Protection Act 1984. The Code does not mention the Home Office in recommending a 'need to know' approach to the new duty of confidentiality under s. 166(2) Housing Act 1996 for information held on the housing register (DoE and DoH, 1996, para. 4.55). It then does not refer to s. 166(2) in discussing contacts with the Home Office (Annex E4).

There are serious implications for data protection in these practices, especially if the data collection is on a sufficiently large scale. Liberty, in exposing the illusory attractions of identity cards to control illegal immigration, pointed out the 'bureaucratic nightmare' of trying to keep a constantly updated database of citizenship and immigration status 'including the five million or so people who come to Britain as visitors every year' (Liberty, 1995, p. 21). Hackney council faced controversy when it was reported in 1995 that details of its black employees had been passed on to the Home Office for immigration investigations (Guardian, 1995). The Code, however, does not appear to contemplate that information might be misused by councils or the government. Instead it concentrates on registering a contact from the housing authority with the Home Office, to stop anyone impersonating either agency (Annex E4). Such complacency must be a worrying sign in itself.

Race Equality

Assumptions may be made on racial grounds about which applicants should be questioned about immigration status. Visible ethnic minorities settled here may as a result be further challenged as to their rights to live in this country and to receive services. Councils need to avoid race discrimination but they also have to go further in promoting good race relations under s. 71 Race Relations Act 1976. The Social Security Advisory Committee pointed out that the related introduction of the habitual residence test into social security benefits

> would lead to arbitrary and inconsistent decision-making, and was likely to introduce problems of actual or perceived discrimination, with attendant risks of damaging community relations and deterring genuine claims from black and Asian British Citizens (SSAC, 1995, p. 28).

There is also a dilemma for good practice in balancing the risk of wrongly leaving someone inadequately housed against the risk that someone's immigration status will be jeopardized by an unnecessary contact with the Home Office. It is extremely difficult to suggest nondiscriminatory ways to implement legislation which is itself discriminatory.

The CRE collaborated on the Refugee Council's 1995 guide to the effects on asylum-seekers of the Asylum and Immigration Appeals Act 1993 (Refugee Council et al., 1995). However, they produced no guidance on categories of immigrant other than asylum-seekers after the *Tower Hamlets* decision in 1993. After the implementation of the 1996 package the CRE cooperated with Shelter to produce guidance dealing in depth with eligible and qualifying persons (Shelter and CRE, 1997). It recommends councils should give full information to applicants, refer applicants for independent immigration advice, and make all efforts to determine immigration status themselves (p. 38–40). However, it recognizes that councils may nevertheless sometimes in practice be forced to contact the Home Office, and it recommends that applicants should be warned of this and given an opportunity to withdraw applications first (p. 41). When combined with the idea that all Home Office contact should go through a nominated officer in the council (see DoE and DoH, 1996, Annex E4), this seems likely to lead to a 'gate-keeping' exercise where people are not passed on through the system rather than being given clear refusals. From the best of motives this could lead to deterrence and denial, although the CRE counter this by recommending ethnic monitoring at all stages of applications (pp. 33–4).

Conclusion

The previous government created an artificial problem, revived a long-standing moral panic, and tagged concerns about illegal immigrants onto the back of the furore about asylum-seekers. This mixture simmered into a draconian response of denial, deterrence and responsibilization. Housing officers are being brought into line with the rest of the welfare state in the handling of immigrants. Under the guise of voluntary checking, the reporting of applicants to the Home Office by housing officers will increase. The result is likely to be a major erosion of civil liberties, and the fuelling of racist stereotypes of immigrants. The purpose behind this viciously exclusionary programme was partly to distract attention from the housing shortage, but also to keep a racist project ticking over and try to win the last two general elections. The complexity and poor drafting of the exclusions makes them very hard to implement, but succeeds in forcing housing authorities into the arms of the Home Office.

It remains to be seen whether New Labour will want to run the risk of appearing 'soft' on 'illegal immigrants' in doing something about the immigration questioning it has inherited. *Inside Housing* reported Labour before the election as having 'stopped short of a commitment to repeal' the 1996 restrictions on council accommodation and housing benefit and saying only that 'asylum procedures would be speeded up' (West, 1996).

Bibliography

Ashford, M. (1993), *Detained Without Trial: a Survey of Immigration Act Detention*, Joint Council for the Welfare of Immigrants, London.

Bhabha, J. and Shutter, S. (1994), *Women's Movement: Women under Immigration, Nationality and Refugee Law*, Trentham Books, Stoke-on-Trent.

Billig, M. and Golding, P. (1992), 'Did the Race Card Tip the Balance?', *New Community*, Vol. 19 (1), pp. 161–63.

Carlen, P. (1994), 'The Governance of Homelessness: Legality, Lore and Lexicon in the Agency-maintenance of Youth Homelessness', *Critical Social Policy*, Vol. 14 (2), pp. 18–35.

Cohen, S. (1972), *Folk Devils and Moral Panics: the Creation of the Mods and Rockers*, MacGibbon and Kee, London.

Cole, I. and Furbey, R. (1994), *The Eclipse of Council Housing*, Routledge, London.

Commission for Racial Equality (1985), *Immigration Control Procedures: Report of a Formal Investigation*, Commission for Racial Equality, London.

Commission for Racial Equality (1989), *Race, Housing and Immigration: A Guide*, Commission for Racial Equality, London.

Commission for Racial Equality (1991), *Code of Practice in Rented Housing*, Commission for Racial Equality, London.
Cook, D. (1997), *Poverty, Crime and Punishment*, Child Poverty Action Group, London.
Cowan, D. (1997), *Homelessness: the (In-)Appropriate Applicant*, Dartmouth, Aldershot.
Department of Environment (1994a), *Access to Local Authority and Housing Association Tenancies: a Consultation Paper*, DoE, London.
Department of Environment (1994b), *Homelessness Code of Guidance for Local Authorities*, HMSO, London.
Department of Environment (1995), *Our Future Homes: Opportunity, Choice, Responsibility: the Government's Housing Policies for England and Wales*, HMSO, London.
Department of Environment (1996), *Allocation of Housing Accommodation by Local Authorities: Consultation Paper Linked to the Housing Bill*, DoE, London.
Department of Environment and Department of Health (1996), *Code of Guidance on Parts VI and VII of the Housing Act 1996: Allocation of Housing Accommodation; Homelessness*, DoE and DoH, London.
Dummett, A. and Nicol, A. (1990), *Subjects, Citizens, Aliens and Others: Nationality and Immigration Law*, Weidenfeld and Nicolson, London.
Ellery, S. (1996), 'Ruling Plunges Asylum Law into Chaos', *Inside Housing*, 11 October.
Evans, A. and Duncan, S. (1988), *Responding to Homelessness: Local Authority Policy and Practice*, HMSO, London.
Garland, D. (1996), 'The Limits of the Sovereign State: Strategies of Crime Control in Contemporary Society', *British Journal of Criminology*, Vol. 36 (4), pp. 445–71.
Goode, E. and Ben-Yahuda, N. (1994), *Moral Panics: the Social Construction of Deviance*, Blackwell, Oxford.
Gordon, P. (1981), *Passport Raids and Checks: Britain's Internal Immigration Controls*, Runnymede Trust, London.
Griffith, J. (1991), *The Politics of the Judiciary*, Fontana Press, London.
Guardian (1995), 'Officials May Break Data Law', 20 July.
Hall, S., Critcher, C., Jefferson, T., Clarke, J. and Roberts, B. (1978), *Policing the Crisis: Mugging, the State, and Law and Order*, Macmillan, Basingstoke.
Home Office (1996a), *Immigration Review Will Save One Hundred Million Pounds*, Home Office Press Release 325/96, 24 October.
Home Office (1996b), *Home Office Circular to Local Authorities in Great Britain: Exchange of Information with the Immigration and Nationality Directorate (IND) of the Home Office*, Home Office, London.
Home Office (1997), *No Desperate Measures On Asylum Backlog Says Mike O'Brien*, Home Office Press Release 242/97, 26 September.
Hudson, B. (1987), 'Collaboration in Social Welfare: a Framework for Analysis', *Policy and Politics*, Vol. 15 (3), pp. 175–82.
Husbands, C. (1994), 'Crises of National Identity as the "New Moral Panics": Political Agenda-setting about Definitions of Nationhood', *New Community*, Vol. 20 (2), pp. 191–206.
Layton-Henry, Z. (1984), *The Politics of Race in Britain*, Allen and Unwin, London.
Liberty (1995), *I-D Cards: a Solution Looking for a Problem*, Liberty, London.
Macdonald, I. and Blake, N. (1995), *Immigration Law and Practice in the UK*, Butterworths, London.
Menski, W. (1996), Review of Hughes and Lowe *Social Housing Law and Policy*, *Immigration and Nationality Law and Practice*, Vol. 10 (3), p. 116.

Paliwala, A. (1995), 'Law and the Constitution of the "Immigrant" in Europe: a UK Policy Perspective' in P. Fitzpatrick (ed.), *Nationalism, Racism and the Rule of Law*, Dartmouth, Aldershot.

Power, A. (1993), *Hovels to High Rise: State Housing in Europe Since 1850*, Routledge, London.

Prescott-Clarke, P., Clements, S. and Park, A. (1994), *Routes into Local Authority Housing: a Study of Local Authority Waiting Lists and New Tenancies*, HMSO, London.

Refugee Council, CRE, ADC, AMA, ALA, and LBA (1995), *Homelessness and Asylum: the Asylum and Immigration Appeals Act 1993, a Guide for Housing Authorities*, Refugee Council, CRE, ADC, AMA, ALA, and LBA, London.

Rutherford, A. (1996), *Criminal Policy and the Eliminative Ideal*, University of Southampton, Southampton.

Sampson, A., Stubbs, P., Smith, D., Pearson, G. and Blagg, H. (1988), 'Crime, Localities and the Multi-agency Approach', *British Journal of Criminology*, Vol. 28 (4), pp. 478–93.

Shelter and Commission for Racial Equality (1997), *The Housing Act 1996 and the Asylum and Immigration Act 1996: Shelter and CRE Guidance on Eligible and Qualifying Persons*, Shelter and Commission for Racial Equality, London.

Social Security Advisory Committee (1995), *Social Security Advisory Committee Tenth Report*, HMSO, London.

Spencer, S. (ed.) (1994), *Immigration as an Economic Asset: the German Experience*, IPPR/ Trentham Books, London.

Storey, H. (1986), 'United Kingdom Immigration Controls and the Welfare State' in A. Dummett (ed.), *Towards a Just Immigration Policy*, Cobden Trust, London.

Tuitt, P. (1996), *False Images – The Law's Construction of the Refugee*, Pluto Press, London.

Vincent, J. (1996), 'Who's Afraid of an Ageing Population? Nationalism, the Free Market, and the Construction of Old Age as an Issue', *Critical Social Policy*, Vol. 16 (2), p. 3.

West, T. (1996), 'Hopes rise for refugees but Asylum Act stays', *Inside Housing*, 4 October.

11 Facing Both Ways at Once? The Effect of the Housing Act 1996 on Legislation and Policy for the Safety of Women and Children Escaping Domestic Violence

ELLEN MALOS AND GILL HAGUE

Introduction

We begin this with some words from a woman who was involved in our recent research on multi-agency responses to domestic violence. Her words were written before the Housing Act 1996 came into effect but when some local authorities were anticipating its provisions. When she was asked for her permission to use it she said she would be honoured to share it in the hope that something might change.

A Woman's Experience

Thank you for listening
Thank you for your time
Thank you for putting your weight behind me

Because no one does
It feels like we are just being abandoned and thrown away
I didn't ask to be a single parent alone with five kids
I didn't do anything to land up in the gutter

Ten years I was with him
It wasn't a careless thing

I had five kids by him
I tried everything I could
Until the violence and the hospitalisation got too much

As a direct result
It'll be our third Christmas homeless

Do you know what it's like to be homeless with five kids
four of them under five?

I am worth something you know
But they just seem to want to dump me
It is as though we're worth nothing
But I know what we're worth
Me and my kids
Thank you for listening

Confusions and Contradictions in Government Policies: the Example of Housing

We would argue that the example of policy and legislation affecting safe housing for women experiencing domestic violence, under the previous government in particular, betrayed confusion and lack of commitment to a coordinated policy of support for women in this situation and their children. This was in contradiction to the guidance issued through the Home Office (1995) on coordinated multi-agency action at local level to provide safety and support for women experiencing domestic violence and their children. The government's statements contrast poignantly with the experiences described above.

The Inter-agency Circular 1995

> ***The Government's Approach***
> The Government's approach is based on the premise that domestic violence is a serious crime which must not be tolerated. The priority must be to stop the violence occurring and services should be provided on that basis ...
> In order to tackle domestic violence action is needed on a number of fronts directed towards:
> encouraging those who are experiencing domestic violence to come forward and address their situation through the help that is available;

addressing the needs of children affected by domestic violence;
the provision of safe accommodation and support services, both emergency and long term, for women and their children who feel compelled to leave the family home;
ensuring adequate legal protection under the civil and criminal law;
bringing perpetrators to justice;
assisting perpetrators to understand and address the reasons for and the consequences of their offending behaviour in order to stop the abuse;
prevention through education and community initiatives including those that condone and reproduce violent behaviour in intimate relationships (Home Office, 1995).

Safe Accommodation and Support Services? The Housing Act 1996

In contrast to these exhortations to local agencies, the government's willingness to coordinate its own actions at a national level appeared to be minimal and did not seem to include any scrutiny of forthcoming legislation or policy for its impact. The Housing Act 1996 is the prime example of this tendency.

One of its most important provisions was to end the duty of local authorities to secure permanent tenancies for homeless households, thus striking a major blow at one of the ways in which women escaping from domestic violence, and especially women with children, have been able to obtain permanent safe alternative housing at a new address not known to their abuser. Under the new law a local authority's specific obligation to homeless people has been limited to a two year renewable duty to provide temporary accommodation to persons who are homeless and in priority need or vulnerable within the meaning of the law.

They would then have a duty to review the case. At this point they may renew the two year accommodation; or decide that other 'suitable' accommodation is now available to the applicant; or that circumstances have otherwise changed so that the duty no longer applies; or they may offer to aid the applicant to obtain an assured shorthold tenancy in the private rented sector in which case the duty will terminate. The Act contains no recognition of the need of homeless families for secure long-term accommodation in which to begin to build a new life. This is a need which our research into domestic violence and housing suggests was paramount for those escaping the trauma of domestic violence. Such a lack of security, especially where there are children in the family, would also apparently contradict the government's duty to families and children in need under other legislation such as the

Children Act 1989.

Fortunately, the previous government accepted the force of some of the criticisms made of the possible effects of an uncritical recourse to assured shorthold tenancies under The Homelessness (Suitability of Accommodation) (Amendment) Order 1996 in force since 1 September 1997 (DoE, 1996):

> accommodation is not to be regarded as suitable unless the local authority are satisfied that it will be available for occupation by the applicant for at least two years beginning with the date on which he secures it.

Subsequently, the Labour Government, although not as yet fulfilling its pre-election promises to repeal the sections of the 1996 Act referring to homelessness, has taken further action by way of regulation and guidance which mitigates some of the worst effects of the new law. Most notably, this has been achieved by making homelessness a matter which will allow reasonable and additional preference to be given in the allocation schemes of local authorities (DoE, 1997).

The Act itself does appear to be potentially beneficial to some women already in local authority tenancies (a significant proportion of women applying as homeless in our research on homelessness and domestic violence: Malos and Hague, 1993). The 1996 Act also introduced further grounds for repossession in cases of nuisance and antisocial behaviour. Domestic violence thus becomes a ground for eviction from secure tenancies and assured tenancies with social landlords (Cowan, 1996; Arden and Hunter, 1997). However, this ground for possession only arises when the couple are married or living together as husband and wife, and the partner leaving is unlikely to return. It therefore does not cover *McGrady* type cases (a procedure, based on case law, used by some councils to allow the woman to return to the tenancy after a notice to quit had been served to joint tenants). It remains to be seen therefore whether the new eviction provision is able to be used creatively to allow women and their children to be transferred to a new tenancy without falling foul of the new homelessness provisions.

Some Key Points of the Act as it Relates to Homelessness and Domestic Violence[1]

Part III, Housing Act 1985 was repealed, thus ending the statutory duty of local authorities to secure permanent accommodation for homeless people.

Local authority allocation policies will be subject to statutory control and local authorities will only be able to allocate permanent housing to those who are on the unified housing register. In the Act, homelessness is not listed as a factor entitling an applicant on the register to 'reasonable preference'. However, this has been amended by regulation of the new government – Allocation of Housing (Reasonable and Additional Preference) Regulations 1997 (which come into force in November 1997) – so that those owed a duty in relation to homelessness under the 1985 or 1996 Acts should be accorded reasonable preference.

The definitions of homelessness and priority need remain as before (with slight amendments) and the local authority will have a two year renewable duty to house persons who are homeless and in priority need. After the two year period the local authority will have to review the case. If the applicant is still homeless and in priority need the two year renewable duty will begin again. But the duty can be discharged either by providing further temporary 'social housing' or by an assured shorthold tenancy in the private sector. If a local authority believes there is suitable accommodation available to homeless applicants they can refuse to house them. The definition of 'suitable accommodation' in the Act does not include the concept of permanence, though the Act has since been amended by regulation to safeguard against short-term lets being regarded as suitable (see above).

Councils do not have to offer emergency assistance to anyone admitted to the UK without the right of recourse to public funds. This covers many women admitted on marriage to a UK resident and applies whether or not the woman is subjected to domestic violence. Anyone, whether a UK citizen or not, with a home in another country would be prevented from obtaining even emergency assistance.

Some Good News

Homelessness in General

Local authorities must set up advice services for the homeless. Assistance to voluntary organizations concerned with homelessness or matters relating to homelessness in the form of grant aid is retained under s. 180. This replaces the former provision which covered the contribution to funding that many refuge groups receive from their local authority.

Domestic Violence

The definition of domestic violence within the concept of 'homelessness' has been broadened to include violence or threats of violence from an 'associated person'. Violence from former cohabitants is included as well as violence from the father of a women's child, whether or not he has lived with her. Violence from relatives of the women or the partner is also included, irrespective of whether the couple have been married. Domestic violence also becomes a ground for possession under certain specified circumstance, for example under provisions about antisocial behaviour.

Some Likely Effects of the New Law on Women and Children Experiencing Domestic Violence

Women escaping domestic violence by implication shared the stigma of all homeless people and single-parent families in the Consultation Paper circulated prior to the passage of the legislation. The law was designed quite explicitly to support government policies to promote the traditional two parent heterosexual, nuclear family. The Consultation Paper made direct reference to young couples attempting to establish a home and family, and being frustrated in so doing by the homeless having an unfair, fast route to rehousing (DoE, 1994, paras 2.8, 2.9 and 3.1). The implications were twofold: first, that 'normal' families should have precedence over others. In this context, this must, for example, by definition have included precedence over single people or 'single parent families', among whom would be women with children escaping domestic violence. The second implication was that the rights of the homeless must be curtailed to such an extent that the possibility of achieving permanent rehousing was to be more or less totally removed except in the most extreme circumstances.

Housing organizations across the board, statutory, voluntary and commercial, including those representing specific groups such as women and children escaping domestic violence, were disturbed and outraged by the proposed legislation. There were more than 9,000 submissions during the consultation process, the overwhelming majority highly critical of the proposals. Responses from a large number of organizations, collated by Shelter, pointed out that the proposals: attacked homeless families; would trap homeless people in short-term housing and create a cycle of deprivation; would deprive homeless people of their existing right to a permanent home. It was also pointed out that the resulting Act could mean that a greater burden would be placed on Social Services in meeting their duties under the Children Act 1989 – for example, in ensuring that children are housed safely and forcing hard-pressed social services departments to consider splitting more children from their families where poor housing or homelessness had been a major factor in their difficulties. In addition, it would force homeless families into the private rented sector where high rents paid by housing benefit would add to the ballooning social security bill (Bradburn, 1994). Concern was also expressed that homeless people would be trapped for increasing lengths of time in unsuitable and inadequate temporary accommodation with resultant implications not only for the people themselves but for other services such as health, and education due to the well documented detrimental effects of living in temporary accommodation and most notably for children (Malos, 1993; Thomas and Niner, 1989).[2]

Despite all such concerns, expressed with almost unprecedented unanimity, the proposals were nevertheless enacted, with only one or two significant concessions (for example on the length of the duty to provide temporary accommodation which was extended to two years from a proposed six months). As noted above, there have been some further developments since the election of the new Labour government. These are welcome in so far as they point local authorities towards a humane interpretation of the legislation, specifically mentioning reasonable preference for those owed a duty as homeless under the previous and current legislation, which includes women experiencing domestic violence and their children, and ruling out the approval of very short-term tenancies as suitable accommodation under the law. However, so far we have seen nothing which approaches their pre-election commitment to repeal or radical revision of the Act, restoring the local authority duty to secure permanent accommodation. Nor have we seen any commitment to give statutory force to the provisions of the Code of Guidance to the Act, so that authorities still retain the wide discretion in their interpretation both of their duties under the law and their observance of the good practice recommended in the code of guidance as documented by researchers on both homelessness and domestic violence (for example, Evans and Duncan, 1988; Thomas and Niner, 1989; Evans, 1991; Bull, 1993; Malos and Hague, 1993; Malos, 1993). Indeed, any such repeal or radical revision would be largely meaningless without a commitment to reverse the decline of social rented housing. In particular, this would require a commitment to restore that form of tenure to its previous provision as a significant proportion of the housing stock which would be available as an option to wide sectors of the population – traditionally the Labour Party's policy – instead of 'targeted' to the poorest and most in need as a stigmatized and inferior form of housing for those with no choice – traditionally the Conservative party's attitude. However, this would necessitate a shift in the current attitude to public expenditure and public ownership and an end to the shibboleth that progressive taxation is a political impossibility.

Domestic Violence and the Previous Law on Homelessness

One significant feature of the previous homelessness legislation, as enacted in 1977, was the inclusion, for the first time, of domestic violence as a cause of homelessness. It thus provided one possible means for women experiencing violence within the home to obtain safe, alternative long-term accommodation (this was particularly important for women with children, who were defined as having a priority need). The existence of this legislation gave women the possibility of being rehoused by the council in an emergency and of moving on from the short-term, emergency and temporary accommodation being gradually developed by the new Women's Aid Groups from the early 1970s onwards.

This inclusion of domestic violence as a ground of homelessness in the legislation was an early achievement of the new Women's Aid Federation. Currently there are Women's Aid Federations, covering England, Scotland, Wales, and Northern Ireland. These are the main bodies in the British Isles which coordinate the provision of refuges for women and their children who are escaping domestic violence, and which campaign nationally against violence in the home. The national Women's Aid Federations monitor both legislation and government policy and also policy and practice in other relevant agencies, as well as lobby for improvements in meeting the needs of abused women and children. They also provide information, resources, training and networking for women involved in Women's Aid groups.

The problem is a large one. Over 100,000 women experiencing domestic abuse contact Women's Aid in England alone for advice each year. Thousands more contact the police and other agencies. Of those made homeless as a result of violence, some seek prosecutions under criminal law, many make use of civil law remedies and obtain injunctions and ouster orders, thus being enabled to return to their own homes. But many others know that, no matter how much they may want to return home, it will never be safe to do so, and that they must leave completely in order to attain safety and security for themselves and their children. Moving back into their original accommodation may well be putting their lives and those of their children literally at risk. Prosecution may exacerbate the violence and prison sentences, where imposed, may offer only temporary respite.

Additionally, courts do not grant injunctions permanently banning a man from his former home, and while they are there the woman and children's whereabouts are known to him. Perpetrators may go to enormous lengths to track down their former partners and there have been many tragic cases of further abuse and violence, including murder, occurring if they are found. Any consideration of the government's new proposals must be set against this very real background of danger and threat (WAFE, 1994). Like other concerned organizations, the Women's Aid Federations campaigned hard against the 1996 legislation, concentrating particularly on its likely impact on women experiencing domestic violence (see, for example, WAFE, 1994, 1996).

Some Shortcomings of the Previous Homelessness Legislation

The effectiveness of the law on homelessness was limited by its own complexities, such as the priority need, intentional homelessness and local connections provisions; the requirements for investigation; and the degree of discretion allowed to local authorities, which were introduced because of opponents' fears that the law would become an easy road into local authority tenancies when it was passed in 1977. Since then, the Conservative governments have drastically reduced the availability of public rented housing, through the policy of changing the role of local housing authorities from that of provider to 'enabler', put into practice by cuts in public housing finance, the right to buy council housing and the transfer of the provider role to housing associations and lately to private housing companies. Together, these have meant that homeless households have had to spend increasingly long periods in temporary accommodation often highly unsuitable for 'priority need' households: families with children and others who were vulnerable within the meaning of the Act. Unfortunately, there is little indication that such policies will be reversed under the current Labour government, although they may be modified. Our research on women who had experienced domestic violence and applied to local authorities for rehousing under the previous homelessness legislation (Malos and Hague, 1993) did not confirm the belief that homelessness offered a 'fast track' to permanent council or housing association housing or conferred 'automatic priority' over households on the waiting list as assumed in the government's consultation paper (DoE, 1994, paras 2.6–

2.9) even for families in priority need and certainly very rarely for others.

The Research Findings: Housing and Domestic Violence under the Homeless Persons' Act

A two year research study into local authority responses to domestic violence by a team in the domestic violence research group at the University of Bristol (supported by the Joseph Rowntree Foundation) documented the continuing need for women experiencing domestic violence for safe permanent housing as well as safe emergency accommodation. It also demonstrated the continuing importance of access to local authority and social rented housing (Malos and Hague, 1993). Women's worse access to better paid work and to financial resources generally, especially when they have children, has been firmly established. This means that they are often less able to afford acceptable housing in the private housing market, either as owners or as tenants (Watson with Austerberry, 1986; Watson, 1984; Logan, 1986; Muir and Ross, 1993). It is, therefore, all the more important for women seeking safety from violent partners that there should be safe emergency or temporary accommodation of a reasonable standard in the short term. If a safe return to their previous home would not be possible, they also need access to an adequate, secure and affordable permanent home in which they and their children can live. Our research demonstrated that, despite the increasing problems it faces, the public housing sector has remained an important, if diminishing, resource for women and children in this situation. In the last 20 years this has often been possible only through the special provisions made for homelessness, with local authority nominations to housing associations as a valuable supplement. In some areas, however, local authority responses reflected the minimum required within the law and, in some cases, even less than that. Therefore, the 1996 Act, which permits and encourages local authorities to discharge their duties to homeless people by referring them to the private rented sector, not only weakens the safety net but creates dangers that that net may be withdrawn altogether in some areas of the country.

Varying Response of Local Authorities

Our research into local authority responses under the previous law considered policy and practice in seven local authorities. In four of these, the research centred on in-depth interviews with women who had experienced domestic violence and were seeking rehousing in each of four local authorities (20 in each authority) with a follow up approximately six months later. Although the majority of the women were or had been in women's aid refuges the study included women from bed and breakfast, local authority homeless hostels, and temporary private accommodation. These four authorities were one rural and one London borough and two urban district authorities. We interviewed workers from a large number of local voluntary agencies in all seven study areas, as well as from women's refuges, housing associations and the local authority housing departments.

The majority of the women interviewed had dependent children and were therefore a priority under the law. The Code of Guidance current at that time advised local authorities to give special consideration to women without dependent children where they had been made homeless through violence. A sizeable proportion of women in the study came from minority ethnic communities. Contrary to recent suggestions, our research provided no evidence that these groups received unfair precedence over other homeless applicants for local authority housing or were given 'fast track' access to permanent tenancies on more favourable terms than others.

The authorities varied in the sympathy of their response but none went significantly beyond the law and the advice of the government's Code of Guidance as to which groups of applicants they accepted for rehousing. Some did show more consideration for the problems faced by women escaping violence in their approach to interviewing women, in the facilities they provided to help ensure a safe and sympathetic interviewing environment, or in allowing them to specify areas in the authority in which they would not wish to be rehoused. Such authorities were often developing written guidelines on policy and practice in relation to domestic violence and were carrying out training programmes for all staff. These practices have continued in many metropolitan boroughs in particular and have been somewhat extended through the development of multi-agency initiatives (Hague et al., 1995, 1996) but are often under pressure as a result of financial constraints.

On the other hand some authorities interpreted their duties very narrowly: for example by adopting a stance of minimum compliance with the law and attempting to deter women from pursuing their applications, or insisting they pursue legal remedies, or refusing to accept women who did not have dependent children with them, or interpreted the 'local connection' clause of the homelessness law more narrowly than the law prescribes in situations involving domestic violence. This might involve the authority attempting to refer women on to another authority even if they were likely to be in danger in that other authority, or keeping them in uncertainty about whether they would be accepted for rehousing for very long periods of time.

Overall, our impressions from the research were that the queues of women waiting for rehousing were lengthening as an effect of the cutback in public housing and the recession, especially in London and the rural authority we studied. There was little evidence that housing associations were making up for the shortfall although they did make a valuable contribution, especially in rehousing single women and women from minority ethnic communities who might otherwise have had special difficulty in some areas.

A significant proportion of women, especially in the London authority and the rural borough, had difficulty in establishing their claim to be accepted for rehousing. The great majority of the women and children spent periods varying from four months to several years in temporary accommodation and in the rural and the London borough most had still not been rehoused at the end of the study.

Our research confirmed the existing evidence that local authority responses vary widely from one area to another, in terms of the use of their discretion under the homelessness legislation to accept or attempt to limit their acceptance of homeless people (see, for example, Evans and Duncan, 1988; Thomas and Niner, 1989; Evans, 1991; Bull, 1993). We found that women who become homeless because of domestic violence are no exception to this pattern. This response is not always explicable in terms of the amount of housing stock the authority controls although, not surprisingly, the length of time that women had to wait for housing once they had been accepted *was* affected by the availability of housing in the area.

In the new situation created by the combination of the continued decline of the public rented sector and the inability of the housing associations to fill the gap, especially in view of current government pressures to force them to borrow in the commercial market, it is even more important than before for local authorities to seek sympathetic and creative use of the human and material resources they do have at their disposal. At the time of our research into local authority responses, housing departments in some areas had begun to examine their practices and policies towards homeless people in general and women escaping domestic violence in particular, developing better informed policies and codes of practice, providing training for staff, as well as developing better facilities. In existing accommodation, for example, the provision of alarms and door phones to control access or easing transfers to other accommodation could lessen the need for women and their children to become homeless in the first place. Changes in the homeless section could also be important, for example through taking a sympathetic, informed and 'believing' approach;

allowing for more privacy in interviews; providing information and interpretation in a variety of languages; and giving clear information of the progress of their application. In some cases these changes took place in conjunction with the development of multi-agency initiatives on domestic violence. Clearly these changes can remain in place, provided that local authority finances are not so squeezed that they fall victim to the myriad of small-scale economies.

Conclusion

The insistence that it can be sufficient to secure accommodation in the private rented sector (Housing Act 1996) ignores the need of families for safe long-term security, which cannot be assured by action under the criminal or civil law, despite recent attempts to strengthen the latter in the Family Law Act 1996 (Barron, 1990; Law Commission, 1992; Malos and Hague 1993; Cretney and Davis, 1996). Ultimately, for many families, the only protection will be their ability to 'disappear' and for that to have any chance of success one of the key needs is for safe permanent housing, often in a different locality altogether. For many women and children this can only be provided through access to 'social rented' housing.

In the coming years, we can probably expect an ever-widening gap between the authorities which will use the legislation to wash their hands of any long-term responsibility and more enlightened and conscientious authorities which will use their 'enabling' powers to the full in order to provide what security they can. Thus the developing policy of multi-agency coordination to secure safety and support for women experiencing domestic violence and their children (Home Office, 1995), despite much innovative work at local level (Hague et al., 1996), may be sabotaged by housing policies condemning women and their children to the notoriously expensive, insecure and often poor standard accommodation of the private rented sector, or else to staying in or returning to danger, for lack of adequate alternatives.

One vital ingredient of a successful policy to maximize support and safety measures for women and their children experiencing domestic violence would be adequate funding for women's refuges and their associated services (helplines, outreach services, services for children, etc.). Another would be the repeal of those sections of the Housing Act 1996 which remove the right of homeless people to permanent social rented tenancies. In order for such policies to be effective in providing the possibility of safety and long-term security for women experiencing domestic violence and for their children, this would need to be combined with policies directed to reversing the decline in housing provision, most notably in the social rented sector, which has led to massively increased homelessness (Social Trends, 1997; Greve, 1991; Malos, 1993) and its restoration to the position it held in the post second world war period as a significant proportion of housing stock and an option for many sectors of the population, rather than as a stigmatized and residual form of accommodation for those who, through experience of poverty, hardship, disaster or violence, have no choice.

Notes

1 This is predominantly contained in Part VII, 1996 Act; as to which, see Women's Aid Federation of England, Housing Briefings 1994 and 1996, Cowan, op. cit., Arden and Hunter, op cit.

2 Clear contradictions were displayed in government policy here. At the same time as the homelessness review implied the need for an increase in housing benefits the DSS was considering further cuts in this expenditure. Thus, housing benefit and other cuts will further effect the ability of poorer people in general and homeless people in particular to obtain satisfactory accommodation.

Bibliography

Arden, A. and Hunter, C. (1997), *Homelessness and Allocations*, Legal Action Group, London.

Barron, J. (1990), *Not Worth the Paper? ... The effectiveness of Legal Protection for Women and Children Experiencing Domestic Violence*, WAFE, Bristol.

Bradburn, H. (1994), *Home Truths: Access to Local Authority and Housing Association Tenancies, Responses to the Consultation Paper*, Shelter, London.

Bull, J. (1993), *Housing Consequences of Relationship Breakdown*, HMSO, London.

Cowan, D. (ed.) (1996), *The Housing Act 1996 – A Practical Guide*, Jordans, Bristol.

Cretney, A. and Davis, G. (1996), 'Prosecuting Domestic Assault', *Criminal Law Review*, March, pp. 162–74.

DoE (1994), *Access to Local Authority and Housing Association Tenancies*, HMSO, London.

DoE (1996), *The Homelessness (Suitability of Accommodation) Order 1996*, The Stationery Office, London.

DoE (1997), *The Allocation of Housing (Reasonable and Additional Preference) Regulations*, The Stationery Office, London.

Evans, A. (1991), *Alternatives to Bed and Breakfast, Temporary Housing Solutions for Homeless People*, National Housing and Town Planning Council, London.

Evans, A. and Duncan, S. (1988), *Responding to Homelessness: Local Authority Policy and Practice*, HMSO, London.

Greve, J. (1991), *Homelessness in Britain*, Joseph Rowntree Foundation, York.

Hague, G. and Malos, E. (1993), *Domestic Violence; Action for Change*, New Clarion Press, Cheltenham.

Hague, G., Malos, E. and Dear, W. (1995), *Against Domestic Violence: Inter-agency Initiatives*, University of Bristol, SAUS Publications, Bristol.

Hague, G., Malos, E. and Dear, W. (1996), *Multi-Agency Work and Domestic Violence: A National Study of Inter-agency Initiatives*, Joseph Rowntree Foundation and Policy Press, Bristol.

Home Office (1995), *Inter-agency Circular: Inter-agency Co-ordination to Tackle Domestic Violence*, Home Office and Welsh Office.

Law Commission (1992), *Family Law, Domestic Violence and the Occupation of the Family Home*, HMSO, London.

Logan, F. (1986), *Homelessness and Relationship Breakdown: How the Law and Housing Policy affects Women*, One Parent Families, London.

Malos, E. (1993), *'You've got No Life': Homelessness and the Use of Bed and Breakfast Hotels*, University of Bristol, School of Applied Social Studies, Bristol.

Malos, E. and Hague, G. (1993), *Domestic Violence and Housing*, Women's Aid Federation England and University of Bristol, School of Applied Social Studies, Bristol.

Muir, J. and Ross, M. (1993), *Housing The Poorer Sex*, London Housing Unit, London.

Social Trends (1997), 27, HMSO, London.

Thomas, A. and Niner, P. (1989), *Living in Temporary Accommodation: a Survey of Homeless People*, HMSO, London.

Watson, S. (1984), 'Definitions of Homelessness: a Feminist Perspective', *Critical Social Policy*, Vol. 11.

Watson, S. with Austerberry, H. (1986), *Housing and Homelessness: A Feminist Perspective*, Routledge and Kegan Paul, London.

For Product Safety Concerns and Information please contact our EU representative GPSR@taylorandfrancis.com
Taylor & Francis Verlag GmbH, Kaufingerstraße 24, 80331 München, Germany

www.ingramcontent.com/pod-product-compliance
Ingram Content Group UK Ltd.
Pitfield, Milton Keynes, MK11 3LW, UK
UKHW022204190926
475702UK00003B/190

* 9 7 8 1 1 3 8 3 2 0 3 1 4 *